Transport Law in Australia

Transport Law in Australia

Third Edition

John Livermore

This book was originally published as a monograph in the International Encyclopaedia of Laws/Transport Law.

Founding Editor: Roger Blanpain
General Editor: Frank Hendrickx
Volume Editor: Eric Van Hooydonk

Wolters Kluwer

Published by:
Kluwer Law International B.V.
PO Box 316
2400 AH Alphen aan den Rijn
The Netherlands
Website: lrus.wolterskluwer.com

Sold and distributed in North, Central and South America by:
Wolters Kluwer Legal & Regulatory U.S.
7201 McKinney Circle
Frederick, MD 21704
United States of America
Email: customer.service@wolterskluwer.com

Sold and distributed in all other countries by:
Air Business Subscriptions
Rockwood House
Haywards Heath
West Sussex
RH16 3DH
United Kingdom
Email: international-customerservice@wolterskluwer.com

ISBN 978-90-411-9315-5

e-Book: ISBN 978-90-411-9347-6
web-PDF: ISBN 978-90-411-9378-0

The Author

John Livermore lives in Hobart, Tasmania, Australia.

He retired in 2002 as Senior Lecturer in Commercial Law in the School of Accounting and Finance, Faculty of Commerce and Economics, University of Tasmania after appointment in 1974. He holds an LLB (Bristol, 1959), a Diploma in Social Studies (Sheffield, 1961), an LLM (Tasmania) 1988, and a Professional Certificate in Arbitration (Adelaide) 2002. He served as Dean of the Faculty of Economics and Commerce 1986–1988.

He is a Fellow of the Chartered Institute of Logistics and Transport and a former Chairperson of the Tasmanian Branch 1992–1994. He is also a Fellow and Certified Practising Marketer of the Australian Marketing Institute, and a Graded Arbitrator with the Resolution Institute of Australia.

He has presented papers on commercial law at Australia and New Zealand universities and on maritime law to the International Congress of Comparative Law Montreal 1990, Athens 1994, Bristol 1998, and papers on aviation policy and law at the Asian Institute of Air and Space Law Taipei 1991, Beijing 1995, Seoul 1997, 2008, Shanghai 1999.

Since 1990 he has been Editor of *Transport: Laws of Australia* with contributing chapters on carriage by road, rail and sea and limitation of liability. Publications include the Australian reports in *Ocean Bills of Lading: Traditional Forms, Substitutes and EDI Systems* (editor Yiannapoulos, AN Kluwer Law International, 1998) and *Multimodal Transport: Carrier Liability and Issues Related to Bills of Lading* (editor Kiantou-Pampouki, A Bruylant, 2000). Other publications include chapters on road, rail, and air carriage in Palmer, N *Bailment* (Law Book Company, 1979), *Exemption Clauses and Implied Obligations in Contracts* (Law Book Company, 1986) and *Marketing Law* (with Clarke, E Law Book Company, 1994).

He enjoys bushwalking, relaxing in the company of family and friends, travelling overseas whenever possible, unravelling historical mysteries, fossicking through second hand bookshops.

E-mail: johnlivermo@bigpond.com
Website: www. johnlivermore.com
Australia

The Author

Table of Contents

Table of Contents

List of Abbreviations

AA	Airservices Australia
ABLR	Australia Business Law Review
ANZMarLJ	Australian and New Zealand Maritime Law Journal
AC	Appeal Cases
ACCC	Australian Competition and Consumer Commission
ACT	Australian Capital Territory
AGPS	Australian Government Printing Service
All ER	All England Reports
ALJ	Australian Law Journal
ALJR	Australian Law Journal Reports
ALR	Australian Law Reports
ALRC	Australian Law Reform Commission
ALT	Australian Law Times
AMSA	Australian Maritime Safety Authority
ARTC	Australian Rail Track Corporation
ATPR	Australia Trade Practices Reporter
ATS	Australia Treaty Series
ATSB	Australian Transport Safety Bureau
BC	British Columbia
BIMCO	Baltic and International Maritime Conference
CA	Court of Appeal
CA (Ont)	Court of Appeal Ontario
CASA	Civil Aviation Safety Authority
CCH	Commercial Clearing House
CCR (Vic)	County Court Reports Victoria
Ch	Chancery Division (Law Reports)
CLR	Commonwealth Law Reports

List of Abbreviations

CPD	Common Pleas Division
Cth	Commonwealth (Australia)
Dist Ct/DC	District Court
DLR	Dominion Law Reports
EEZ	Exclusive Economic Zone
ER	English Reports
FCA	Federal Court of Australia
FLR	Federal Law Reports
HC	High Court
HCA	High Court of Australia
HL	House of Lords
IASC	International Air Services Commission
IATA	International Air Transport Association
ICLQ	International Commercial Law Quarterly
IMDG	International Maritime Dangerous Goods Code
Imp	Imperial
IR	Irish Reports
ITOPF	International Tanker Owners Pollution Federation
JBL	Journal of Business Law
JCL	Journal of Contract Law
JMLC	Journal of Maritime Law and Commerce
KB	King's Bench Division
Lloyd's Rep	Lloyd's Law Reports
LOF	Lloyd's Open Form
LMCLQ	Lloyd's Maritime and Commercial Law Quarterly
LT	Law Times
Mal LR	Malaysian Law Review
MIA	Agreement on Measures to Implement the IATA Intercarrier Agreement
Mod LR	Modern Law Review
NRC	National Rail Commission
NTC	National Transport Commission
NSW	New South Wales
NSWLR	New South Wales Law Reports
NT	Northern Territory
NYPE	New York Produce Exchange

NZ	New Zealand
NZLJ	New Zealand Law Journal
NZLR	New Zealand Law Reports
P	Probate Division
PC	Privy Council
QB	Law Reports, Queen's Bench Division
QBD	Queen's Bench Division
Qld	Queensland
SA	South Australia
SALR	South Australian Law Reports
SASR	South Australian State Reports
SC	Supreme Court
SDR	Special Drawing Rights
SR(NSW)	State Reports of New South Wales
St RQ	State Reports (Queensland)
Tas	Tasmania
TR	Tasmanian Reports
TLR	Times Law Reports
Vic	Victoria
VR	Victorian Reports
WA	Western Australia
WALR	Western Australian Law Reports
WLR	Weekly Law Reports
WN	Weekly Notes (Law Reports)

List of Abbreviations

Preface

I would wish to acknowledge, in the completion of this work, those who have made it possible.

To my wife Netta who has been supportive of me during what seemed a long process of arriving at the final version. Second, to Catherine Roberts of Thompson Laws of Australia, Sydney who initially secured permission for me to include material from 'Carriage' in *Transport: Laws of Australia* of which I am Editor and draw on my entry under 'Shipping' in the same publication. Readers are referred to *Transport: Laws of Australia* as fuller reference for Australian transport law. I am grateful to Professor Marc Huybrechts and Joeri Lauwers for continued support for updating this entry for the International Encyclopaedia of Laws. I am honoured by the original request (at the suggestion of Dr Kristian Bernauw to Professor Blanpain) to produce the original Australian contribution.

I also wish to thank Debra Bowring, Head Librarian, Law School, University of Tasmania, for help in accessing research facilities and Thomson Reuters for assistance in using the Westlaw database.

No one ever produces any written work without the support and criticism of friends and colleagues. I have been fortunate to have attended international conferences where I could meet other specialists in this complex but vital field of research. To them I owe a great debt of gratitude for their good humour and encouragement. I would particularly mention Professors Doo Hwan Kim, Yianapolous, Aliki Kiantou-Pampouki, and Bin Cheng.

The law as stated is this July 2017.

General Introduction

§1. Background Information on the Country

I. Geography and Climate

1. Australia is situated between the Indian, Pacific, and Southern Oceans, and lies between latitudes 10 41'S (Cape York) and 43 39'S (South East Cape), and longitudes 113 09'E (Steep Point) and 153 39'E (Cape Byron). The latitudinal distance between the two points is 3,680 km and the longitudinal distance about 4,000 km. The overall area of Australia is almost as great as that of the continental United States of America and thirty-two times greater than the United Kingdom. By far, the greatest land area of the country is made up of the largest island, 'the mainland'. However, other significant islands off the coast are the State of Tasmania (Tas), Kangaroo Island in South Australia (SA), Melville Island in the Northern Territory (NT), and Fraser Island in Queensland (Qld). There are also a large number of out-lying islands, including Christmas Island, Macquarie Island, and Norfolk and Lord Howe Islands.

2. A wide range of climatic zones are present in Australia, from the tropical north, the dry interior, to the temperate south. Eight per cent of Australia has a median rainfall of less than 600 mm per year, with 50% having less than 300 mm The rainfall pattern is strongly seasonal, with a winter (May–October) regime in the south, and a summer (November–April) regime in the north. Fluctuations in temperature can be great, from above 50°C to well below freezing. However, average annual air temperatures range from 28°C along the Kimberley coast of Western Australia (WA) to 4°C in the alpine areas of South-eastern mainland Australia. The absence of extensive mountainous terrain and the surrounding oceans prevent minimum temperatures dropping to levels recorded elsewhere. However, droughts, floods, cyclones, and bushfires are all common in Australia due to Australia's physical geography and climate.

II. The Economic Setting

3. Australia's geographic setting means that it is crucially dependent on international shipping for the bulk of its exports.[1] Reforms in the transport sector have been

1. For current export statistics *see* Australian Bureau of Statistics www.abs.gov.au under International Trade Statistics.

closely tied with government economic policies such as the full sale of Qantas by the Federal Government. Related measures included the sale of Federal airports, and on the waterfront a package of measures designed to enhance the efficiency and international competitiveness of the Australian shipping industry. In relation to the road network, the introduction of charges for heavy vehicles was designed to ensure the application of user pays principles.[2]

III. The Constitutional, Political, and Legal Systems

4. Australia is a constitutional monarchy with parliamentary government under the Westminster tradition. The Australian Constitution of 1901 established a Federal Parliament and the six Australian colonies transferred specified powers to it while retaining residual powers for State responsibility.[3] Most of the Federal powers are contained within section 51 of the Constitution. The Commonwealth (Federal) Parliament is one of three branches of government established by the Constitution. The Executive and Judicature are the other two branches. A division of powers exists between the three branches. The scheme of government was, therefore, broadly based on the Westminster model of responsible government.

5. The Parliament of the Commonwealth exercises the legislative power of the country. The Parliament itself consists of the Queen's representative (the Governor-General), the Senate and the House of Representatives. The Senate is the Upper House, an elected body with each State electing an equal number of Senators regardless of electorate size. The House of Representatives is the Lower House and is elected by the people of the entire nation. By convention both the Prime Minister and Leader of the Opposition are drawn from this House. The size of the House of Representatives must be as close as possible to twice that of the Senate. This excludes Territory Senators who have the same terms of office as Representatives, and was designed to maintain the relative strength and importance of the Senate.

6. The Senate largely exercises a review function over the House of Representatives, although there are limitations on its power over financial matters. In order to give it a degree of independence from the Lower House, Senators have a longer term of office than Representatives, and that office is rotated. Therefore, the term of office of State Senators is twice that of Representatives, and half the Senators for each State retire on 30 June every three years. Like the House of Representatives also, since 1949 the Senate has been elected under a system of proportional representation. This operates to give voice to a wide range of views across the entire community. Voting is compulsory in Federal elections.

---

2. *See* Ch. 2.
3. *See Commonwealth of Australia Constitution Act* 1900 (Imp); for the legislative powers of the Commonwealth *see* s. 1, the executive power *see* s. 61, the judicial power *see* s. 71. *See also* the *Statute of Westminster Adoption Act* 1942 (Cth) and the *Australia Act* 1988 (Cth). *See also* Australian Government Publishing Service, *Final Report of the Constitutional Commission* (Canberra 1988).

7. With the exception of Qld, all of the States mirror the Federal Parliament in being bicameral legislatures. In addition, each of the States has a representative of the Queen, the Governor. However, since 1986 the Parliament of the United Kingdom has ceased to exercise any powers over the Commonwealth, and the Australian electorate is becoming aware of its right to choose an Australian Head of State in the future to replace the Queen. At present the Queen's role is primarily limited to the exercise (through the Governor-General and Governors, and on the advice of the respective governments), to give Royal Assent to Acts passed by the Commonwealth and State and Territory Parliaments. However, under certain specified conditions, the Governor-General may dissolve both Houses if the Senate fails to pass a Bill from the House. The possible exercise of this power has generated great national debate in relation to Australia's ties with the British Crown and the issue of Australia becoming a republic.[4]

8. Australia is a Common Law jurisdiction. The most important sources of the law consist of Acts passed by the Commonwealth Parliament, together with regulations, rules and orders made under those Acts; Acts passed by the State and Territory Parliaments, together with regulations, rules and orders made thereunder; some common law or statute law of England still applicable to Australia and un-revoked by domestic legislation; and common law principles developed by Australian judicial decisions.

9. Under the Australian Constitution, the Commonwealth of Australia is empowered to make laws in relation to matters specified, such as trade and commerce, taxation, defence and external affairs. Some of these matters may be exercised by either the Commonwealth or the States and Territories. With regard to some matters the Commonwealth's power is absolute, and Commonwealth laws are binding on the States and Territories if exercised within the area of federal jurisdiction. States and Territories retain independent legislative power on a wide range of matters, however, it is this statute and common law that has the greatest impact upon the majority of Australians.

10. The High Court of Australia (HCA) is the highest court in the land, exercising both original and appellate jurisdiction. Original jurisdiction may be exercised in respect of treaty matters, suits between States or relating to States, suits by the Commonwealth or relating to the Commonwealth, or writs of mandamus or prohibition. The High Court (HC) can also remit matters to other courts, and is the Court of Disputed Returns. Appellate jurisdiction permits the High Court (HC) to grant leave to appeal from decisions of the State Supreme Courts (SCs), State courts exercising federal jurisdiction, the Federal Court of Australia, and the Family Court of Australia. It is, therefore, the final Court of Appeal (CA) in Australia. The Federal Court of Australia (FCA) was created in 1976. As is necessary, it sits in each State

---

4. The issue of the Vice Regal (Governor-General's) power has already been actively discussed since the dismissal of the Whitlam Government in 1975 by the then Governor-General Sir John Kerr. For the current law-making powers of the Federal Parliament acting for a sovereign independent nation *see* the *Australia Act* 1986 (Cth); Australia Act 1988 (UK).

and Territory. Concurrent with the High Court, it is also able to deal with matters in which a writ of mandamus or prohibition or an injunction is sought, where these are against an officer of the Commonwealth of Australia. It also exercises a limited appellate function, for example, in relation to the decisions of individual judges of the Court.

11. Specialist courts at the Federal level include the Family Court of Australia, being established under the *Family Law Act 1975* to deal with matrimonial and related proceedings. The Administrative Appeals Tribunal is another specialist court. It was created as an independent body to review the decisions made by Commonwealth Ministers and authorities.

12. In the States and Territories, courts have original jurisdiction on all matters brought under State and Territory laws and matters under federal laws where jurisdiction has not been reserved to the courts of federal jurisdiction. Within each State and Territory there are courts with general, appellate and specialist jurisdiction. The Federal Constitution gives Federal Parliament power to create Federal courts or to invest a state court with jurisdiction.[5] The *Jurisdiction of Courts (Cross Vesting) Act* 1987 (Cth) in 1988 provided a cross vesting scheme between the States and Commonwealth. However, in 1999 the High Court declared the scheme invalid under the Constitution in *Wakim; ex parte McNally* (1999) 73 LJR 839.[6] Cross vesting can only be resorted by an amendment to the Constitution by a national referendum or reference of powers by the States to the Commonwealth in certain areas.

IV. The Road and Rail Systems

13. Australia is a physically vast country with large sparsely settled inland area and population concentrated around the coast. The road system is in three categories; federal highways, state highways and local roads. The road network totals 913,000 km (353,330 km sealed, 559,669 km unsealed).[7]

Australia has the second highest car ownership in the world and has nine times more road length per capita than Asia.

Canberra and Darwin have only bus based public transport as the other capital cities have multimodal networks. Light rail has been developed in Adelaide, Gold Coast, Melbourne, Perth, and Sydney. Canberra is in the process of planning light rail as is Hobart.

14. The large rail network totals 35,819 km of which 2,450 km is electrified. All mainland capital cities are linked by standard gauge rail. Interstate rail services include the Great Southern Railway, owned by Serco Asia Pacific which operates

5. Constitution s. 77(iii).
6. *See* P. Latimer, *Australian Business Law* 14–15 (20th ed., CCH 2001).
7. For infrastructure statistics *see* Australian Infrastructure Statistics-Yearbook 2017 at Department of Transport and Regional Services at www.dotars.gov.au.

the Indian Pacific (Sydney-Adelaide-Perth), the Ghan (Adelaide-Alice Springs-Darwin), and the Overland (Melbourne-Adelaide). Country Link services link Brisbane, Canberra, and Melbourne via Sydney. Tasmania through Tasrail owns and operates a government freight only service since 2009.

15. State and city services are operated by both government and private companies. These include V/Line (regional trains and buses in Victoria (Vic)); Metro Trains Melbourne operates the Melbourne rail network; RailCorp runs passenger rail services in NSW, including Sydney Trains and Country Link; Queensland Rail (QR) operates the City train network, SE Queensland passenger network Translink, and Transwa operates train and bus services in Western Australia.

High Speed Rail in Australia has been under investigation since the 1980s. The Australian Government has undertaken a study of implementation of high speed rail on the east coast of Australia, linking Melbourne, Canberra, Sydney, and Brisbane. A feasibility study into the project began in 2010. Perth and the Gold Coast have light rail systems with one planned for Canberra.

V. Australian Transport Safety Bureau

16. The Australian Transport Safety Bureau (ATSB) contributes to transport safety by independently investigating, analysing, and openly reporting on transport safety matters.[8] The ATSB was established by the *Transport Safety Investigation Act* 2003 (Cth) and conducts its investigations in accordance with the Act's provisions which allow the ATSB to investigate transport safety matters in the aviation, marine, and rail transport modes within the Australian Government's jurisdiction.[9]

Under the *Transport Safety Investigation Act*, it is not a function of the ATSB to apportion blame or provide a means for determining liability. The ATSB does not investigate for the purpose of taking administrative, regulatory, or criminal action. The independence of the ATSB is integral to the Bureau's safety investigations. The Act allows the ATSB to investigate transport safety matters in aviation, marine, and rail transport modes within the Australian Government's jurisdiction. The Act contains powers for the release of transport safety information, including investigation reports that detail the findings and significant factors that led to a particular safety occurrence.

The ATSB is a member of key safety bodies which include the International Transportation Safety Association, the International Society of Air Safety Investigators, the Flight Safety Foundation, and the Marine Accident Investigators' International Forum.

---

8. *See* website www.atsb.gov.au.
9. *See* G. Heilbronn, *Aviation Regulation and Licensing* 101–123 (Thomson: Law Book Co 2008) for a detailed account of the ATSB's functions and powers in relation to air accident and safety investigation.

VI. Inland Waterways

17. The longest river system in Australia is the Murray-Darling that drains part of Qld, the major part of NSW, and a large part of Vic. It finally flows into an arm of the sea called Lake Alexandria, on the eastern side of the South Australian coast. The Murray is about 2,520 km long, and the Darling and Upper Darling are collectively about 2,000 km long. There are also other rivers of considerable size, including those of the north-west coast of Australia, and rivers in the NT and Qld. The largest of the Australian lakes are drainage sumps for its rivers. There are, however, many other types. Australia is affected by both droughts and floods which impact upon the inland waterways. With south-eastern Australia containing about 75% of the nation's population, droughts affecting this region have a severe effect on the economy. Widespread flood rainfall is particularly common in the north and eastern coastal areas and is most economically damaging along the eastern uplands eastward towards the seaboard of Qld and NSW. Floods also occur in the great Fitzroy and Burdekin river basins of Qld, and the Murray itself is often affected by flood rains. As a consequence of these natural conditions and the location of the population and port facilities, most of Australia's inland waterways are not used for transport and traffic is essentially that of private recreational craft.

VII. Airports and Civil Aviation

18. Airports are all now privatized or held by local authorities or locally based boards. In 1990, the Federal Government deregulated the domestic airline market. This market is currently dominated by three companies, Qantas, Jetstar, and Virgin Airlines, all of which also operate international airlines. Tiger Airlines is a minor domestic operator.

VIII. Pipelines

19. Natural gas pipelines are some of the more significant in Australia. These include those running from Bunbury to Dampier through the Perth and Carnarvon Basins in WA; from the Amadeus Basin, near Alice Springs, to Darwin in the NT; from the Cooper Basin near Moomba in SA to Adelaide and Whyalla, and from there also to the NSW coast; and from Wallumbilla to Brisbane and Gladstone. In general, infrastructure investment in the gas industry has been small except for the construction of the North-West Shelf to Perth pipeline in the early 1980s and the Moomba pipeline in 1976. The construction of the North-West Shelf to Perth pipeline in the early 1980s has been followed by a large export contract for liquefied gas from the North-West Shelf to China.[10] The pipeline systems carry crude oil (2,500 km);petroleum products (500 km); natural gas (5,600 km). Water is carried

10. For current energy statistics (including gas) *see* Australian Bureau of Statistics at www.abs.gov.au.

in pipelines; Perth to Kalgoorlie-Goldfields Water Supply Scheme; Morgan on the Murray River to Adelaide, Wyalla, Port Lincoln; Waranga Western Channel, near Colbainabbin to Bendigo and Ballarat-Goldfields Superpipe. Other completed water pipelines in Vic link the Goulburn River to Melbourne, Melbourne to Geelong, Wimmera to Malle and the Hamilton-Grampians pipeline.

Part I. Introduction

§1. Institutions Regulating the Transport System

I. The Department of Transport and Regional Development

20. The Department of Transport and Regional Services administers the Government's domestic and international aviation policies. Previously the Department of Transport and Communications, it has taken on functions of regional development also.[11]

II. The Australian Transport Advisory Council

21. This comprises the Commonwealth, State, and Territory ministers responsible for transport, roads, marine, and ports matters. Its main role is to review and coordinate particular aspects of transport policy, development, and administration. It does this through biannual meetings, initiating discussion, and reports on issues raised by members. It thereby provides advice on policies which will promote better coordination and development of transport in Australia.

III. The Bureau of Transport and Communications, Economics

22. This is a centre for applied economic research in the Department of Transport and Regional Services.[12] It undertakes research to contribute to greater understanding of these industries. It is particularly concerned with the factors influencing the efficiency and growth of the transport and communications sectors, and the development of effective transport and communications policies. It has been involved in a number of matters recently, including studies of the international air industry and shipping reform.

IV. Australian Maritime Safety Authority

23. Established under the *Australian Maritime Safety Authority Act* 1990 (Cth), it is responsible for maritime safety activities in Australia, and for providing the

11. For current Federal Government transport policy and information *see* www.dotars.gov.au.
12. *See* http://btre.gov.au.

Australian maritime navigational aids network. It operates the Maritime Rescue Coordination Centre, which coordinates major maritime search and rescue activities in Australian waters. It is also responsible for pollution prevention and clean-up, and for the registration of Australian ships.[13]

V. Australian Transport Safety Bureau

24. The ATSB contributes to transport safety by independently investigating, analysing, and openly reporting on transport safety matters.[14] The ATSB was established by the *Transport Safety Investigation Act* 2003(Cth) and conducts its investigations in accordance with the Act's provisions which allow the ATSB to investigate transport safety matters in the aviation, marine, and rail transport modes within the Australian Government's jurisdiction.[15]

Under the *Transport Safety Investigation Act*, it is not a function of the ATASB to apportion blame or provide a means for determining liability. The ATSB does not investigate for the purpose of taking administrative, regulatory, or criminal action. The Act contains powers for the release of transport safety information, including investigation reports that detail the findings and significant factors that led to a particular safety occurrence.

The ATSB is member of key safety bodies which include the International Transport Safety Association, the International Society of Air Safety Investigators, the Flight Safety Foundation, and the Marine Accident Investigators' International Forum.

VI. The National Transport Commission

25. Established as a result of legislation agreed at the Special Premiers Conference in 1991, the National Transport Commission (NTC) has responsibility for road vehicles, drivers, other road users, and related matters. It is concerned with developing uniformity in road transport law, and for improvements in road safety and transport efficiency. It is also concerned to see reductions in the cost of the administration of road transport. The Commonwealth has power to legislate in relation to interstate road transport pursuant to the trade and commerce power in the Constitution, section 51(i), subject to the restriction of section 92 that provides that trade and commerce between the States shall be absolutely free.

26. The Special Premiers Conference of 1991 envisaged the development of uniform and consistent road transport law by the Commission, to overcome the inconsistencies that different State and Territory legislation had brought. The Commission is created by the Act, together with the Ministerial Council for Road Transport

---

13. *See* www.amsa.gov.au.
14. *See* website www.atsb.gov.au.
15. *See* G. Heilbronn, *Aviation Regulation and Licensing* 101–123 (Law Book Co 2008) for a detailed account of the ATSB's functions and powers in relation to air accident and safety investigation.

(below). The Act, therefore, defines the legal status of the Commission and sets out its functions in relation to the Ministerial Council. Following legislation enacted for the Australian Capital Territory (ACT) by the Commonwealth, it was agreed that each of the States and the NT would pass legislation providing for the automatic repeal, amendment, or modification of existing legislation to avoid conflict with the Act. Other incidental powers were designed to ensure its further effective functioning. Until that time, however, the States and the NT will continue to exercise powers under their existing legislation.

VII. The Ministerial Council for Road Transport

27. The Ministerial Council, as created under the Act, is required to perform four main functions: it is required to consider and where appropriate disallow legislative proposals made by the Commission (within two months); it has the power to allow exemptions for certain jurisdictions from particular aspects of the package, which are known as Application and Emergency Orders; it is required to make decisions as to budget and funding; and it is required to oversee the administration of the legislation by the States and Territories.

VIII. The Australian Road Transport Advisory Committee

28. The Australian Road Transport Advisory Committee was established in April 1990 as part of continuing reforms to the road transport sector. Its role is to provide the Minister for Transport and Regional Services with direct industry-based advice on all aspects of the road transport industry. Its specialist advice also helps in the task of integrating road and rail with other types of transport.

IX. Austroads

29. Austroads is a national association of road and traffic authorities, which provides strategic direction for the development, management, and use of Australia's road system through consultation with stakeholders. It coordinates research, prepares guides and standards, and is concerned with improvements in and harmonization of practices within an agreed national policy framework.[16]

X. The Australian Road Research Board

30. The Australian Road Research Board is a non-profit making national group owned by the Department of Transport and Communications, the State and Territory authorities, and the Local Government Association. As well as conducting

16. *See* www.austroads.com.au.

research into all aspects of roads and their use, it also provides an information service to government in general, industry, educational and research organizations and the general public.

XI. The National Rail Corporation

31. The National Rail Corporation was established by the Commonwealth Government to achieve coordinated development of the national rail system, replacing the National Railways Commission which was established in 1983. In 1991 an agreement was made between the Commonwealth, NSW, Vic, Qld, and WA which was given effect by the *National Rail Corporation Agreement Act* 1992 (Cth). This Act set up the National Railway Corporation which took over the assets of the Australian National Railway Commission which were assets of the Commonwealth and other assets acquired by the company under the 1991 Agreement. The National Rail Corporation carried out its operations over the interstate network to Sydney, Melbourne, Brisbane, Perth, and Alice Springs. The great majority of the National Rail Corporation's shares were owned by the Commonwealth Government. This reflected that most of the shares transferred to the National Rail Corporation consisted of interstate rail freight operations of the Australian National Railways Commission. The National Rail Corporation was wound down and sold by the *Australian National Railways Commission Sale Act* 1997 (Cth) which repealed the *Australian National Railways Commission Act* 1983 (Cth). The 1997 Act provided for the assets of the Australian National Railway Commission to pass to the Commonwealth. While the Commonwealth does not have direct constitutional power over railways (other than for military purposes), it can acquire and construct railways in a State either by agreement or with its consent.

XII. Airservices Australia

32. The Civil Aviation Authority (CAA) was established by the *Civil Aviation Act* 1988 (Cth) which was set up to deal with the safety regulation of civil aviation in Australia and of Australian registered aircraft overseas. It also provided air traffic control, search and rescue, and other facilities to the industry. It was replaced by Airservices Australia (AA) in 1995 under the *Air Services Act* 1995 (Cth). The *Civil Aviation Legislation Amendment Act* 1995 (Cth)[17] transferred the assets, liabilities and staff to the new body. Airservices Australia continues to provide the functions of the CAA in a cost-effective way. Although it regards the safety of air navigation as its most important consideration, it is also required to act in a manner that ensures, as far as practicable, that the environment is protected from the effects of aircraft operations. There are three operating divisions: Air Traffic Services, Rescue and Fire Fighting Service, and Facilities Management. There are also five support divisions.

---

17. For a detailed description of AA and its administrative and legal status *see* G. Heilbronn, *Aviation Regulation and Licensing* 54–57 (Law Book 2008).

XIII. Civil Aviation Safety Authority

33. The Civil Aviation Safety Authority (CASA) established in July 1995 by the *Civil Aviation Act* 1988 (Cth) is the most important aviation safety regulatory body in Australia. It shares with Airservices Australia AA most of the functions previously carried out by the now defunct CAA and the Federal Airports Corporation (FAC) which CASA and AA replaced in 1995 under the responsibility of the relevant Commonwealth department. This is now the Department of Infrastructure, Transport, Regional Development, and Local Government which retains more or less direct powers over air accident investigation and aviation security. In 2007, CASA acquired the regulatory authority that AA previously exercised over airspace, and CASA now exercises regulatory supervision over most AA functions, importantly airports and air traffic control. CASA has taken over the only remaining regulatory role that AA previously exercised in airspace regulation and administration. As a result, CASA has been responsible since mid-2007 for designation of air routes and controlled and prohibited areas.[18]

XIV. The International Air Services Commission

34. This body was set up under the *International Air Services Commission Act* 1992 (Cth). It is an independent body with the duty of allocating international aviation capacity and route entitlements among Australian international carriers. The Commission works with wide-ranging public benefit criteria set by the Minister for Transport and Regional Services. In 2003, the Federal Government made changes to the *International Air Services Commission Act* 1992 (Cth) and issued new regulations. The Minister also issued a new policy statement to the Commission. The main aim of the new regulations was to:

(a) make the object of the Act focus more strongly on competition benefits; and
(b) speed up decision-making by providing for the delegation of Commission powers and functions to an officer of the Department of Transport and Regional Services (the delegate) in circumstances set out in the regulations.

Under these arrangements, the delegate can make a range of determinations previously made by the Commission. However, the more complex matters continue to be dealt with by the Commission.[19]

---

18. For a detailed description of CASA's administrative context and legal status *see* G. Heilbronn, *Aviation Regulation and Licensing* 45–53 (Law Book Co 2008).
19. The object of the *International Air Services Commission Act* 1992 (Cth) is to promote economic efficiency through competition in the provision of international air services resulting in: (1) increased responsiveness by airlines to the needs of consumers, including an increased range of choices and benefits; (2) growth in Australian tourism and trade; and (3) the maintenance of Australian carriers capable of competing effectively with airlines of foreign countries. For the IASC website *see* www.iasc.gov.au.

§2. OUTLINE OF CHAPTERS

35. Chapter 1 provides a concise account of carriage of goods by sea. The contractual arrangements provided by demise, time, and voyage charter parties are illustrated by reference to standard clauses litigated over time and put in the context of common shipping practice. The principal features of bills of lading are outlined and the main issues confronting the shipper, the carrier, and the consignee are dealt with. The problem of third-party liability under a bill of lading is appraised in the light of key cases. The provisions of the Hague-Visby Rules enacted in Australian municipal law by the *Carriage of Goods by Sea Act* 1991(Cth) are noted as modernizing the Australian maritime carriage liability regime. The chapter concludes with a summary of statutory provisions governing the regulation of overseas liner shipping by the Commonwealth.

36. Chapter 2 concisely reviews aspects of the general law relating to shipping which deals with the operation of maritime vessels. The chapter gives the constitutional context of the role and powers of the Commonwealth to regulate shipping. Shipping registration and the coverage of the *Shipping Registration Act* 1981(Cth) are noted, as is the right of shipowners, managers, operators, and salvors to limit their liability. Marine pollution, which has increased both in its potential for environmental and economic loss, is largely regulated by a range of international conventions to which Australia is party. The National Plan to Combat Pollution of the Sea by Oil 1973 provides a coordination of Commonwealth and State resources to deal with specific oil pollution threats and actual spills. Collision is governed by international convention given effect by the *Navigation Act* 2012(Cth). Salvage, apart from some statutory provisions, is generally regulated by private standard form agreements.

37. Admiralty law is only briefly summarized regarding its provisions dealing with actions against vessels under the *Admiralty Act* 1988 (Cth).This reform in Australian admiralty law replaced and repealed the *Colonial Courts of Admiralty Act* 1890 (Imp) and provided a more modern statute and much needed reform.

38. Chapter 3 deals with carriage by road. The law of carriage by road is regulated by standard form contracts between the parties and increasingly, by Federal legislation and enacted international conventions. In the early law of carriage, the position of the common carrier was crucial. Although the common carrier has ceased to exist for all practical purposes in the regime of land, sea, and air transport, the distinction between common and private carriers has moulded the law significantly. Modern standard form contracts provide a detailed framework for the law of carriage and the rules governing such contracts are those that apply to standard form contracts and exemption clauses. The general position is that once the courts accept a document as contractual in nature and its terms protect the carrier from a range of liabilities, then the consignee will normally bear the risks of carriage. However, statute has made inroads into this principle, particularly in relation to consumer protection under the *Competition and Consumer Act* 2010 (Cth).

39. The impact of Federal legislation on road transport has been significant. This is illustrated by the *Interstate Road Transport Act* 1985 (Cth), the *Interstate Road Transport Charges Act* 1985 (Cth), the *National Road Transport Commission Act* 1991 (Cth), the *Road Charges (ACT) Act* 1993 (Cth), and the *Road Transport Reform(Vehicles and Traffic) Act* 1991 (Cth).The development of the Uniform Road Transport Law on a cooperative basis between the Federal, State, and Territory Governments is accordingly set out. The laws of the States and Territory are referenced to Laws of Australia: Transport.

40. Chapter 4 provides an account of the law of rail carriage. The role of the Commonwealth was strengthened by the creation of the National Railways Commission in 1983 and its successor, the National Rail Corporation (since wound down) with increased power to the Commonwealth as a result of the *National Rail Corporation Agreement* Act 1992 (Cth), a cooperative agreement between the Commonwealth Government and the States. In 1998 the Australian Rail Track Corporation (ARTC) was formed which took over the National Rail Corporation. As a result the Commonwealth has retreated from direct rail management in Australia.

41. Chapter 5 is concerned with the framework of air carriage law, with particular reference to the provisions of the amended *Warsaw Convention* implemented to establish various liability regimes by the Commonwealth and related State legislation. The position of the air carrier is detailed with reference to the issues of liability for loss of and damage to cargo (including baggage), delay, wilful misconduct, required air ticket and waybill provisions, and time limits for claims. Air carriage, while still in its technological infancy, was subjected to an early attempt to secure uniformity of law affecting the liability of air carriers to passengers and shippers in the shape of the *International Convention for the Unification of Certain Rules relating to International Carriage by Air (Warsaw Convention* Warsaw 1929. Since then the law governing air carriage has grown in coverage and complexity. These developments in Australia have occurred against a background of transport deregulation, including the domestic airline system, the rise of the international airline' megacarriers' and national economic reform in general.

42. The *Civil Aviation (Carrier's Liability Act* 1991(Cth) ratified the Montreal Protocols Three and Four. These Protocols raised the limit of a carrier's liability to international carriage of passengers by air and cargo and registered baggage. In relation to liability for passenger injury and death, which has seen much litigation, the position has changed radically with the adoption by a large number of International Air Transport Association (IATA) carriers (including Qantas) of the Intercarrier Agreement on Passenger Liability and the supplemental agreement to it outlined in the chapter.

Part II. Maritime Law

Chapter 1. Carriage by Sea

§1. General

43. The carriage of goods by sea may be conducted by adopting one of two courses. The first course is that the services of a ship and its crew may be chartered for a specified time or voyage and arrangement made for the carriage of goods by that ship. This hire of services is often loosely referred to as 'the hire of the ship', an expression more accurately confined to demise charter parties.[20] Second, and more commonly, the cargo owner may seek space in a general ship, that is, one which will carry the goods of all who so wish, and they will generally employ a forwarding agent to find the space.[21] The forwarding agent will arrange this with a loading broker acting on behalf of a shipowner or, where the ship is under charter, on behalf of the charterer.[22] Although not normally in possession of the goods, the forwarding agent will often arrange for them to be placed on board the ship, taking in return from the master a mate's receipt, which will be subsequently exchanged for the document of title (a bill of lading), again issued by the master. The bill of lading, as a document of title, may be sold several times over while the goods are in transit, thereby altering the relationship of the various parties concerned in the transaction. It is necessary to pay careful attention to the times of passing of property and of risk and the need to insure the goods.[23]

20. *See Tankexpress A/S v. Compagnie Financière Belges des Petroles SA* [1949] AC 76 [[1949] 2 All ER 939], considered in *Empresa Cubana de Fletes v. Lagonisi Shipping Co Ltd* [1971] 1 QB 488 [[1971] 2 WLR 221; [1971] 1 All ER 193; [1971] 1 Lloyd's Rep 7] (CA), applied in *Mardorf Peach & Co Ltd v. Attica Sea Carriers Corporation of Liberia (The Laconia)* [1976] QB 835 [[1976] 2 WLR 668; [1976] 2 All ER 249; [1976] Lloyd's Rep 395] (CA). Less usually, where the master and crew are to be agents of the charterer the contract will be for the hire or demise of the ship as opposed to its services only. *See also* S. Boyd, S. Berry, A. Burrows, B. Eder, D. Foxton & C. Smith, *Scrutton on Charterparties and Bills of Lading* [A28]–[A29] (21st ed., Sweet & Maxwell 2008).
21. *Heskell v. Continental Express Ltd* [1950] 1 All ER 1033 (KB); *Texada Mines Pty Ltd v. The Afovos* (1972) 46 ALJR 476 [[1974] 2 Lloyd's Rep 168] (HC).
22. Bill of lading '[A] document issued by a shipping company recording particulars of a contract for the carriage of goods by sea. It serves three purposes: (a) it serves as receipt of goods carried; (b) it is a contract to carry goods; and (c) it is a document of title to the goods': *The CCH Macquarie Dictionary of Law* (rev ed., (1990)), 20.
23. *See* generally K.C.T. Sutton, *Sales and Consumer Law in Australia and New Zealand* Ch. 26 (3d ed., LBC 1983).

44. A sea carrier's common law obligations are of limited relevance because liability is governed in practice by contract and statute. At common law a shipowner who carries goods is absolutely bound to provide a seaworthy ship at the commencement of the voyage,[24] to proceed on the voyage with reasonable despatch[25] and without unreasonable deviation.[26] It is not clear whether a carrier by sea is absolutely liable to deliver goods at the port of destination in exactly the condition it received them, subject to recognized defences at common law, or whether a carrier is liable only to exercise due care and diligence. Much will depend on whether or not the shipowner is a common carrier. In such a case, the carrier is absolutely liable. A common carrier must engage regularly in the carriage trade for reward, employing its ship, or at least part of it, as a general ship. It is not clear whether a carrier must ply regularly between fixed places or whether it should habitually carry for the public. Part of the difficulty in determining the nature of a sea carrier's liability originates in doubt as to whether a sea carrier can be sued for refusing to take goods offered to it as in the case of a common carrier, and whether in the absence of such a liability the shipowner's liability for carriage is similar to that of a common carrier.[27] The common law defences – act of God, loss caused by the monarch's enemies, inherent vice, defective packing, loss due to sacrifice (such as a jettison of cargo to save the common venture) – were limited and could be denied if a shipowner contributed to the loss or damage by negligence,[28] deviation,[29] or by providing an unseaworthy ship.[30]

24. *Steel v. State Line Steamship Co* (1877) 3 App Cas 72; *Hyman v. Nye* (1881) 6 QBD 685, J. Mathews at 690. *See also Hong Kong Fir Shipping Co Ltd v. Kawasaki Kisen Kaisha Ltd* [1962] 2 QB 26 [[1961] 2 WLR 716; [1961] 2 All ER 257; [1961] 1 Lloyd's Rep 159] (CA), L.J. Diplock at 71. The statutory modification of this obligation requires due diligence only. *see Carriage of Goods by Sea Act 1991*(Cth) s. 17. *See also* S. Garvin, *Exempting Clauses and the Obligation to Provide a Seaworthy Vessel at Common Law* [2004] LMCLQ 29.
25. *Anglo-Saxon Petroleum Co Ltd v. Adamastos Shipping Co Ltd* [1957] 2 QB 233 (CA) (reversed on other grounds in *Adamastos Shipping Co Ltd v. Anglo-Saxon Petroleum Co Ltd* [1959] AC 133); *Universal Cargo Carriers Corporation v. Citati* [1957] 2 QB 401 [[1957] 2 WLR 713; [1957] 2 All ER 70]. Note that the master's utmost despatch is typically a requirement under a time charter party: *see* Baltic and International Maritime Council *BIMCO Uniform Time-Charter (as revised 2001) (Baltime 1939)*(BIMCO 2001) Cl. 9 *see* http://www.bimco:Association of Ship Brokers and Agents (USA) Inc, *New York Produce Exchange Form (NYPE 93)*(ASBA, 1993) Cl. 8(a) *see* http://www.bimco.org.
26. *Scaramanga & Co v. Stamp* (1880) 5 CPD 295 (CA).
27. *See Belfast Ropework Co v. Bushell* [1918] 1 KB 210, J. Bailhache at 212; *Hill v. Scott* [1895] 2 QB 371, C.J. Lord Russell at 376. *See Liver Alkali Co v. Johnson* (1948) LR 9 Ex 338, J. Brett at 344. It has been doubted that there are now any common carriers left and if the distinction is of any present validity or relevance. *See* G. McBain, *Time to Abolish the Common Carrier*, JBL 545, 591–596 (2005).
28. *The Freedom v. Simmonds* (1871) LR 3 PC 594; *Notara v. Henderson* (1872) LR 7 QB 225. Act of God '[An] unforeseeable and/or irresistible action of natural forces, such as to exclude any human responsibility for loss suffered. Examples to include tornado, tidal wave, high water, flood and earth movement' *The CCH Macquarie Dictionary of Law* (rev ed., CCH 1996), 4.
29. *Internationale Guano v. MacAndrew* [1909] 2 KB 360; *James Morrison & Co Ltd v. Shaw Savill & Albion Co Ltd* [1916] 2 KB 783 (CA); *Davis v. Garrett* (1830) 6 Bing 716 [130 ER 1456]. But *see Hain Steamship Co Ltd v. Tate & Lyle Ltd* [1936] 2 All ER 597 (HL); *Trade & Transport Incorporated v. Iino Kaiun Kaisha Ltd (The Angelia)* [1973] 1 WLR 210 [[1973] 2 All ER 144] (QB).
30. *Lyon v. Mells* (1804) 5 East 428 [102 ER 1134]; *Steel v. State Line Steamship Co* [1877] 3 App Cas 72. *see* Lord Cairns at 77, L.J. Blackburn at 86; *Connor v. Spence* (1878) VLR 812 at 819.

45. A shipowner may expressly limit its liability by contract, subject to implied duties under the contract. It is customary for a shipowner to include in a contract the common law defences but, given the wide range of standard contractual exceptions, a shipowner's obligations are said to have been reduced to merely receiving the freight.[31] A shipowner may exclude liability for loss or damage caused by strikes,[32] perils of the sea,[33] and even negligence of itself and its crew.[34] However, a carrier may lose the benefit of the exceptions where it is in breach of its implied duties under the contract of affreightment[35] to provide a seaworthy ship,[36] to proceed without unreasonable delay,[37] and not to deviate.[38]

46. The liability of a sea carrier has been significantly modified by statute. By virtue of their superior bargaining power, shipowners were often able to reduce their liabilities so as to effectively reverse the common law relationship between shipper and carrier.[39] Essentially, the shipper could either ship the goods on the terms offered or not at all. An additional problem was that the usefulness of bills of lading was reduced by their varied and complex characters and by their restricted usefulness to third parties.

Following legislative reform in the United States,[40] an attempt to overcome these difficulties resulted in the recommendation by an international conference at Brussels in 1924 of a uniform set of rules for the carriage of goods by sea, commonly

---

31. But *see Empresa Cubana de Fletes v. Lagonisi Shipping Co Ltd* [1971] 1 QB 488 [[1971] 2 WLR 221; [1971] 1 All ER 193; [1971] 1 Lloyd's Rep 7] (CA), J. Donaldson at 494.
32. *See Williams Bros (Hull) Ltd v. WH Naamlooze Vennootschap WM Berghuys Kolenhandel* (1915) 21 Com Cas 253, Sankey at 257; *J Vermaas' Scheepvaartbedrijf NV v. Assoc Technique de l'Importation Charbonniere (The Laga)* [1966] 1 Lloyd's Rep 582 (QB). But *see Caltex Oil (Australia) Pty Ltd v. Howard Smith Industries Pty Ltd* [1973] 2 NSWLR 89 [[1973] 1 Lloyd's Rep 544] (CA).
33. *Thomas Wilson, Sons & Co v. Owners of the Cargo of The Xantho* (1887) 12 App Cas 503; *Charles Goodfellow Lumber Sales Ltd v. Verreault, Hovington & Verreault Navigation Inc.* [1971] 1 Lloyd's Rep 185 (SC Can).
34. *See* K. Sutton, *Sales and Consumer Law* Ch. 26 (4th ed., LBC Information Services 1995); F. Hannah & R. Grime, *Sea Carriage Documents* in *Australian Maritime Law* [4.4]–[4.5.2] (M. White ed., 2d ed., The Federation Press 2000).
35. Contract of affreightment: 'A Contract Made by a Shipowner to Carry Goods for Payment': *The CCH Macquarie Concise Dictionary of Modern Law* (CCH 1988).
36. *Connor v. Spence* (1878) 4 VLR (L) 243; *Peyton, Dowling & Co v. Houlder Bros* (1890) 16 VLR 812 [12 ALT 121] (FC).
37. *M'Andrew v. Adams* (1834) 1 Bing NC 29 [130 ER 1028]; *Anglo-Saxon Petroleum Co Ltd v. Adamastos Shipping Co Ltd* [1957] 2 QB 233 (CA) (reversed on other grounds in *Adamastos Shipping Co Ltd v. Anglo-Saxon Petroleum Co Ltd* [1959] AC 133); *Suisse Atlantique Société d'Armement Maritime SA v. Rotterdamsche Kolen Centrale* [1967] 1 AC 361 [[1966] 2 WLR 944; [1966] 2 All ER 61; [1966] 1 Lloyd's Rep 533] (CA). *See also* Hague-Visby Rules, Art. 4 r. 4 (reproduced in Sch. 1 of the *Carriage of Goods by Sea Act* 1991 (Cth)); *Thiess Bros (Queensland) Pty Ltd v. Australian Steamships Pty Ltd* [1955] 1 Lloyd's Rep 459 (SC NSW).
38. *Southcote's Case* (1601) 4 Co 83b [76 ER 1061]; *Russell v. Niemann* (1864) 34 LJCP 10; *Duncan v. Koster (The Teutonia)* (1872) LR 4 PC 171; *Internationale Guano v. MacAndrew* [1909] 2 KB 360.
39. *See* F. Hannah & A. Phillipides, *Carriage of Goods by Sea*, in *Australian Maritime Law* [3.1] (M. White ed., 2d ed., Federation Press 2000).
40. *See Carriage of Goods by Sea Act 1893 Stat* (US) commonly known as the *Harter* Act which provided a model for the *Carriage of Goods by Sea Act* 1904 (Cth) (now repealed). *See* F. Hannah & A. Philipides (above) at [3.1] who suggested that one reason for the former British colonies such as

known as the *Hague Rules*.[41] However, dissatisfaction arose concerning issues such as the limitation of carrier's liability instanced by unit liability limits set in relation to boxes, bales or bundles, during a time when international trade was increasingly occurring through the use of standardized shipping containers.[42] As a result in 1968 the *Visby Rules*, amending the *Hague Rules* were signed.[43] These amended rules received further modification through the *SDR Protocol*,[44] which substituted 'francs' with 'Special Drawing Rights' (SDRs)[45] producing the *Amended Hague Rules*.[46]

The purpose of the *Hague-Visby Rules* is to establish a balance between the shipper and the shipowner, the latter being obliged to accept certain listed liabilities in return for enumerated qualifications on its liability. In this sense, the *Hague-Visby Rules* represent a compromise between the positions under common law and under contract.[47]

The *Hague-Visby Rules* have been given wide effect internationally and enacted into Australian domestic law (with some modification) in the *Carriage of Goods by Sea Act* 1991(Cth).[48]

I. Charter Parties

47. A contract of charter is known as a charter party. It will not necessarily contain terms which can be referred to a shipment of cargo. In other words, not all charter parties are contracts of carriage.[49] The main function of a charter party is to

---

Australia on attaining nationhood favouring the *Harter* Act was that these nations tended to have cargo-owning interests that did not coincide with the established ship-owning network of the UK and Europe. *See also* M. Davies & A. Dickey, *Shipping Law* 169 (3d ed., Lawbook Co 2004).

41. *International Convention for the Unification of Certain Rules of Law Relating to Bills of Lading (Hague Rules) (1924) 120 LNTS 187; [1956] ATS 2.* Australia adopted the *Hague Rules* by enacting the *Carriage of Goods by Sea 1924* (Cth) (now repealed).
42. *See* F. Hannah & A. Phillpides at [3.1].
43. Protocol to Amend the International Convention for the Unification of Certain Rules Relating to Bills of Lading (Visby Rules) (1968) 1412 UNTS 127: [193] ATS 23.
44. Protocol (SDR Protocol) Amending the International Convention for the Unification of Certain Rules of Law relating to Bills of Lading of 25 Aug. 1924 (Hague Rules) as Amended by the Protocol of 23 Feb. 1968(Visby Rules) (SDR Protocol) (1979) 1412 UNTS; [1993] ATS 23.
45. A 'Special Drawing Right' (SDR) is the unit of account of the International Monetary Fund (IMF). The SDR's value is derived from a weighted basket of major currencies containing the United States Dollar, the European Union Euro, the Japanese Yen, and the British Pound. The present value is updated on a daily basis at the IMF's website, *see* http://www.imf.org/external/np/fin/data/rms_five.aspx.
46. As the *Amended Hague Rules* do not fundamentally alter the liabilities of sea carriage participants compared with the *Hague-Visby Rules* judicial decisions discussing that *Hague-Visby Rules* remain generally accurate and current with the exception of liability changes introduced by the *SDR Protocol.*
47. *Gosse Millerd Ltd v. Canadian Government Merchant Marine Ltd (The Canadian Highlander)* [1929] AC 223, Viscount Sumner at 236.
48. *See Carriage of Goods by Sea Act* 1991(Cth), s. 4 (definition of 'amended Hague Rules'), ss 7–8, 10, Sch. 1-1A.
49. *See* generally S. Boyd, S. Berry, A. Burrows, B. Elder, D. Foxton & C. Smith, *Scrutton on Charterparties and Bills of Lading* [A28]–[30] (21st ed., Sweet & Maxwell 2008); S. Derrington, *Charterparties*, in *Australian Maritime Law* Ch. 6 (M. White ed., 2d ed., The Federation Press 2000); M. Davies & A. Dickey, *Shipping Law* Chs 13–14 (3d ed., Lawbook Co 2004).

obtain a vessel or its services for a number of uses by the charterer. In the event that a charterer requires a shipowner to carry cargo, the charter party usually includes the terms of carriage. Both common law and maritime codes, such as the Hague-Visby Rules, reproduced in Schedule 1 of the *Carriage of Goods by Sea Act* 1991 (Cth), classify a body of law by reference to the charter party, as it is a standard type of commercial contract.

48. Three principal types of charter party have been recognized by the courts.[50] These are:

(1) the demise or 'bareboat' charter which is in the nature of a lease whereby the charterer takes possession and control of the ship for an agreed period.[51] Here, the charterer assumes liability as a carrier if the charterer contracts to transport cargo for third persons and the charterer's liability will be determined by the individual contracts of shipment independently of the charter party;
(2) the voyage charter, where the exclusive use and services of the ship are obtained on designated voyages; and
(3) the time charter, which is similar to the voyage charter but expressed for a prescribed period.

A hybrid of a voyage and time charter party is what is commonly termed a 'mixed' charter party. Sometimes a charter in the form of a time charter party is expressed to be for a voyage or a round voyage. The effect may be to maintain the contract in the form of a time charter as the basis and method of payment by time with the essence of a voyage charter incorporated to make the prescribed voyage the main part of the contract, the length of time of the voyage being used to measure the period of chartered service and payment of chartered hire.[52] Alternatively, a charter party may be so drafted, in connection with consecutive voyages, to operate as a voyage rather than a time charter.[53] Such mixed charter parties may be regarded as a sub-category of voyage charters.[54]

49. Where a charterer wishes to reserve the ship for the carrying of its own cargo, the charter party will include terms dealing with the shipment. In such a case, the shipowner acts as a carrier and the charterer is cast in the role of the shipper. If the charterer subcontracts the ship to third parties, this subcontract will govern the relations between the charterer and the third parties. As an alternative arrangement,

50. *See* M. Davies & P. Anderson, *Bareboat Charters* (2d ed., Lloyds of London Press 2005). *See* P. Gram, *Chartering Documents* (Lloyd's of London Press 1981).
51. For a decision in which the scope and nature of demise charters was discussed *see Kaleej International Pty Ltd v. Gulf Shipping Lines Ltd* (1986) 6 NSWLR 569 (CA).
52. *Vsesojuznoje Objediheni Sovfracht v. Temple SS Co* (1945) 62 TLR 43 (HL), 45.
53. *See Anglo-Saxon Petroleum Co Ltd v. Adamastos Shipping Co Ltd* [1957] 2 QB 233. *See also* S. Derrington, *Charterparties*, in *Australian Maritime Law* [6.11] (M. White ed., 2d ed., The Federation Press 2000); S. Boyd, S. Berry, A. Burrows, B. Eder, D. Foxton & C. Smith, *Scrutton on Charterparties and Bills of Lading* [A28]–[A29] (21st ed., Sweet & Maxwell 2008).
54. For a detailed discussion of hybrid charters *see* L. Gorton & R. Ihre, *A Practical Guide to Contracts of Affreightment and Hybrid Contracts* (Lloyd's of London Press 1986).

the shipper may reserve space for cargoes over prescribed routes or periods under a contract of affreightment.[55] Charter is commonly used where liner services are unsuitable, either because the destination is not travelled to regularly by the liners concerned, or the cargo is not suited to general carriage. Since Australia is economically dependent on revenue from bulk shipments of oil, ore, and grain, it is significant that these are usually shipped under charter for the reasons given in the preceding sentence.

§2. Demise Charter Parties

50. A demise charter party is the effective lease of a ship by a charterer.[56] This occurs when the shipowner provides the charterer with full possession and control of the vessel.[57] The charterer assumes liability as a carrier (if the charterer contracts to transport cargo for third persons) and the charterer's liability will be determined by the individual contracts of shipment independent of the charter party. Although this form of charter party is generally uncommon in contracts of carriage by sea, it may occur for particular purposes such as financing the charterer's purchase of the vessel.[58]

Occasionally a distinction may be drawn between a charter by demise of a ship without master and crew (called a 'bareboat charter party') and a demise charter party that includes the services of the master and crew (although there is a tendency for the terms to be used interchangeably). In the case of bareboat charter parties a

55. Contract of affreightment: 'A Contract Made by a Shipowner to Carry Goods for Payment': *The CCH Macquarie Concise Dictionary of Modern Law* (Sydney, 1996), 7. *See* M. Davies & A. Dickey, *Shipping Law* 342 (3d ed., Law Book Co 2004), 'Strictly speaking, any contract for the carriage of goods is a contract of affreightment. In practice, though, the expression is mainly used to describe a contract of such large quantities of goods that several voyages are needed.' The authors give example of a specialized standard form contract of affreightment: *see* now Baltic and International Maritime Council, *BIMCO Standard Contract of Affreightment for the Transportation of Bulk Dry Cargoes (GENCOA)*(BIMCO, 2004 (available at http://www.bimco.org).

56. S. Boyd, S. Berry, A.A. Burrows, B. Eder, D. Foxton & C. Smith, *Scrutton on Charterparties and Bills of Lading* [A28] (21st ed., Sweet & Maxwell 2008); S. Derrington, *Charterparties*, in *Australian Maritime Law* [6.4] (M. White ed., 2d ed., The Federation Press 2000); M. Davies & A. Dickey, *Shipping Law* 42 (3d ed., Lawbook Co 2004). *See also* M. Davies & P. Anderson, *Bareboat Charters* (2d ed., Lloyd's of London Press 2005). On construction of demise charterparties *see Strang Patrick Stevedoring Pty Ltd v. Owners of MV 'Stetten'* (1992) 38 FCR 501. *See also Ship Hako Endeavour v. Programmed Total Marine Services Pty Ltd* [2013] FCAFC 21 where Rares & Buchanan JJ at [56] cited Lord Herschell LC in *The Baumwell Manufactuing Von Carl Scheiber v. Christopher Furness* [1893] AC 8 at 14 who explained 'that the use of the word "demise" is descriptive of the plenary ambit of those rights in which the charterer has become … during the terms of the charter, the owner of the vessel, when one is considering the rights and liabilities which arise from the acts of the master, and the crew of the vessel, who during that time are the servants of the charterer, appointed and paid by him.' *See* S. Baughen, *Summerskill on Laytime* (5th ed., Sweet & Maxwell 2013).

57. *Baumwell Manufacturing Von Carl Scheiber v. Furness* [1892] 1 253(CA), Lord Esher MR at 259 (affirmed by *Baumwell Manufacturing Von Carl Scheiber v. Furness* [1893]8), *Australasian Steam Navigation co Ltd v. Shipping Control Board* (1945) 71 CLR 508, Latham CJ at 521, *Laemthong International Lines Co Ltd v. BPS Shipping Ltd* (1997) 190 CLR 181, 72 ALJR 129, 149 ALR 675, J. Toohey at 192 (CLR).

58. M. Davies & A. Dickey, *Shipping Law* 42 (3d ed., Lawbook Co 2004).

commonly used standard form is the *BIMCO Standard Bareboat Charter (Barecon 2001)*.[59]

In either case, a key distinction between demise (whether bareboat or otherwise) and time charter parties is that demise charter parties do not contain an off hire clause: the charterer is obliged to pay hire for the full term of the charter.[60] As a demise charter party places the ship under the complete control and possession of the charterer, standard form charter parties are carefully worded to place the full obligations of operating the vessel on the charterers.[61]

> In *Socoft Stream v. CMC (Australia) Pty Ltd* [2001] (FCA) 961, the vessel's owner gave notice to the charterer Sovcomflot on default of payment of hire to re-deliver the vessel to a safe port to be nominated by the owner. The vessel subsequently took on cargo in Singapore and Malaysia. The vessel was later arrested by the owner in Brisbane. On the issue of whether there had been a failure to deliver within a reasonable dispatch on appeal to the Federal Court it was held that delay by the arrest of the vessel was material. CMC was entitled to treat the delay as unreasonable, and make its own arrangements to transport the cargo from Brisbane by other means. The charterers Sovcomflot had created the delay occasioned by the arrest even though this had an adverse effect on CMC, the owner of the goods.[62]

---

59. *See* Baltic and international Maritime Council, *BIMCO Standard Bareboat Charter (Barecom 2001)* (BIMCO 2001) at http://www.bimco.org. *See also* R. Barnes, 'Barecon 2001, *Barecon 2001* Bareboat Charter Revisited' [2002] LMCLQ 528.
60. *Barecon 2001* Cl. 11(b) provides that '[h]ire shall be paid continuously throughout the Charter Period'.
61. Compare *Barecon 2001*, Cl. 10(b) with Baltic and International Maritime Council, *BIMCO Uniform Time-Charter (as revised 2001) (Baltime 1939)* (BIMCO, 2001) Cl. 9 at http://www.bimco.org and Association of Ship Brokers and Agents (USA) Inc, *New York Produce Exchange Form* (NYPE 93) 9ASBA, 1993) Cl. 8(a) at http://www.bimco.org. *See* A. Stewart, *The Owner's Vulnerability to the Liability of the Demise Charterer*, 29(2) Austl & NZ Mar LJ 85 (2015).
62. *Socoft Stream v. CMC (Australia) Pty Ltd* [2001] FCA 961, Ryan, Tamberlin & J.J. Conn at [75]. *See* earlier action in the Federal Court: *CMC (Aust) Ltd v. Socoft Stream* [2000] FCA 1681. J. Mason at [67] holding that 'where the charter party authorized the master to sign the bill of lading without prejudice to the charterparty, it operated as a mere receipt for the goods or as a document of title and had no impact on the charterparty' citing *Sanko Steamship Co Ltd v. Sumitomo Australia Ltd [No 2]* (1995) 63 FCR 227. J. Sheppard at 267. On the implied term of a contract of goods by sea that the vessel will proceed between ports of loading and discharge with reasonable dispatch *see* [74] of the FCA appeal judgment *Socoft Stream v. CMC (Australia Pty Ltd* [2001] FCA 961. Ryan, Tamberlin & J.J. Conn at [74] citing *Fyffes Group Ltd v. Reefer Express Lines Pty Ltd (The Krti Rex)* [1996] 2 Lloyd's Rep 171, Moore-Back at 191. *See* F.D. Rose (ed.), *International and Commercial Law Year Book 2010* (Lloyd's List Law 2010) p. 1 for comment on termination of a demise charter in *APc Marine Pty Ltd v. APC Aussie 1* [2009] FCA 690.

§3. VOYAGE CHARTER PARTIES

I. 'Gencon' Provisions

51. Voyage charter parties are often entered into on standard terms. These standard form documents such as the 'Gencon'[63] voyage charter may be amended by the parties so that only general principles can be laid down. The following provisions are found in most voyage charter parties:

(1) the shipowner agrees to provide a ship and states her position, capacity, and class on the register;
(2) the shipowner promises that the ship will proceed with reasonable despatch;
(3) the shipowner undertakes that the ship is seaworthy;
(4) the shipowner undertakes to carry the goods to their destination;
(5) the charterer agrees to provide a full cargo;
(6) the charterer agrees to pay freight;
(7) Excepted perils are listed;
(8) the manner of loading and discharge is laid down with particular reference to time for these operations, and the rate of demurrage;
(9) the charterer is given the right to cancel the contract if the ship does not arrive at a certain port on a given date;
(10) a clause incorporating the Hague-Visby Rules (reproduced in Schedule 1 of the *Carriage of Goods by Sea Act* 1991 (Cth)), known as a 'general paramount clause';
(11) the amended 'Jason' clause, concerning general average;[64]
(12) a 'both to blame' collision clause;
(13) an arbitration clause;[65]

63. *See* generally M. Davies & A. Dickey, *Shipping Law* (3d ed., Lawbook Co 2004) Ch. 13, S. Derrington, *Charterparties*, in *Australian Maritime Law* [6.3.1]–[6.3.16] (M. White ed., 2d ed., The Federation Press 2000); J. Cooke, T. Young, J. Kimball, D. Martowski & L. Lambert, *Voyage Charters* (3d ed., Informa 2007). *See* Baltic and International maritime Council, *Uniform General Charter (as revised 1922, 1976, and 1994 (Gencom))* (BIMCO, 1994) *see* http://www.bimco.org. In *Dampskibsselskabet Norden v. A/S v. Gladstone Civil Pty Ltd* [2013] FCAFC 109 it was held that the voyage charter party in the case at issue was not a sea carriage document for the purposes of the *Carriage of Goods by Sea Act 1991*(Cth) s. 11(a) (*see* 189, 108). In relation to the settlement of disputes, including charter parties by arbitration that policy was upheld by the HCA in *TLC Air Conditioner (Zhongshan) Co Ltd v. The Judges of the Federal Court of Australia* (2013) 295 ALR 596 at [10] and [45]. *See* the definition of a 'contract of carriage' in the *Sea Documents Act 1997* (NSW) s. 5. (*see* 204, 115–1160).

64. 'General average' is the proportionate bearing of all loss arising as a result of extraordinary sacrifices made or expenses incurred in preserving the ship and cargo: *See* S. Boyd, S. Berry, A. Burrows, B. Eder, D. Foxton & C. Smith, *Scrutton on Charterparties and Bills of Lading* [A1.34] (21st ed., Sweet & Maxwell 2008); J. Gilman & R. Merkin, *Arnold's Law of Marine Insurance* and Average (17th ed., Sweet & Maxwell 2008); J. Cooke & Cornah, *Lowndes and Rudolf: The Law of General Average and the York-Antwerp Rules* (13th ed., Sweet & Maxwell 2008). *See also Marine Insurance Act 1909*(Cth), 272.

The use of the general paramount clause in the 'Congenbill' is contemplated under Gencon Cl. 10.

65. *See* A Nair *A Note on Norden: Voyage Charterparties, the Hague Visby Rules and Enforcing Foreign Arbitration Awards*, 27(2) AANZMarLJ 90–95 (2013).

(14) a clause governing payment of commission to the broker for negotiating the charter party;
(15) a 'cesser' clause which purports to relieve the charterer from paying demurrage;[66] and
(16) a war clause.[67]

52. In a voyage charter party, the shipowner makes three implied undertakings: to provide a seaworthy ship for the voyage, to proceed without unjustifiable deviation, and to proceed with reasonable despatch. A ship must be seaworthy at the commencement of the voyage for that particular voyage and for the cargo carried.[68] A shipowner's duty to provide a seaworthy ship includes a duty to have its loading and discharging tackles available for the ordinary purposes of loading and discharging. This will be the case even where a charter party provides that stowing, trimming, and discharging are to be paid for by the charterers.[69] An express clause in a voyage charter party that the ship is to be 'tight, staunch, and strong, and in everyway fitted for the voyage' relates to the preliminary voyage to the port of loading. It refers to the time at which the contract is made,[70] or to the time of sailing from the port of loading. The express undertaking does not displace the undertaking implied by law (i.e., to provide a seaworthy ship for the voyage).[71]

In *STX Pan Ocean Co Ltd v. Bowen Basin Coal Group Pty Ltd (No2)* [2010] FCA 1240 STX entered into a contract in an Americanised Welsh Coal Charter (AMWELSH 93 form of charter party) for two voyage charters for each carrying coal of 42,000 tonnes from Kwinana in WA to ports in the People's Republic of China. Bowen Basin made a significant commercial loss on the first cargo and defaulted on payment of hire and demurrage to STX. After the second vessel had been at Kwinina ready to load for about one month STX terminated the charter party.

STX proceeded against Thomson, sole shareholder and director of Bowen Basin. The basis of STX's claim was that Thomson had allegedly represented, expressly or

---

66. Charter parties usually contain a clause to the effect that the charterer's liability shall cease on shipment of cargo.. It is usually inserted in consideration of the granting to the shipowner of a lien, which the shipowner would not otherwise have, on the cargo for demurrage and dead freight: *see Gencon* Cl. 8 In the absence of this clause a shipowner would not otherwise have a lien for these expenses: S. Boyd, S. Berry, A. Burrows, B. Eder, D. Foxton & C. Smith, *Scrutton on Charterparties and Bills of Lading* [A190]–[A191].[196] (21st ed., Sweet & Maxwell 2008). A cesser clause purports to relieve the charterer from paying demurrage, *see Scrutton* [A92]. To receive this protection the charterer would need to inert a cesser clause under *Gencon. See also* S. Baughen, *Charter party Bills of Lading-Cargo Interests' Liabilities to the Shipowner,* in *The Evolving Law and Practice of Voyage Charterparties* 217–250 (D. Rhidian Thomas ed., Informa 2009).
67. An express term is often included in a charter party providing for its variation or cancellation on the outbreak of war or some other contingency. On the meaning of 'an act of war'. *See Avery v. Bowden* (1856) 25 LJQB 49; *Kawasaki Kisen Kabushiki Kaisha v. Bantham Steamship Co Ltd (Hire)* [1939] 2 KB 544 [[1939] 1 All ER 819] (CA). *See Gencom* 17. *See* 78–81.
68. *Stanton v. Richardson* (1874) LR 9 CP 390.
69. *Hang Fung Shipping & Trading Co Ltd v. Mullion & Co Ltd* [1966] 1 Lloyd's Rep 511 (QB).
70. *Scott v. Foley* (1899) 5 Com Cas 53.
71. *Seville Sulphur & Copper Co v. Colvils* (1888) 25 SLR 437 (Sess. Ct). Exceptionally, an inference of unseaworthiness may be raised: *see Fiumana Società Di Navigazione v. Bunge & Co Ltd* [1930] 2 KB 47.

impliedly, he was ready to perform the charter party by providing cargoes under the charter party and pay freight and demurrage under its terms. In addition STX claimed that fraudulently Bowen Basin was ready, willing and able to perform its obligations under the charter party to induce STX to continue its tender of performance and not to exercise its then accrued rights to terminate for Bowen Basin's breaches.[72]

STX claimed that by making this representation Bowen Basin had engaged in conduct that was misleading or deceptive, or likely to do so, in breach of section 52(1) of the *Trade Practices Act 1974* (Cth).[73]

The Federal Court found that on the evidence provided it was not persuaded anyone in STX who made the decision to enter the charter party relied on anything beyond the written terms of the contract and STX's internal assessment of Bowen Basin's creditworthiness. Nor was the Court satisfied that the ready, willing, and able representation was made to STX. STX was prepared to take the commercial risk that Bowen Basin would earn sufficient from the sale of the two coal cargoes, or would be able to sub-charter or otherwise pay to meet its obligation.[74]

Rares J noted 'A shipowner is well aware of the likelihood of the possibility before entering a charterparty, that the charterer may default in payment of freight. That is why, as here, standard form charterparties like AMWELSH 93 (in Cl 21) or the NYPE 1046 form (in Cl 18) all provide for owners to have a lien on all cargoes, sub-freights and sub-hires for amounts due by the charterer. If the shipowner wants more protection he can negotiate appropriate terms to add to the charterparty'.[75]

53. The voyage must be completed without unjustifiable deviation. The terms of the voyage charter party often give the shipowner the right to call at ports off the ordinary trade route. A clause will normally give liberty to the vessel to tow or assist vessels, or both, in all situations, and to deviate for the purpose of saving life or property or both, and to comply with any orders given by the government of the nation under whose flag it sails, or by any other government.[76] It is also common for goods to be covered by item or floating policies under an Institute of London Underwriters clause (known as an 'Institute clause'), which holds the goods covered in the event of delay and deviation.[77] Voyage charter parties generally include a deviation clause which allows a limited right to deviate from the voyage route. A charter party normally stipulates that the vessel will also some other similar

72. 73 STX also relied on s. 51A of the *Trade Practices Act* 1974 (Cth) on the basis the representation at issue was with respect to future matters, Now *see Competition and Consumer Act* 2010 (Cth).
73. At [6] Rares J.
74. At [76] Rares J.
75. At [84] Rares J.
76. Clause 3. *See also Luigi Monta of Genoa v. Cechofracht Co* [1956] 2 QB 557 [[1956] 3 WLR 480; [1956] 2 All ER 769; [1956] 2 Lloyd's Rep 97].
77. *See* London Institute of Underwriters, *CLR382 Institute Cargo Clause A* (LIU 2009) Cl 8.3 at http://www.iua.co.uk. *See* D. Creamean, *Marine Insurance*, in *Australian Maritime Law* [5.4]–[5.9] (M. White ed., 2d ed., The Federation Press 2000). *See also Marine Insurance Act* 1909(Cth) s. 35.

expression. The common law obligation to be diligent is not generally extended by these stipulations.[78]

54. The principal implied undertaking by a charterer under a voyage charter party is that it will not ship dangerous goods.[79] A charterer will be liable for any loss or damage caused even by the master's acceptance of dangerous goods on board, unless the master has acted unreasonably in carrying them. A charter party may expressly prohibit the loading of dangerous goods, although an express term may entitle a charterer to load provided due notice is given to the master. Goods may be dangerous not only because they may create a danger to the vessel,[80] but also because they are liable to cause detention of the ship by authorities.[81]

II. The 'Near' Clause

55. An undertaking by a shipowner to perform a voyage is usually expressed in the charter party in terms of a 'near' clause in relation to the specified port for loading and discharging cargo. The 'near' clause is usually expressed in the following terms:

> [T]he said vessel shall proceed to … (loading port) or so near thereto as she may safely get and lie always afloat and there load … and being so loaded the vessel shall proceed to … (loading port) or so near thereto as she may safely get and lie always afloat and there deliver the cargo.[82]

A charterer is obliged to furnish the required orders to the ship's master to proceed within the time specified or within a reasonable time if none is specified. If a charterer does not give orders within the required time then the ship has to await orders until the delay is such to constitute frustration of the voyage. Until frustration occurs, the ship's master is not entitled to proceed to a port of the master's own

---

78. *Forest Oak Steam Shipping Co v. Richard* (1899) 5 Com Cas 100; *Nelson v. Dundee Shipping Co* [1907] This is typically under a time charter party; *see* Baltime and Maritime International Maritime Council. *BIMCO Uniform Time-Charter (as revised 2001) (Baltime 1939)*(BIMCO, 2001) Cl. 9 *see* http://www.bimco.org. Gencom Cl. 2 provides the shipowner with a wide exclusion of liability. *See* S. Baughen, *Does Deviation Still Matter*?, 2 LMCLQ 70 (1991).
79. '[D]angerous goods' are defined by the *Navigation Act* 2012 (Cth) to mean goods listed in the *International Maritime Dangerous Goods Code* (IMDG) issued by the International Maritime Organisation (IMO). *See* s. 14 and Division 4 ss B. *See also* P.E. King, *The Carriage of Dangerous and Nuclear Cargoes*, 86 ABLR 14 (1986).
80. *Micada Compania Naviera SA v. Texim* [1968] 2 Lloyd's Rep 57 (QB); *Health Stelle Mines v. The Erwin Schroeder* [1969] 1 Lloyd's Rep 370 (Ex Ct Can) (copper concentrate).
81. *Mitchell, Cotts & Co v. Steel Bros & Co Ltd* [1916] 2 KB 610 (rice cargo bound for port where discharge forbidden).
82. Baltic and International Maritime Council, *Uniform General Charter (Gencon)* (BIMCO 1994) Cl. 1 *see* http://www.bimco.org.

choice.[83] If a ship is required to proceed to a port of call for orders as to a port of discharge, and if at the port of call the charterer will only name a port that is impossible to get into, the charterer then commits a breach of contract. The shipowner, accordingly, on discharging the goods at the port of call, if that is a reasonable place for discharge, can claim freight under a quantum merit and damages for any detention of the ship at the port of call due to the charterer's refusal to nominate a proper port.[84] This rule will only apply if the port is impossible or subject to delay which will frustrate the commercial object of the undertaking. The charterer, in selecting a port, does not have to consider the shipowner's convenience.[85] The main purpose of the 'near' clause – 'or so near thereto as she may safely get and lie always afloat' – is to give the shipowner the option of refusing to proceed further than to a point where the vessel will not be in danger. It also entitles the shipowner to substitute an alternative destination. Thus, the clause qualifies the shipowner's duty to bring the vessel to an agreed place. A vessel, chartered to unload at a named port, dock, or berth, subject to such a clause, is bound to wait a reasonable time before adopting the alternative place of loading or discharge, if by waiting the vessel can enter the named location.[86] What constitutes a reasonable time is determined by commercial considerations and by the nature of the voyage in which the vessel is employed. In determining what would be reasonable from a commercial point of view, the interests of both parties have to be considered.[87]

56. The issues involved in assessing a 'near' clause hinge on foreseeability, the nature of the obstacle and an alternative port or ports. Questions arise as to whether the hindrance is known to the shipowner or could reasonably have been foreseen by the shipowner, and whether and to what extent it has a duty to inquire about the conditions of the port. Where the port, berth, or location is to be specified in the charter party, the shipowner is usually considered to be under a duty to ascertain the condition of the place before it undertakes to bring the vessel there. Where a shipowner had knowledge, actual or implied, of the obstacle or hindrance then it is doubtful whether the shipowner has the protection of the 'near' clause.[88] Where neither of the parties knew or ought to have known of the obstacle, a distinction should be made between charter parties with a clause designating a general area (such as 'East

83. *Zim Israel Navigation Co v. Tradex Export Co (The Timna)* [1970] 2 Lloyd's Rep 409 (QB). *See* S. Boyd, S. Berry, A. Burrows, B. Eder, D. Foxton & C. Smith, *Scrutton on Charterparties and Bills of Lading* [A69] (21st ed., Sweet & Maxwell 2008); M. Davies & A. Dickey, Shipping Law 282–288 (3d ed., Lawbook Co 2004).

84. *Aktieselskabet Olivebank v. Dansk Svoulsyne Fabrik* [1919] 2 KB 162 (CA).

85. *Dobell v. Green* [1900] 1 QB 526 (CA); *Bulman v. Fenwick* [1894] 1 QB 179 (CA); *Reardon Smith Line v. Ministry of Agriculture* [1962] 1 QB 42 [[1961] 3 WLR 110; [1961] 2 All ER 577; [1961] 1 Lloyd's Rep 385] (CA).

86. *See also Dahl v. Nelson* (1861) 6 App Cas 38; *Fornyade Rederiaktiebolaget Commercial v. Blake & Co (The Varing)* [1931] P 79 (CA). *See* S. Boyd, S. Berry, A. Burrows, B. Eder, D. Foxton & C. Smith (above) [A 69].

87. *The Athamas v. Dig Vijay Cement Co* [1963] 2 Lloyd's Rep 287 (CA). For a comment on the 'near' clause and *The Athamas v. Dig Vijay Cement Co* in particular *see* J. Marston, *The 'Near' Clause in Charter Parties*, 42 JBL (1966); *See* S. Bord, S. Berry, A. Burrows, B. Eder, D. Foxton & C. Smith at [A 71].

88. *See* J. Marston, *The 'Near' Clause in Charter Parties*, JBL 42, 43 (1966).

Coast, United States') known as an 'order' clause and those which state a simple port or nominate a narrow range of ports. In this first case, the 'near' clause is of commercial value as a shipowner cannot be expected to have knowledge of every port to which it could be ordered at short notice. By contrast, where a limited number of ports are included in the charter party, a shipowner can usually discover the existence of any obstacles in advance. In this situation, it may be argued that the courts will only permit a shipowner to invoke the 'near' clause when the obstacle would have come into existence after it had accepted the port of destination and be one that it could not have reasonably foreseen.[89] Therefore, shipowners are advised to make careful enquiries before accepting a port and are warned not to use the 'near' clause to protect themselves from the consequences of faults within their own lines of information.[90]

57. No distinction is made in English (or Australian) law between local obstacles, which are within a charterer's ambit of responsibility and against which the 'near' clause protects a shipowner, and marine obstacles, which are within a shipowner's expectation of risk. An obstacle may be of a physical nature, such as ice or lack of draught, or refusal of port authorities to allow the ship to proceed or dock. Insufficient draught, as an obstacle, has been the subject of much litigation. Where insufficient draught is temporary, as when tides are low, the ship has to wait until the water rises.[91] The length of time an obstacle is likely to exist is also of importance.[92] The shipowner appears to be under no other duty than to proceed to the place nearest the primary destination that the ship can safely reach, whether or not loading or discharging facilities are available.[93] It is usual for most charter parties to cover this eventuality by the addition of the words 'and there load' or 'and there deliver'.

III. Safe Ports

58. Where it is unsafe to load or discharge cargo in the port specified in the charter party, the alternative port or destination must be a place where safe facilities exist for loading or discharging.[94] Where it is often the practice, as in Asia and Africa, for cargoes to be loaded from or discharged into lighters at open anchorages, the problem is less of a practical one. In such cases, the charterers could maintain that the vessel must proceed as near to the primary destination as it can safely get and

89. J. Marston, *The 'Near' Clause in Charter Parties*, JBL 42, 43–44 (1966).
90. J. Marston, *The 'Near' Clause in Charter Parties*, JBL 42, 43 (1966), citing *The Athamas v. Dig Vijay Cement Co* [1963] 2 Lloyd's Rep 287 (CA).
91. In *Schilizzi v. Derry* (1855) 4 El & Bl 873 [119 ER 324], a vessel reached the mouth of the River Danube at a time when it was known that it would have to wait for late December tides to clear the bar and proceed to its destination 90 miles further on. The court held that the vessel had not gone as near as it could safely get.
92. *Metcalfe v. Brittania Ironworks Co* (1876) 1 QBD 613.
93. *Bremner v. Burrill* (1877) 4 SC (4th) 934.
94. *See The Athamas v. Dig Vijay Cement Co* [1963] 1 Lloyd's Rep 287 (CA). *See* Q.A. Rares, *Safe Port Promise by Charterers: Rethinking Outstanding Complications*, 29(2) AANZMLJ b111–121 (2015).

there use lighters. It would not be enough for the vessel to stop at the nearest safe port.[95] In *The Athamas v. Dig Vijay Cement Co* [1963] 2 Lloyd's Rep 287, the vessel in question was chartered on a Gencon form:

> [To] proceed to one safe berth or place Saigon, always afloat, where the vessel is to discharge part cargo … and to enter and discharge the balance of the cargo at one safe place, always afloat, Pnom Penh, or so near thereto as she may safely get and lie always afloat and there deliver the cargo on being paid freight.[96]

The vessel arrived at Saigon in mid-March where it discharged its cargo for that port. Because it could not fulfil a minimum speed restriction on the River Mekong, the pilotage authority refused to pilot the vessel to Pnom Penh, 250 miles away in Kampuchea, until mid-August. The Pnom Penh cargo was, therefore, discharged at Saigon and the shipowners claimed demurrage (*see* paragraph 69) for the time occupied in discharging it. In the English Commercial Court, McNair J, held that the vessel had gone as near as it might safely get. Applying the principle to the facts of the case, McNair J found that under the circumstances of the particular voyage Saigon was within the ambit of Pnom Penh.[97]

In the earlier arbitration, the Arbitrators had found that no one had suggested that an alternative port was open, so that discharge had to take place at Saigon or Pnom Penh; that there was nowhere on the route between Saigon and Pnom Penh where the cargo for the latter port could be discharged; and that the insistence of the pilotage authority on minimum speed was unforeseen and could not have been reasonably foreseen until it was declared. The decision was upheld in the English CA (finding for the charterers).[98]

59. In *Tage Berglund v. Montoro Shipping Corporation (The Dagmar)* [1968] 2 Lloyd's Rep 563, a vessel was chartered for a voyage from St Lawrence ports to West Italy. Under a clause in the charter party the vessel was to be employed 'only between good and safe ports or places … where vessels of similar size and draft are accustomed to lie in safety'. The charterers ordered the vessel to Cape Chat to load timber. The vessel was moored to a pier at Cape Chat; the wind and swell increased, the vessel's after-mooring parted; and it swung round and was driven aground. The shipowner claimed damages, arguing that Cape Chat was not a safe port in that the pier gave no shelter from northerly winds, there was no means of communicating adverse weather forecasts to the vessel, and that the charterers had failed to warn the master of the approach or risk of bad weather. In the Commercial Court of the Queen's Bench, Mocatta J, noted that the non-receipt of the relevant marine weather forecast was important and held that Cape Chat was unsafe for the vessel on the following basis: unless a vessel up to the size of The Dagmar ordered

95. J. Marston, *The 'Near' Clause in Charter Parties*, JBL 42, 47–48 (1966).
96. *The Athamas v. Dig Vijay Cement Co* [1963] 1 Lloyd's Rep 287 (CA), L.J. Sellers at 291–292. Compare with the present clause in the form: Baltic and International Maritime Council, *Uniform General Charter (Gencom)*(BIMCO) 1994 Cl. 1 at http://www.bimco.org.
97. *The Athamas v. Dig Vijay Cement Co* [1962] 2 Lloyd's Rep 121 (Comm Ct), J. McNair at 130.
98. *The Athamas v. Dig Vijay Cement Co* [1963] 1 Lloyd's Rep 287 (CA).

to load at Cape Chat was specifically warned that, first, no weather information would be received by the vessel from the shore but only by its own resources, and second, it was unsafe to remain in the place during strong winds and seas, then such a place is unsafe within the meaning of the relevant clause unless the charterers either passed on, or caused to be passed on, all relevant weather forecasts. The first warning was given, but not the second, and the charterers did not pass on weather forecasts. Therefore, Cape Chat was not a safe port for the vessel.[99]

60. A port will not be safe unless, in the relevant period of time, the particular ship can reach it, use it, and return from it without, in the absence of some abnormal occurrence, being exposed to danger which cannot be avoided by good navigation and seamanship.[100] The dangers which a vessel may encounter in a port are many, and a port will be unsafe not only on account of physical and natural causes such as sea swells, exposure, winds, and insufficient draught, but also as a result of political conditions. Where the charterer is given the option of nominating a port or berth of its choice, the loading or discharging port shall be safe.[101]

If the weather is so unpredictable that it would be unreasonable for the master to endanger the vessel in the port, for example, by the suddenness of high winds, then the port is not safe.[102]

61. On the basis that the giving of an order to sail to an unsafe port, or load or discharge at an unsafe berth, is a breach of contract, the person giving that order is liable in damages for the consequences, subject to the ordinary rule of remoteness.[103] In *Reardon Smith Line Ltd v. Australian Wheat Board* [1956] AC 266 [93 CLR 577; 30 ALJ 34; [1956] 2 Weekly Law Reports (WLR) 403; [1956] 1 All ER 456],[104] a vessel was to proceed under a voyage charter 'to one or two safe ports in Western Australia' and there load 'at such [a] safe dock, pier, wharves, and/or anchorage as ordered' by the charterers. At the port nominated, Geraldton, a hauling-off buoy (for use in keeping vessels off the wharf in northerly winds) and 50 feet of fender on the wharf, was missing. During a gale, the vessel rolled and damaged itself and the wharf. The shipowners claimed damages from the charterers for breach of their contractual obligation to nominate a safe port and berth. On

---

99. *Tage Berglund v. Montoro Shipping Corporation (The Dagmar)* [1968] 2 Lloyd's Rep 563 (QB), J. Mocatta at 569.
100. *Leeds Shipping Co v. Société Française Bunge* [1958] 2 Lloyd's Rep 127 (CA), L.J. Sellers 131. L.J. Sellers's statement was based upon a similar one in *Compañia Naviera Maropan v. Bowaters Ltd* [1955] 2 QB 68 [[1954] 3 WLR 894; [1954] 3 All ER 563] (CA), L.J. Morris at 105. *See Tage Berglund v. Montoro Shipping Corporation (The Dagmar)* [1968] 2 Lloyd's Rep 563 (QB).
101. *See* the standard forms in the grain trade that stipulate a sole alternative that the loading and discharging ports are to be nominated within a certain range: *see* Centrecom, Cl. 4. Centrecom is a charter party form.
102. *Tage Berglund v. Montoro Shipping Corporation (The Dagmar)* [1968] 2 Lloyd's Rep 563 (QB), J. Mocatta at 569.
103. *GW Grace & Co v. General Steamship Navigation Co Ltd* [1950] 2 KB 383 [[1950] 1 All ER 201].See C.W.B. Yim '*Port Promise by Charterer: Rethinking Outstanding Complications*' NZMarLJ (2016) 30(2) 1.
104. *Reardon Smith Line Ltd v. Australian Wheat Board* [1956] AC 266 [93 CLR 577; 30 ALJ 34; [1956] 2 WLR 403; [1956] 1 All ER 456], reversing the majority decision of the HCA in *Reardon Smith Line Ltd v. Australian Wheat Board* (1954) 91 CLR 233.

appeal from the High Court, that found for the charterers, the Privy Council (PC), finding for the shipowner, held that,[105] since the master had acted reasonably, and the port was unsafe at the time of nomination and when the damage occurred, the charterers had broken their undertaking to nominate a safe port or wharf, and were liable for damages to the vessel which stemmed from the breach.[106]

62. In *Kodros Shipping Corporation of Monrovia v. Empresa Cubana de Fletes (The Evia) [No. 2]* [1983] 1 AC 736 [1982] 3 WLR 637; [1982] 3 All ER 350],[107] the House of Lords (HL) held, in the case of a vessel under a time charter trapped at Basrah in the Shatt el Arab waterway after the outbreak of the Iran-Iraq war, that a port was not safe unless, in the relevant period of time, the particular ship could reach it, use it, and return from it, without, in the absence of some abnormal occurrence, being exposed to damage which could not be avoided by good navigation and seamanship. In exercising its right to order a ship to go to a particular port or place of loading or discharge, the charterer's contractual promise regarding the safety of that intended port or place related to the characteristics of the port or place, and meant that when the order was given, that port or place was prospectively safe for the ship to get to, stay at, so far as necessary, and, in due course, leave.[108] So long as those characteristics were, at the time the order was given, such as to make that port or place prospectively safe in that way, the sudden subsequent occurrence of some unexpected and abnormal event which created conditions of unsafety which resulted in the delay, damage, or detention of the vessel would not extend the charterer's contractual promise to make it liable for any resulting loss or damage, physical or financial.[109]

63. Where a charterer is to give orders for the port of discharge at the port of loading, the port must be named without unreasonable delay.[110] When a charterer has named the port, it is not entitled afterwards to change the destination.[111] The time within which orders are to be given at a port of call is often stated in the charter party. If this is fixed, then the charterer must give the order within a reasonable

105. *Reardon Smith Line Ltd v. Australian Wheat Board* [1956] AC 266 [93 CLR 577; 30 ALJ 34; [1956] 2 WLR 403; [1956] 1 All ER 456], the Court at 281–282, approving dicta of J. Devlin at 77 in *Compania Naviera Maropan v. Bowaters Ltd* [1955] 2 QB 68 [[1954] 3 WLR 894; [1954] 3 All ER 563] (CA).

106. In the HC's decision in *Reardon Smith Line Ltd v. Australian Wheat Board* (1954) 91 CLR 233, Dixon CJ's dissenting judgment at 242 stressed the predicament of the master who considers a port unsafe and may subsequently be found to be wrong and noting the master's theoretical choice to refuse to comply with directions as outside the terms of the charter.

107. For comment on the case *see* C. Baker & P. David, *The Politically Unsafe Port*, 112 LIMCLQ 1 (1986).

108. *Kodros Shipping Corporation of Monrovia v. Empresa Cubana de Fletes (The Evia) [No. 2]* [1983] 1 AC 736 [[1982] 3 WLR 637; [1982] 3 All ER 350], Lord Diplock at 749.

109. *Kodros Shipping Corporation of Monrovia v. Empresa Cubana de Fletes (The Evia) [No. 2]* [1983] 1 AC 736 [[1982] 3 WLR 637; [1982] 3 All ER 350], L.J. Roskill at 757.

110. *Procter Garrett v. Oakwin SS Co* [1926] 1 KB 244 (CA), L.J. Bankes at 251–252 (L.J. Warrington agreeing), L.J. Scrutton at 253–254.

111. Particularly if bills of lading given for that already-named port are outstanding: *see Davidson v. Gwynne* (1810) 12 East 381 [104 ER 149]; but *see Tank of Oslo A/S v. Agence Maritime L Strauss of Paris* (1939) 55 TLR 139 (CA), where the charter party provided that the ship was to proceed

time after the vessel's arrival there. If improper delay occurs the charterer is then liable in damages for the ship's detention. If a master has received no orders at the port of call, the master may, after waiting a reasonable time for them, act on his or her own judgment, and take the ship to any one of the ports of discharge permitted by the charter party. The master is not bound to communicate with the charterer before doing so,[112] but should notify of the vessel's arrival, if having a reasonable opportunity at the port of call, to the charterer or its agent.[113]

64. The word 'freight'[114] denotes the remuneration payable for the carriage of goods in a vessel or for the use of a vessel.[115] Payment of the freight is the main obligation of a charterer under a charter party.[116] The freight clause in a charter party usually contains provisions, varying in detail, covering the payment of freight and its calculation. Most standard charter parties stipulate that the freight due is to be paid 'on unloading' or 'on delivery of the cargo' (known as 'freight collect' clauses), less such advance on the freight as the charterer may be requested to pay at the port of loading to cover the vessel's ordinary disbursements at that port.[117] In practice, however, the parties often prescribe a different regulation of the freight payment. It is common, for instance, to stipulate payment in advance of the entire freight 'on completion of loading' or 'on signing bills of lading'.

65. Any time during which a vessel is not working and earning, represents a loss in freight for a shipowner, since fixed overheads continue to accrue irrespective of whether the vessel is actually employed. The time factor is, therefore, of considerable importance to the shipowner. In relation to the performance of a charter voyage, time is of particular relevance where the vessel's stay in port is prolonged. The

---

'as ordered on signing of bills of lading to one safe port' and gave the charterers the option of discharging at two safe ports. It was held that the mistaken signing of a bill of lading for one port only did not affect the earlier exercise of the charterer's option to discharge at two ports.

112. *Procter Garrett v. Oakwin SS Co* [1926] 1 KB 244 (CA).
113. *Procter Garrett v. Oakwin SS Co* [1926] 1 KB 244 (CA).
114. *See* T. Carver, *Carriage of Goods by Sea* Ch. 18 (13th ed., Stevens 1982); A.A. Mocatta, M.J. Mustill & S.C. Boyd, *Scrutton on Charterparties* 331–358 (19th ed., Sweet & Maxwell 1984). In *Itex Export SA v. Care Shipping Corp (The Cebu) [No. 2]* [1993] QB 1, 3 WLR 609, [1992] 1 All ER 91. J. Steyn at 10–14(QB) stated that 'freight' and 'hire' now have distinctly separate meanings in the context of chartering documents. *See also* S. Boyd, S. Berry, A. Burrows, B. Eder, D. Foxton & C. Smith, *Scrutton on Charterparties and Bills of Lading* Ch. 15 (21st ed., Sweet & Maxwell 2008); M. Davies & A. Dickey, *Shipping Law* 340–342 (3d ed., Lawbook Co 2004).
115. *See* the objection to the use of 'freight' in the latter sense in *Federal Commerce & Navigation Ltd v. Molena Alpha Inc.* [1978] QB 927 [[1978] 3 WLR 309; [1978] 3 All ER 1066] (CA), M.R. Lord Denning at 973, who sought to justify a rigid distinction. T. Carver, *Carriage of Goods by Sea* para. 1164 (13th ed., Stevens 1982), regards it as unfortunate if such a distinction were to be drawn between 'freight' and 'hire'; but now *see* above.
116. Where a charterer also undertakes to compensate the shipowner for delay in the loading or discharging port by payment of demurrage, this is sometimes referred to as a supplement to the freight. *See* Baltic and International Maritime Council, *BIMCO Standard Contract for the Transportation of Bulk Dry Cargoes (GENCOA)* (BIMCO), 2004 and *(Gencon)* (BIMCO, 1994) Cl. 4(a),(c) *see* http://www.bimco.org.
117. *See* Gencon, Cl. 4 in, *Australian Maritime Law* Appendices (M.W.D. White ed., Federation Press 1991). *See Profinda Pte Ltd v. Abani Trading Pte* [2013] SGHC (Singapore). *See* in case comment 'Laytime and Demurrage Provisions in Sales Contracts' [2013] LMCLQ 150.

shipowner will incur overheads for each day the vessel is detained, thereby reducing its profit. The charterer has to have the vessel available for long enough to carry out the loading and discharge of cargo efficiently and economically.

IV. Loading

66. An appropriate period of time in respect of port stay is usually allowed for in standard charter parties to cover loading and discharge. This is generally termed 'laytime'. Demurrage is a sum named in the charter party to be paid by the charterer as liquidated damages for delay beyond laytime. It is an exceptional circumstance if no fixed time for loading or unloading is set down in the charter party. If this occurs, an agreement on the part of the charterer is implied at common law to load or discharge the cargo within a reasonable time.[118] The effect of the clause '[t]ime lost in waiting for berth to count as loading time'[119] has been extensively litigated. However, recent English decisions on what is an 'arrived ship',[120] which widens the geographical area within which a vessel is deemed to have arrived, has widely reduced the practical importance of the clause. In *Aldeberan Compania Maritima SA v. Aussenhandel AG (The Darrah)* [1976] 3 WLR 320 [[1976] 2 All ER 963; [1976] 2 Lloyd's Rep 359], the HL held that in computation of time lost in waiting for a berth, there were to be excluded all periods that would have been left out in the computation if the vessel had actually been in berth.[121]

67. The problem of when a vessel is regarded as an 'arrived ship' seems to have been resolved in *EL Oldendorff & Co GmbH v. Tradax Export SA (The Johanna Oldendorff)* [1974] AC 479 [[1974] 3 WLR 382; [1973] 3 All ER 148; [1973] 2 Lloyd's Rep 285] where Lord Reid laid down the following test:

> Before a ship can be said to have arrived at a port she must, if she cannot proceed immediately to a berth, have reached a position within the port where she is at the immediate and effective disposition of the charterer. If she is at a place where waiting ships usually lie, she will be in such a position unless in some extraordinary circumstances proof of which would lie in the charterer.[122]

118. *See* generally S. Boyd, S. Berry, A. Burrows, B. Eder, S.D. Foxton & C. Smith, *Scrutton on Charterparties and Bills of Lading* [A73]–[A81] (21st ed., Sweet & Maxwell 2008); M. Davies & A. Dickey, *Shipping Law* 339–340 (3d ed., Lawbook Co 2004); S. Derrington, *Charterparties*, in *Australian Maritime Law* [6.3.6]–[6.3.7] (M. White ed., 2d ed., The Federation Press 299); J. Schofield, *Laytime and Demmurage* (5th ed., Lloyd's of London Press 2005); D. Davies, *Commencement of Laytime* (4th ed., Lloyd's of London Press 2006).
119. Gencon, Cl. 6; *see Australian Maritime Law* Appendices M.W.D. White ed., Federation Press (1991).
120. *See The Martha Envoy* [1977] 2 Lloyd's Rep 301.
121. *Aldeberan Compania Maritima SA v. Aussenhandel AG (The Darrah)* [1976] 3 WLR 320 [[1976] 2 All ER 963; [1976] 2 Lloyd's Rep 359, Lord Diplock at 324.
122. *EL Oldendorff & Co GmbH v. Tradax Export SA (The Johanna Oldendorff)* [1974] AC 479 [[1974] 3 WLR 382; [1973] 3 All ER 148; [1973] 2 Lloyd's Rep 285] (CA), Lord Reid at 535, the phrase 'within the port' is given a broad meaning 'within the legal, fiscal and administrative limits'. *See*

The effect of this test is that time waiting for a berth counts as laytime.[123] The test is applied by a 'Whether In Berth Or Not' (WIBON) clause in a charter party.[124]

V. Demurrage

68. When laytime has expired, a vessel will come 'on demurrage',[125] which accrues and becomes due for every day on which the vessel is delayed. This includes Sundays and holidays as well as days that would be expected during the period of laytime. However, demurrage will not be paid for delays due to the shipowner's fault or for the shipowner's convenience. In the case of most standard form charter parties, no fixed demurrage period is laid down. In this case the common law permits the charterer, unless it has definitely refused to provide cargo, to detain the vessel on demurrage for a period limited only by the common law doctrine of frustration.[126] The actual demurrage rate is normally laid down in the charter party and is not normally the subject of contention. The amount may be expressed in various terms, either as a fixed amount per day, or pro rata for part of a day, or as a given amount per cargo ton or ton of vessel gross or net registered tonnage, per day or pro rata for part of a day.

69. In *Dampskibsselskabet Torm A/S v. Australian Wheat Board* [1981] VR 145, the owners of a vessel claimed demurrage from the charterer in respect of a three-month delay suffered by the vessel at the Port of Geelong. The vessel was chartered by the Australian Wheat Board and was prevented from loading by a tug operators' strike and related industrial action by the Storemen and Packers' Union. Under Clause 16 of the charter party, demurrage was not payable when cargo could not be loaded 'by reason of a strike … of any class of workmen essential to the berthing

---

J. Trappe, *Laytime Problems and Comparison of Law*, 25 LIMCLQ 2, 251 (1986). *See also Nereide SA di Navigazione v. Bulk Oil International Ltd (The Laura Prima)* [1981] 3 All ER 737 [[1982] 1 Lloyd's Rep 1] (HL).

123. This is commonly provided for in standard form charter parties. *See* Baltic and Maritime International Council, *Uniform General Charter (Gencon)* Cl. 6 'Time used in moving from the place of waiting to the loading/discharging berth shall not count as laytime' *see* http://wwwbimco.org. However, the parties are always free to agree to different terms regarding the operation of laytime under the charterparty.

124. *See*, regarding the WIBON clause, M. Davies & A. Dickey, *Shipping Law* 295–296 (3d ed., Lawbook Co 2004). *See also* P. Mcarter, 'Re-defining the Function(s) of the Notice of Readiness' [1997] LMCLQ 483.

125. Demurrage: '[a] charge by way of damages for such delay, stipulated in the charter party' *The CCH Macquarie Dictionary of Law* (rev ed., CCH 1996), 52. *See* generally S. Boyd, S. Berry, A. Burrows, B. Eder, D. Foxton & C. Smith, *Scrutton on Charterparties and Bills of Lading* Ch. 14 (21st ed., Sweet & Maxwell 2008); M. Davies & A. Dickey, *Shipping Law* 315–321 (3d ed., Lawbook Co 2004); S. Derrington, *Charterparties,* in *Australian Maritime Law* [6.3.8] (M. White ed., 2d ed., The Federation Press 2000); J. Schofield, *Laytime and Demurrage* (5th ed., Lloyd's of London Press 2005). S. Baughen, *Laytime Definitions for Charterparties*, 19(5) J Intl Mar L 363 (2014).

126. *See Reardon Smith Line v. Ministry of Agriculture* [1962] 1 QB 42 [[1961] 3 WLR 110; [1961] 2 All ER 577; [1961] 1 Lloyd's Rep 385] (CA), considered and distinguished in *Trade & Transport Incorporated v. Iino Kaiun Kaisha Ltd (The Angelia)* [1973] 1 WLR 210 [[1973] 2 All ER 144] (QB), applied by J. Mocatta in *Venizelos ANE of Athens v. Société Commerciale de Cereales et Financière SA of Zurich (The Prometheus)* [1974] 1 All ER 597 [[1974] 1 Lloyd's Rep 350] (QB).

of the vessel or to the loading of the cargo'. Although permission was given by a local board to berth the vessel without tugs while the strike was still pending, the Full Court of the Supreme Court of Vic held that during the entire period of the tug operators' strike the vessel could not be loaded as the operators were essential to the berthing and the loading of the vessel. Under Clause 16 of the charter party demurrage was not payable during the entire period of the tug operators' strike.[127] In *Stolt-Nielsen Australia Pty Ltd v. Ausstar Commodity and Marketing Pty Ltd* [2013] FCCA 602 there were two shipments one of ten containers and a second of four tank containers were sent by the applicant company from Sydney to Chittagong. The intended receiver of the cargo failed to take delivery and both consignments remained in storage at the time of the hearing the case. On a claim from Stolt Neilsen for demurrage the respondent company Ausstrar did not protest about that entitlement. The Court upheld that the bills of lading contained a provision for payment of demurrage and that the bills constituted a contract of carriage. The negotiations between the parties on the payment of demurrage O'Dwyer held (at [45] did not bar Stott Neilsen from claiming more than the discounted amount.

In *Thomsom v. STX Pan Ocean Co Ltd* [2012] FCAFC 5 Bowen Basin (of which Thomson was sole shareholder and director) entered into a voyage charter party by which STX was to supply two vessels it would nominate. These voyage charter parties were for the carriage of coal from Kwinana, WA to ports in the People's Republic of China. Bowen Basin made significant losses on the sale of the first cargo. After the second vessel had been at Kwinana ready to load for about one month STX terminated the charter party on 17 May. STX claimed it delayed terminating the charter party in the eleven days before 17 May because Thomson had made representations to STX on behalf of Bowen Basin that it was ready to perform the charter party (when in fact Bowen Basin was insolvent). At first instance STX obtained judgment for AUD 2,483,296 against Bowen Basin and then proceeded against Thomson as an accessory on the basis of his representations.

The Federal Court found that Thomson as Bowen Basin's managing director had made representations that the company was ready and willing to perform and would do so once finance (said to be imminent) was available. The Court upheld the primary judge's finding that STX's delay in terminating the charter relied on Thomson's representation.

The Federal Court, upholding the primary judge, found that STX was entitled to recover its loss as a result of the payments made on the two vessels it chartered. It also held that STX entering the obligation to charter the vessels was not caused by any actionable breach by Thomson. The breach found against Thomson was the post contractual breach by which time liability to meet these payments (for the charter) had already been incurred.[128]

---

127. *See Dampskibsselskab et Torm A/S v. Australian Wheat Board* [1981] VR 145 (FC), J. O'Bryan at 151. Compare the present wider form of AWB's Limited's (the corporate successor to the Australian Wheat Board) strikes and blockades clause: AWB Limited, *Australian Wheat Charter 1990 (amended 1991) (Austwheat 1990)* (AWB Limited 1991) Cl. 17 *see* http:// www.bimco.org.

128. *See Thomson v. STX Pan Ocean Co Ltd* [2012] FCAFC 15 at [40]. For a detailed examination of the cases illustrating the range of possibilities of measuring damages in relation to the inability to use a potentially profit earning ship *see* H. McGregor, *McGregor on Damages* [32.023]–[32.037] (Thomson Reuters 2009).

§4. TIME CHARTER PARTIES

I. General Provisions

70. Under a time charter, a charterer assumes various costs and risks connected with a vessel's employment. The 'Baltime' and 'New York Produce Exchange' (NYPE) forms are the two most important examples of time charters.[129] It follows that since the time charterer is particularly dependent on the specific characteristics of the vessels the description of the vessel given by the shipowner in the charter party is a fundamental part of the contract.

The charter party usually contains statements regarding the vessel's name and flag, ownership, class, gross, and net tonnage, cargo capacity, indicated horse power and speed, and bunker consumption. As a general rule, the charter party contains a statement in respect of the general condition of the vessel, for example, its seaworthiness.[130] The charter party may contain further details concerning the vessel's technical characteristics, machinery, and equipment.

71. The time freight is calculated on the basis of a certain rate per time unit, usually thirty days or a calendar month per ton of vessel deadweight. The time charter usually provides that the freight shall be payable in advance at regular intervals during the currency of the charter.[131] Both Baltime and NYPE forms provide, with regard to payment of freight, that, in the event of default in punctual payment by the charterer, the shipowner is entitled to withdraw the vessel. This requirement lays a strict liability on the charterer to pay on time.[132] Even a minor delay beyond the prescribed date gives entitlement to withdrawal. The shipowner is not entitled to withdraw if the payment is late due to a method of payment which has been used with the shipowner's approval for payment of earlier instalments in place of those expressly required under the charter party.[133] In *BHP Freight Pty Ltd v. Cosco Oceania Chartering Pty Ltd(No. 3)*[2009] FCA 1087 BHP Freight Pty Ltd(BHPB) was

129. *See* M. Wilford, T. Coghlin & N.J. Healy, *Time Charters* (3d ed., Lloyd's of London Press 1982). *See* generally S. Boyd, S. Berry, A. Burrows, B. Eder, D. Foxton & C. Smith, *Scrutton on Charterparties and Bills of Lading* Ch. 16 (21st ed., Sweet & Maxwell 2008); M. Davies & A. Dickey, *Shipping Law* Ch. 14 (3d ed., Lawbook Co 2004); S. Derrington, *Charterparties*, in *Australian Maritime Law* [6.2.1]–[6.3.10] (M. White ed., 2d ed., The Federation Press 2000); T. Coghlin, A. Baker, J. Kenny & J. Kimball, *Time Charters* (6th ed., Informa 2008).

130. *See* Baltime Cl. 1 and New York Produce Exchange, lines 41–43 reproduced in M. Wilford, T. Coghlin & N.J. Healy, *Time Charters* (3d ed., Lloyd's of London Press 1982). *See Baltime 1939* Cl. 1, *NYPE* Cl. 2.

131. *See* Baltime, Cl. 6 (thirty days) and New York Produce Exchange, Cl. 5 (semi-monthly) reproduced in M. Wilford, T. Coghlin & N.J. Healy, *Time Charters* (3d ed., Lloyd's of London Press 1982). *See* Baltic and International Maritime Council *(BIMCO Uniform Time Charter)*(BIMCO 2001) Cl. 6 (thirty days in advance); Association of ship Brokers and Agents (USA) Inc, *New York Produce Exchange Form (NYPE 93)* (ASBA 1993) Cl. 11(a) (fifteen days in advance)*see* http://www.bimco.org.

132. *Baltime 1939 cl6, NYPE 93 cl 11(a).*

133. *Tankexpress A/S v. Compagnie Financière Belge des Petroles SA* [1948] 2 Lloyd's Rep 43; *Scandinavian Trading Tanker Co v. Flota Petrolera Ecuatoriana (The Scaptrade)* [1981] 2 Lloyd's Rep 425; *Mardorf Peach & Co Ltd v. Attica Sea Carriers Corporation of Liberia (The Laconia)* [1977] AC 850 [[1977] 2 WLR 286; [1977] 1 All ER 545; [1977] 1 Lloyd's Rep 315]; *China National*

the disponent owner of 'Global Hawk' a Panamanian flagged bulk carrier. The vessel had been chartered by her owners to Inui Steamship Company Ltd (Inui) and then time chartered to BHP. The vessel was then purportedly sub-chartered to New Century Leasing Co Ltd (NCL) following negotiations between BHPB's shipbroker Braemar Seascape Pty Ltd and Cosco Ocean Chartering Pty (Cosco) the shipbroker BHPB believed was acting for NCL. The vessel was delivered into charter service on 14 October 2004 not to NCL but to Nera Shipping Co Ltd (Nera). Nera only paid a small proportion of the hire.

72. A division of BHPB, Handy Pacific Chartering, purchases, and sells freight on behalf of the BHP Billiton group, one of the largest users of dry dock shipping. On 3 September 2004 Handy Pacific Chartering sent an email to several shipbrokers, including Seawise (now known as Braemar Seascope Pty Ltd) advising that the 'Global Hawk' would become 'open' (available for hire)on the 12 October 2004 at the PRC port of Lianyungang and requesting the brokers to propose candidates for business. Cosco made a 'firm' offer for the vessel for the account of NCL for delivery at that port and redelivery in Singapore or Japan.

73. BHPB had not previously dealt with NCL. Lloyd's MIV Company Research gave NCL a clean bill of health and a Jack Cao (Jacky) was designated by Mr Lui of Cosco as the PIC (person in charge). As a result of negations between Handy Pacific Chartering and Jacky the vessel was 'fixed on subs' (i.e., a fixture subject to certain conditions being met by NCL). The vessel was to be delivered at Lianyungang on 11 October 2004 the hire at USD 24,500 per day, the full voyage time charter hire to be paid in advance. As Jacky was shown to be the PCI on the documents received by Handy Pacific Chartering he was assumed to be the agent and charterer for the NCL.

74. After redelivery of the vessel to BHPB on 27 November 2004 NCI was invoiced for USD 353,514 which was paid in part after arbitration proceedings against Nera in London.

Foreign Trade Corporation v. Evlogia Shipping Co SA of Panama (The Mihalios Zilas) [1976] 3 Lloyd's Rep 303 (HL); *Awilco of Oslo (A/S) v. Fulvia sp A di Navigazione of Cagliari (The Chikuma)* [1981] 1 WLR 314 [[1981] 1 All ER 652; [1981] 1 Lloyd's Rep 371] (HL). *See* F. Rose, *Withdrawal Clauses in Time Charters*, Cur Leg Prob 30. English courts have no jurisdiction to award equitable relief against forfeiture in this situation: *Scandanavian Trading Tanker Co AB v. Flota Petrolera Ecuatoriana (The Scaptrade)* [1983] 3 WLR 203; [1983]2 All ER 763. Compare *Mardorf Peach & Co Ltd v. Attica Sea Carriers Corp of Liberia (The Laconia)* [1977] AC 850[1977] 2 WLR 289, L.J. Simon at 874(AC), observing that equitable principles might have application to charter parties as 'English law develops by applying an established rule of law to new circumstances which are analogous in the circumstances in which the established rule was framed … and it has been only recently said that equity is not to be presumed to be of an age past child bearing. If so, as presently advised I can *see* no reason why demographic trends should be halted at the bounds of parish of St Mary Axe.' *See Grand China Logistics Holding (Group) Co Ltd v. Spar Shipping AS* [2016] FWCA 982 where an alleged breach of condition to pay hire punctually under a time charter was held not to be so but an obligation the breach of which did not entitle Spar to claim damages for loss of bargain. (at [16]–[21] per Hamblen LJ on appeal from [2015] EWHC 718 Popplewell J HC QB.)

75. BHPB claims against Cosco included that Cosco had breached section 52 of the *Trade Practices Act 1974*(Cth) by engaging in false or misleading conduct. The cause of action by BHPB was that Cosco had wrongly warranted that it had the authority of NCI to conclude the charter party.

76. Finkelstein J in the Federal Court held that Jacky had never acted for NCL which appeared to be a reputable organization. Jacky, on the other hand, was rogue as he had been using Cosco's services in an attempt to charter a vessel for a variety of charterers other than NCL (at FCA[43]) The judge held that BHPB (through Seawise) was induced to enter into a charter party in the belief that the arrangements were with NCL. BHPB had satisfied itself that NCI was a reputable party with which to do business. The identity of NCL and, therefore, Cosco's authority to represent NCL was important to BHPB in its decision to enter into the charter party. Cosco was also held to have breached section 52 of the *Trade Practices Act 1974* (Cth)[134] as it represented to Seawise it was acting for NCL when it was not. The representation induced the negotiations and subsequently the agreement with Jacky and as a result BHPB suffered damage.[135]

77. In *Daebo Shipping Co Ltd v. The Ship Go Star* [2012[FCAFC 156;294 ALR 635 Go Star Maritime Co SA the owners of the 'Go Star' in June 2007 entered into a time charter with Breakbulk Marine Services Ltd (BMS) for a period of thirty-forty months plus or minus one month at the charterer's option. The head charter was made on the 1981 Absaltime NYPE form. In July 2007 BMS sub-chartered the vessel to Bluefield Shipping Co (Bluefield) for a twenty-three–twenty-five month period at Bluefield's option on substantially back to back terms. On 27 July Bluefield entered into a further sub-charter of the vessel to Daebo Shipping Co Ltd (Daebo) a South Korean company on terms similar to that with Bluefield. In December 2008 Daebo entered into another time sub-charter with Nunyuan Shipping Co Ltd another South Korean company. On 4 January 2009 Daebo issued an invoice for the first hire payment and for the value of the bunkers.

78. By this time BMS had fallen into arrears of payment of hire to the owners under the head charter which by Clause 15 provided for the withdrawal of the vessel if this occurred. Before Nanyuan had paid Daebo's invoice the owner's agent Evalend Shipping Co SA advised Nanyuan that the owners intended to exercise their rights and withdraw the ship from hire. On 8 January 2009 Nanyuan purported to cancel or withdraw from its sub-charter with Daebo and did not pay Daebo's invoice and arranged alternative transport for its cargo. Nanyuan on 13 January 2009 confirmed its decision on the basis from Evalend that the owners proposed to exercise their rights under a lien to demand payment of sub-hire from Nanyuan. On

134. Cosco was also found to have breached the *Trade Practices Act 1974* (Cth) s. 53(bb) by falsely representing that it was supplying shipbroking services to NCI. That representation J. Finkelstein held induced BHPB to conclude the hire of the vessel with Jacky (FCA) [53].

135. J. Finkelstien found that Seawise did not breach its retainer with BHPB and was not negligent (FCA) at [79].

this ground Nanyuan claimed that the ship had never been lawfully delivered to them by Daebo because it had not been 'lawfully ready in all respects without any restriction'.

79. On 15 January the owners withdrew the ship from BMS' service and chartered her to Medstar Lines Inc. On 29 January 2009 the vessel arrived at Albany, WA and on that date Daebo demanded delivery of the bunkers. The owners refused and credited the bunkers' value as an offset against BMS' unpaid hire. Daebo then commenced proceedings again at the 'Go Star' in the Federal Court of Australia claiming damages in conversion and detinue in respect of the ship's bunkers. Daebo also claimed damages for loss of hire under the sub-charter party and the loss of repayment of the bunkers on the ground that the owners had unlawfully interfered with Daebo's contractual relations with Nanyuan.

80. The primary judge and the Federal Court (on appeal) found that as the law of China does not recognize the tort of unlawful interference in contractual relations and this law applied as the 'Go Star' was in Chinese territorial waters when the notice was made to withdraw the vessel for non-payment of hire.

81. The Federal Court held that under the NYPE time charter property in the bunkers on board at the time of delivery pass, at that time, to the charterers,[136] delivery under the time charter places the vessel at the charterer's disposal but marks the time of the charterer's obligation to pay hire.[137]

82. The Federal Court noted that the nature of a shipowner's lien under a time charter containing a clause similar to Clause 18, 1981 is unsettled. However, that was not regarded as an issue in the current case as the owners had not given notice to a claim that they had a lien over any sum owed by Daebo or Nanyuan. The Federal Court found that Daebo was entitled to recover the value of the bunkers at the rate set down in the sub-charter party.[138]

---

136. *See* the *Span Terza (No. 2)* [1984] 1 WLR 27; [1984]Lloyd's Rep 119 at 31G-32A; at 122 per Lord Diplock; *The Saetta* [1993] 2 Lloyd's Rep 269 at 273 per J. Clarke *See also The Madeleine* [1967] 2 Lloyd's Rep 224 per J. Roskill at 228; *The Niizuru* [1996] 2 Lyod's Rep 66 at 68 per J. Mance *See* T. Coglin, A. Baker, J. Kenny, J.D. Kimball, *Time Charters* [7.29], [7.33] (6th ed., Informa 2008); *see* Cl. 4 (lines 96–101) 1981 NYPE.

137. *See Federal Commerce & Navigation Co Ltd v. Molena Alpha[Inc (The Nanfri)* [1978] 3WLR 911 at 1004F where Lord Russell suggested that the shipowner's lien on sub-freights operated as an equitable charge on what was due from a shipper to the charterer and to be effective, required an ability to intercept the sub-freight by notice of claim before it was paid by the charterer by the shipper. However, Lord Millett (giving the advice of a strong Judicial Committee of the Privy Council; Lords Bingham, Nicholls, Hoffmann and Hobhouse) observed that the lien was not a creation of common law or equity but originated in maritime law based on the shipowner's lien on cargo.

138. *See Daebo Shipping Co Ltd v. The Ship GO Star* [2012] FCAFC 156 at [106]–[110].*See ENE 1 Kos Ltd v. Petroleo Brasileiro SA Petrobas (The Kos)* [2012] UKSC 17 case note in [2012] LMCLQ 343 'Withdrawal with cargo still on board'.

II. Anti-technicality Clauses

83. It has become the practice for charterers to include 'anti-technicality' clauses to prevent what may be regarded as unfair withdrawals of vessels. These often take the form of requiring shipowners to give charterers a prescribed period of notice within which to pay before the vessel may be withdrawn. In *Afovos Shipping Co SA v. Pagnan (The Afovos)* [1983] 1 WLR 195 [1983] 1 All ER 449; [1983] 1 Lloyd's Rep 335],[139] the charter party, on the NYPE form, provided by Clause 31 that if the hire was not received when due, the shipowners were to give the charterers forty-eight hours notice to rectify the default before exercising the right of withdrawal. Although the charterers had a history of punctual payment, they missed an instalment due on 14 June because of a bank error. At 4:40 p.m., on 14 June the shipowners' agents sent a telex to the charterers stating that they had been instructed that in the event of not receiving the due hire on that day the agents were to give notice to the charterers under Clause 31 of withdrawal of the vessel. The instalment due was not received by the shipowners within forty-eight hours of the telex, and accordingly the shipowners claimed to be entitled to withdraw the vessel. The HL upheld the CA decision that the giving of forty hour's notice under Clause 31 did not arise until the charterers were in default. Applying the principle that where a party was obliged to do a particular act on or before a particular day, it was not in default until the end of that day, the charterers were, therefore, not in default until midnight on 14 June. The shipowners' notice was, therefore, premature and ineffective, and they were not entitled to withdraw the vessel from the charterers.[140]

III. Cessation of Hire

84. Time charters usually provide 'off-hire' clauses for hire to cease in certain specified events.[141] These clauses operate as exceptions to a charterer's primary

139. *Afovos Shipping Co SA v. Pagnan (The Afovos)* [1983] 1 WLR 195 [[1983] 1 All ER 449; [1983] 1 Lloyd's Rep 335] (HL). *See also Italmare Shipping Co v. Ocean Tanker Co Incorporated (The Rio Sun)* [1982] 1 WLR 158 [[1982] 1 All ER 517] (CA); *Tropwood AG v. Jade Enterprises Ltd (The Tropwind) [No. 1]* [1977] 1 Lloyd's Rep 397 (QB); *Telfair Shipping Corporation v. Athos Shipping Co SA (The Athos)* [1981] 2 Lloyd's Rep 74 (QB). *See*, e.g., Association of Ship Brokers and Agents (USA) Inc *(NYPE 93)*)(ASBA, 1993) Cl. 11(b) at http://www.bimco.org.

140. *See Italmare Shipping Co v. Ocean Tanker Co Inc (The Rio Sun)* [1982] 1 WLR 158; [1982] 1 All ER 517(CA). *See Tropwind AG v. Jade Enterprises Ltd (The Tropwind) [No. 1]* [1977] 1 Lloyd's Rep 397(QB); *Telfair Shipping Corp v. Athos Shipping Co SA (The Athos)* [1981] 2 Lloyd's 397(QBD) affirmed in part by *Telfair Shipping Corp v. Athos Shipping Co SA (The Athos)* [1983] 1 Lloyd's Rep 127(CA). On the apparent conflict on the two lines of authority *see* T. Coghlin, A. Baker, J. Kenny & J. Kimball, *Time Charters* [16.94] (6th ed., Informa 2008).

141. *See* T. Carver, *Carriage of Goods by Sea* paras 1781–1972 (13th ed., Stevens 1982); A.A. Mocatta, M.J. Mustill & S.C. Boyd, *Scrutton on Charterparties* 368–371 (19th ed., Sweet & Maxwell 1984); M. Wilford, T. Coghlin & N.J. Healy, *Time Charters* 244–256, 401–403 (3d ed., Lloyd's of London Press 1982). *See* S. Body, A. Burrows, B. Eder, D. Foxton & C. Smith, *Scrutton on Charterparties and Bills of Lading* [A 176] (21st ed., Sweet & Maxwell 2008); T. Coghlin, A. Baker, J. Kenny & J. Kimball, *Time Charters* [25.1]–[25.74] (6th ed., Informa 2008).

obligation to pay hire continuously throughout the charter period. It is for a charterer to prove that the off-hire clause operates in the relevant circumstances. A charterer must bring itself within the exceptions. Where there is doubt as to the meaning of the words in the off-hire clause, they will be read down in favour of the shipowner because the charterer, by invoking the off-hire clause provisions, is attempting to cut down the shipowner's right to hire.[142]

85. Time must be lost as a consequence of the incidents specified in the off-hire clause. Therefore, a breakdown of the ship's propulsion will not put the vessel off-hire if it occurs and is remedied during loading or discharge of cargo. Off-hire will arise where the breakdown affects the particular work the ship is required to do at the relevant time. So a ship may be off-hire due to a propulsion breakdown at sea, but on-hire when such a breakdown has no effect on the service required by the charterers, such as unloading.[143]

In *Hogarth v. Miller* [1891] AC 48,[144] the vessel's charter included an off-hire clause which stated:

> [I]n the event of loss of time from deficiency of men or stores, breakdown of machinery, want of repairs, or damage, whereby the working of the vessel is stopped for more than forty-eight consecutive working hours, the payment of hire shall cease until she be again in an efficient state to resume her service.[145]

The vessel's high-pressure engine broke down while carrying cargo from Africa to Hamburg, and had to put in to Las Palmas. As repairs could not be carried out there the vessel was towed to Hamburg, with some help from its low-pressure engine. At Hamburg the cargo was discharged, with all the vessel's cargo-handling machinery working efficiently. The HL held that the vessel was off-hire during the tow between Las Palmas and Hamburg as it was not fully efficient during the period of the tow. At the time for, and during discharge, the vessel came on-hire again, as she was efficient for what was required.[146]

86. A distinction needs to be drawn between 'net loss of time' and 'period' off-hire clauses. The off-hire clause in *Hogarth v. Miller* established a clear-cut period of similar off-hire. The modern tanker forms contain similar provisions. By contrast, the Baltime and NYPE clauses are net loss off-hire clauses. In *Canadian Pacific (Bermuda) Ltd v. Canadian Transport Co Ltd (The HR Macmillan)* [1974]

---

142. *See Royal Greek Government v. Minister of Transport (The Ilissos)* [1949] 1 KB 525 [[1949] 1 All ER 171], L.J. Bucknill at 530. *See BIMCO Uniform Time-Charter* (BIMCO 2001) Cl. 11.
143. *Hogarth v. Miller* [1891] AC 48.
144. *See also Canadian Pacific (Bermuda) Ltd v. Canadian Transport Co Ltd (The HR Macmillan)* [1974] 1 Lloyd's Rep 311 (CA); *Tynedale Steam Shipping Co Ltd v. Anglo-Soviet Shipping Co Ltd* [1936] 1 All ER 389 (CA).
145. *Hogarth v. Miller* [1891] AC 48, Lord Morris at 67.
146. *Hogarth v. Miller* [1891] AC 48, L.C. Halsbury at 56–57, Lord Watson at 60, Lord Herschell at 64–65, Lord Morris at 66, Lord Bramwell (disagreeing) at 63. *See* T. Coglhlin, A. Baker, J. Kenny & J. Kimball, *Time Charters* [25.44]–[25.51] (6th ed., Informa 2008); S. Boyd, S. Berry, A. Burrows, B. Eder, D. Foxton & C. Smith, *Scrutton on Charterparties and Bills of Lading* [A 176] fn. 102 (21st ed., Sweet & Maxwell 2008).

1 Lloyd's Rep 311, M.R. Lord Denning in the CA indicated that applying Clause 15 of the NYPE form meant that, in the case before him, the breakdown of one of the vessel's cranes would not result in off-hire as the remaining cranes were able to do the work required so that no time was lost.[147] The provision 'deficiency of men' is strictly construed by the courts. In *Royal Greek Government v. Minister of Transport (The Ilissos)* [1949] 1 KB 525 [[1949] 1 All ER 171], the phrase was held to relate to numerical deficiency and not their unwillingness to work.

IV. Speed Warranties

87. Where speed warranties are provided, the courts draw a distinction between speed loss due to accidental fouling and that arising from natural causes. Speed warranties are contained in both the Baltime and NYPE off-hire clauses. In *Cosmos Bulk Transport Incorporated v. China National Foreign Trade Transportation Corporation (The Apollonius)* [1978] 1 All ER 322 [[1978] 1 Lloyd's Rep 53], a vessel was chartered on the Baltime form for carriage of cargo between ports in Japan and South America. The charter party warranted that 'fully loaded [the vessel was] capable of steaming about 141/2 knots in good weather and smooth water on a consumption of about 38 tons of oil-fuel'.[148] At the date of the charter party, the vessel was capable of steaming at the speed warranted. While the vessel was in Whampoa, China, discharging its cargo, the hull became encrusted with a thick coat of molluscs. It was unusual for molluscs to be found in the fresh water there, at the mouth of the Yangtse River, as the creatures normally preferred salt water. When the vessel sailed from Whampoa it had a foul bottom. The vessel was still fouled when it sailed for Argentina at a diminished speed due to the encrustations. Mocatta J in the Queen's Bench Division (QBD) held that for the purposes of Clause 11(A) of the charter party 'damage to hull or other accident' an 'accident' meant something unexpected or out of the ordinary. The mollusc encrustation at Whampoa was both of these and did amount to an accident within the meaning of the clause. Mocatta J held that the charterers were entitled to refuse to pay for the four-and-a-half days lost as a result. The speed warranty applied not only at the date of the charter party but also to the date of the delivery of the vessel.[149]

---

147. *Canadian Pacific (Bermuda) v. Canadian Transport Co (The HR Macmillan)* [1974] 1 Lloyd's Rep 311 (CA), Lord Denning at 314.

148. *Cosmos Bulk Transport Incorporated v. China National Foreign Trade Transportation Corporation (The Apollonius)* [1978] 1 All ER 322 [[1978] 1 Lloyd's Rep 53] (QB), J. Mocatta at 326. *See Santiren Shipping Ltd v. Unimarine SA (The Chrysovalandou-Dyo)* [1981] All ER 340 (QBD); *See* S. Baughen & N. Campbell, 'Hull Fouling – Charterparty Issues' [2006] LMCLQ 129. *See Bimco Uniform Time-Charter* (BIMCO), 2001 box 12, lines 10–15; Association of Ship Brokers and Agents (USA) Inc *(NYPE 93)(ASBA 1993) lines 18–29* both at http://ww.bimco.org.

149. *Cosmos Bulk Transport Incorporated v. China National Foreign Trade Transportation Corporation (The Apollonius)* [1978] 1 All ER 322 [[1978] 1 Lloyd's Rep 53] (QB), J. Mocatta 337. *See* S. Boyd, S. Berry, A. Burrows, B. Eder, D. Foxton & C. Smith, *Scrutton on Charterparties and Bills of Lading* [A49] (21st ed., Sweet & Maxwell 2008); M. Davies & A. Dickey, *Shipping Law* 349 (3d ed., Lawbook Co 2004); S. Derrington, *Charterparties*, in *Australian Maritime Law* [6.2.2] (a) (M. White ed., 2d ed., The Federation Press 2000). For a case involving speed reduction due to fouling *see Santa Martha Baay Scheepvaart & Handelsmaatschappij NV v. Scanbulk A/S (The*

88. In *Santa Martha Baay Scheepvaart & Handelsmaatschappij NV v. Scanbulk A/S (The Rijn)* [1981] 2 Lloyd's Rep 267, the issue of speed reduction due to fouling also arose. The vessel was chartered under the NYPE form and her hull became fouled by marine growth during a long period of waiting for, and loading, cargo. The charterers claimed that the vessel was off-hire for the time lost as a result under Clause 15 as the fouling was 'any other cause preventing the full working of the vessel'. Deduction from hire was also claimed on the basis that speed had been reduced 'by defect in … her hull'. Both these claims were rejected by Mustill J, who observed:

> The draftsman cannot possibly have intended that hire should cease in every circumstance where the full working of the vessel is prevented. This reading would be commercial nonsense, and would make the second half of the clause redundant. In my judgment, only those causes qualify for consideration which are fortuitous, and are not the natural result of the ship complying with the charterers' orders … I am bound to say that I find it hard to visualise the accumulation of marine growth during the contract service as a 'defect' in the hull. But even if it were, the defect arose as a natural consequence of the way in which the charterers chose to employ the ship. I do not consider that the loss of time thus caused should be deducted from the amount of time for which hire is payable.[150]

89. Where hire is expressed to cease when time is lost by 'any other cause', it will only do so if that cause prevents the full working of the vessel. This term is expressed in Clause 15 of the NYPE form. In *Court Line Ltd v. Dant & Russell Inc.* [1939] 3 All ER 314, a vessel chartered in 1937 under an NYPE form charter party was trapped in the Yangtse River when the Chinese Government placed a boom across the river to prevent the entry of hostile Japanese forces. Branson J held, *inter alia*, that the off-hire clause did not apply where the ship was in every way sound but was prevented by outside forces from continuing its voyage.[151] The off-hire clause may not operate where the event which would otherwise cause it to come into effect stems from a breach by the charterer.[152]

Rijn) [1981] 2 Lloyd's Rep 267 where the charterers claimed the vessel was of hire under NYPE Cl. 15 as the fouling by marine growth was 'any other cause preventing the full working of the vessel'. J. Mustill rejected this claim and another alleged defect in the hull.' I am bound to say I find it hard to visualize the accumulation of main growth during the contract service as a 'defect' in the hull. The defect arose as a natural consequence of the way in which the charterers chose to employ the ship. I do not consider the loss of time thus caused should be deducted from the amount of time for which hire is payable (at 272).

150. *Santa Martha Baay Scheepvaart & Handelsmaatschappij NV v. Scanbulk A/S (The Rijn)* [1981] 2 Lloyd's Rep 267 (QB), J. Mustill at 272.

151. *Court Line Ltd v. Dant & Russell Inc.* [1939] 3 All ER 314 (KB), J. Branson at 319. *See also Sidermar SpA v. Apollo Corporation (The Apollo)* [1978] 1 Lloyd's Rep 200 (QB) (vessel held to be off-hire due to health check and disinfection by port health authorities). *Actis Co Ltd v. Sanko Steamship Co Ltd (The Aquacharm)* [1982] 2 All ER 390 (CA) (a vessel which was overloaded and requiring offloading and reloading through the Panama Canal was held fit to carry and not off-hire).

152. *Lensen Shipping Co Ltd v. Anglo Soviet Shipping Co Ltd* (1935) 40 Com Cas 320 (CA); *see* M. Wilford, T. Coghlin & N.J. Healy, *Time Charters* 255 (3d ed., Lloyd's of London Press 1982).

90. The charterer may deduct from payments of hire certain amounts (such as advances for wages and port charges), irrespective of whether or not the terms of the charter party specifically so allow.[153] The charterer may deduct from hire by way of equitable set off in respect of counter claims, whether or not there is express provision in the charter party for the right to deduct. In *Seven Seas Transportation Ltd v. Atlantic Shipping Co SA* [1975] 2 Lloyd's Rep 188, the vessel was chartered under the New York Produce form. Hire was paid punctually for the full period of the charter up to 19 November 1974, but no payment was made between then and redelivery on 10 December 1974. The owners claimed a total unpaid hire of USD 97,000 and the charterers put in a cross-claim of USD 150,000 which they held could be set up against the hire claim. Donaldson J held that the charterers could, in principle, set off the cost of diesel oil used for domestic consumption and, under the off-hire clause, could set off their claim for loss of time during the first four voyages. On the basic point as to whether and to what extent charterers could use cross-claims as a defence to a claim for unpaid hire, Donaldson J was not prepared to accept that this was permissible, on the ground that hire was to be treated in the same way as freight against which there was no right to set off. Additionally there was the consideration that if an alleged claim for breach of the charter, when proved, could be set off against hire, there would be total confusion as to when hire was due and the vessel could be withdrawn.[154]

V. Redelivery

91. A charterer will normally not be in breach of a charter party in sending a vessel on a final voyage which may be expected to allow redelivery within or outside the charter period unless the charter party expressly imposes an absolute obligation to redeliver the vessel by a certain date.[155] If the vessel cannot be redelivered until after the expiry of the charter period, the charterers will be obliged to pay hire at the agreed charter rate until the date of actual redelivery.[156] In *London & Overseas Freighters Ltd v. Timber Shipping Co JA (The London Explorer)* [1971] 1

153. *Seven Seas Transportation Ltd v. Atlantic Shipping Co SA* [1975] 2 Lloyd's Rep 188 (QB). *See* S. Baughen, *Off-Hire Claim and Arrest of Ship*, 20(5) J Intl Mar L 319 (2015).

154. *Seven Seas Transportation Ltd v. Atlantic Shipping Co SA* [1975] 2 Lloyd's Rep 188 (QB), J. Donaldson at 190. *See also Compania Sud Americana de Vapores v. Shipmair BV (The Teno)* [1977] 2 Lloyd's Rep 289 (QB); *Lake Port Navigation Co Panam SA v. Anonima Petroi Italiana spA (The Olympic Brilliance)* [1981] 2 Lloyd's Rep 176 (CA); *Federal Commerce & Navigation Ltd v. Molena Alpha Inc.* [1978] 1 Lloyd's Rep 581 (QB).

155. *London & Overseas Freighters Ltd v. Timber Shipping Co JA (The London Explorer)* [1971] 1 Lloyd's Rep 523. *See* S. Boyd, S. Berry, A. Burrows, B. Eder, D. Foxton & C. Smith, *Scrutton on Charterparties and Bills of Lading* (21st ed., Sweet & Maxwell 2008); M. Davies & A. Dickey, *Shipping Law* 362–369 (3d ed., Lawbook Co 2004); S. Derrington, *Charterparties*, in *Australian Maritime Law* [2.10] (M. White ed., 2d ed., The Federation Press 2000).

156. *The Dione* [1975] 1 Lloyd's Rep 115. *Torwald Klaveness A/S v. Arni Maritime Corp (The Gregos)* [1994] 1 WLR 1465; [1994] 4 All ER 998(hl), L.J. Mustill at 1474 (WLR) (Ackner, Stynn & L.J.J. Woolf concurring). *See* F. Reynolds, *Legitimate Last Voyage*, LMCLQ 173 (1991).

Lloyd's Rep 523,[157] the vessel was chartered on the New York Produce form for 'twelve months fifteen days more or less in charterers option' with the preceding word 'about' deleted. The vessel was considerably delayed by strikes on its final voyage beyond its usual redelivery date. The freight rate had fallen in the interim and the charterers set out to establish that they were in breach. This would make them liable to pay damages for the period of overlap at the then market rate instead of the higher rate as stipulated under the charter. The HL held that there was no breach of contract by the charterers. The orders for the final voyage were valid and held despite the unexpected delays. Under the charter party, in any case, hire was payable until redelivery at the charter rate.

92. A shipowner may be entitled to be indemnified by the charterers against loss sustained as a result of the charterers' acts or of loss sustained by the shipowner carrying out the charterers' orders. Time charters usually contain express indemnity clauses. Clause 9 of the Baltime form provides that indemnity clauses may be implied where such clauses are not present, as the case of the New York Produce form.[158]

93. A charterer's liability for delay in delivery and for damage to the vessel and cargo on the basis of negligence may be explicitly regulated by the charter party. Clause 13 of the Baltime form makes such express provision. Financial loss is included in the term 'damage' in Clause 13, and the term is not limited to loss or damage to goods. In *The Nippon Yusen Kaisha v. Acme Shipping Corporation* [1972] 1 WLR 74 [[1972] 1 All ER 35; [1972] 1 Lloyd's Rep 1],[159] the vessel was chartered on the Baltime form. Although the vessel was ordered by the charterers to discharge cargo at a particular port, the master refused. The charterers claimed

---

157. *London & Overseas Freighters Ltd v. Timber Shipping Co JA (The London Explorer)* [1971] 1 Lloyd's Rep 523. *See also Attica Sea Carriers Corporation v. Ferrostaal Poseidon Bulk Reederei GmbH (Puerto Buitrago)* [1976] 1 Lloyd's Rep 250 (CA); *Arta Shipping Co v. Thai Europe Tapioca Service Ltd (The Johnny)* [1977] 1 Lloyd's Rep 257 (QB). Regarding the early redelivery of a vessel *see Ocean Marine Navigation Ltd v. Koch Carbon Inc (The Dynamic)* [2003] 2 Lloyd's Rep 695 applying *White& Carter (Councils) Ltd v. McGregor* [1962] AC 413. *See also Golden Strait Corp v. Nippon Yusen Kubishika Kaisha (The Golden Victory)* [2007] 2 AC 353 (damages for early delivery). *See* D. Foxton, *Damages for Late or Early Redelivery under Time Charterparties*, LMCLQ 461 (2008).

158. *Strathlorne Steamship Co Ltd v. Andrew Weir* (1934) 40 Com Cas 168 (CA); *Royal Greek Government v. Minister of Transport (The Ann Strathatos)* (1950) 83 Ll L Rep 228. *See Chiswell Shipping and Liberian Jaguar Transports Inc v. National Iranian Tankers Co (The World Symphony and The World Renown)* [1992] 2 Lloyd's Rep 115(CA) (*Shelltime 3* time charter party permitted the FTD (final terminal date) to be extended, covering a voyage that would otherwise have been illegitimate). Compare *BIMCO Uniform Time-Charter* (BIMCO 2001) Cl. 7 requiring the payment of hire at market rate if exceeding the contract rate for a last legitimate voyage exceeding the FTD.

159. *The Nippon Yusen Kaisha v. Acme Shipping Corporation* [1972] 1 WLR 74 [[1972] 1 All ER 35; [1972] 1 Lloyd's Rep 1] (CA). *See Cosmos Bulk Transport Incorporated v. China National Foreign Trade Transportation Corporation (The Apollonius)* [1978] 1 All ER 322 [[1978] 1 Lloyd's Rep 53] (QB); *Tor Line A/B v. Altrans Group of Canada (The TFL Prosperity)* [1982] 1 Lloyd's Rep 617 (QB).

damages for loss of time and for expenses incurred by the master's refusal. The CA held that Clause 13 effectively protected the owners.[160]

VI. Cancelling Clauses

94. A cancelling clause in a time charter party gives a charterer the automatic right to cancel the charter in certain express circumstances. It will operate independently of breach of the contract.[161] The option to cancel by a charterer when a vessel was not available at a specified date, together with other issues, including anticipatory breach, was considered by the English CA in *Maredelanto Compania Naviera SA v. Bergbau-Handel GmbH (The Mihalis Angelos)* [1971] 1 QB 164 [[1970] 3 WLR 601; [1970] 3 All ER 125]. Under the Gencon voyage charter party, it was provided that the Mihalis Angelos 'now trading and expected ready to load under this charter about 1 July 1965' would proceed to Haiphong in North Vietnam and there load a cargo of apatite. Clause 11 of the charter provided that should the vessel not be ready to load on or before 25 July, the charterers had the option of cancelling the contract. The vessel arrived at Hong Kong on 23 June but did not complete discharge of cargo until 23 July. She had to have a special survey which would have taken two days with a further two days to sail to Haiphong. The charterers had discovered that there was no apatite awaiting at Haiphong, which they understood was due to American bombing of the railway to the port. On 17 July, the charterers informed the owners that they had cancelled the contract on the grounds of force majeure.[162] The owners accepted this information as a repudiation of the charter.

The CA,[163] held that the 'readiness to load' clause could properly be described as a condition of the charter party and was an assurance by the owners that they honestly expected on reasonable grounds that the vessel would be ready to load on 1 July. Accordingly, when the charterers discovered the falsity of the owners' assurance, they were entitled to cancel the charter immediately. Even if the charterers had not been entitled to terminate the charter on 1 July under Clause 1, the owners would have been granted only nominal damages for wrongful repudiation by the charterers. This was because the charterers would have later been entitled to cancel under Clause 11, which they would have done on grounds of delay and this would

160. *The Nippon Yusen Kaisha v. Acme Shipping Corporation* [1972] 1 WLR 74 [[1972] 1 All ER 35; [1972] 1 Lloyd's Rep 1] (CA), M.R. Lord Denning at 78–79 (Cairns and L.J.J. Roskill agreeing).

161. For liability for delay in delivery and damage to a vessel or its cargo *see BIMCO Uniform Time-Charter* (BIMCO 2001) Cl. 9. Compare Association of Ship Brokers and Agents (USA) INC *(NYPE 93)*(ASBA 1993) Cl. 8(a) both at http://www.bimco.org indicating that the charterers perform certain activities 'at their risk and expense'.

162. Force majeure clause: '[a] contractual clause excluding liability where a party's failure to perform is caused by forces (either natural or human) beyond his/her control': *TheCCH Macquarie Dictionary of aw* (rev. ed., CCH. 1996), 73.

163. *Maredelanto Compania Naviera SA v. Bergbau-Handel GmbH (The Mihalis Angelos)* [1971] 1 QB 164 [[1970] 3 WLR 601; [1970] 3 All ER 125] (CA) (reversing J. Mocatta's decision in *Maredelanto Compania Naviera SA v. Bergbau-Handel GmbH (The Mihalis Angelos)* [1970] 1 All ER 673 (QB)).

have had to be taken into account as reducing the owners' loss. Megaw LJ stated that breach of an expected readiness clause in a charter party should be regarded as sufficient grounds to validly repudiate the contract.[164] M.R. Lord Denning dissented, holding that Clause 11 did not entitle the charterers to cancel on 17 July because, on strict construction of the clause the option to cancel could not be exercised before 20 July, even though it was clear before that date that the vessel would not be ready to load on the date.[165] In practice cargo claims under the New York Produce Exchange Form *(NYPE 93)* are settled in accordance with a form of the *Inter-Club New York Produce Exchange Agreement.* It is an agreement between major protection and indemnity associations (P&I club) which insure a variety of marine risks. The aim of the agreement is to simplify marine arbitration by apportioning liability between the charterers and shipowners for cargo claims (and associated costs) arising from unseaworthiness, bad stowage, or handling and damage from shipment. Clause 27 of *NYPE 93* incorporates the 1984 version of the Agreement and subsequent amendments. Where applicable, the Agreement will, for example, apportion liability equally between the charterer and the shipowner for a short delivery claim.[166]

§5. Special Clauses and Frustration

I. War, Ice, and Penalty Clauses

95. The rights and obligations of the parties under a charter party in the event of war or armed conflict may be governed by stipulations in the charter party known as 'war clauses'. These clauses are framed to address the risks and dangers to a vessel and cargo that may prevent the vessel from carrying out the contract voyage. War clauses are commonly found in time charters. Those of particular note are Genorecon, Baltime, the Chamber of Shipping, NYPE clauses.[167] These clauses and others of a similar function are essentially drafted to prevent the charterer from ordering the vessel to a port or place rendered hazardous by war.

---

164. *Maredelanto Compania Naviera SA v. Bergbau-Handel GmbH (The Mihalis Angelos)* [1971] 1 QB 164 [[1970] 3 WLR 601; [1970] 3 All ER 125] (CA), L.J. Megaw at 205.
165. *Maredelanto Compania Naviera SA v. Bergbau-Handel GmbH (The Mihalis Angelos)* [1971] 1 QB 164 [[1970] 3 WLR 601; [1970] 3 All ER 125] (CA), M.R. Denning at 195.
166. The *Inter-Club New York Produce Exchange Agreement* was revised in 1996, partially in response to the decision in *Inverans Rederei A/S v. MS Holstencruiser Seeschiffahrts GmbH & Co KG (The Holstencruiser)* [1992] 2 Lloyd's Rep 378 (QBD), For a reproduction of the Agreement *see* S. Boyd, S. Berry, A. Burrows, B. Eder, D. Foxton & C. Smith, *Scrutton on Charterparties and Bills of Laing* App. IV (21st ed., Sweet & Maxwell 2008). *See also*, M. Davies & A. Dickey, *Shipping Law* 389–391 (3d ed., Lawbook Co 2004); S. Baughen, *Shipowners' Implied Indemnity for Cargo Claims*, LMCLQ 15 (1996). *See* on cargo claims *Kamilla Hans-Peter Eckhoff KG v. AC Oersleff's EFTF A/B (The Kamilla)* [2006] 2 Lloyd's Rep 238; [2006] EWHC 509(Comm.)(unseaworthiness and cargo loss). *See also* S. Baughen *Withdrawal with Cargo Still on Board; the Kos*, LMCLQ 343 (2012). and S. Baughen, L 248 (2004).
167. *See BIMCO Uniform Time-Charter (1994 Gencom)*(BIMCO 1994) Cl. 17; Cl. 20; Association of Ship Brokers and Agents (USA) Inc *(NYPE 93)* Cl. 31(e), 32 at http://www.bimco.org.

96. The significance and construction of the Baltime war clause, was considered, among other aspects of the Baltime form, in *Ocean Tramp Tankers Corporation v. V/O Sovfracht (The Eugenia)* [1964] 2 QB 226 [[1964] 2 WLR 114; [1964] 1 All ER 161; [1963] 2 Lloyd's Rep 381]. Under a time charter party concluded on 9 September 1956, The Eugenia was chartered, when at Genoa, for a 'trip out to India via Black Sea'. The Suez Canal had been nationalized by the Egyptian Government on 26 July 1956. Both parties to the charter party realized that intervention by English and French forces might lead to the Canal's becoming impassable to shipping. The charter party provided (under Clause 21) that The Eugenia should not, unless the owners agreed, be used on any service which would bring the vessel within a zone which was dangerous as the result of actual or threatened warlike operations. If the vessel was brought within such a zone the owners could, among other matters, insure their interests in the vessel, the charterers being obliged to refund the premium on demand. On 25 October the vessel sailed from Odessa and arrived at Port Said on 30 October, the Suez Canal still being the customary route. On that date Egyptian artillery were in action and bombing of the Canal by Franco-British forces commenced on 31 October. On that date, the vessel had already entered the Canal and the Egyptian Government had blocked the waterway at both ends by scuttling vessels. The Eugenia, as a result, was trapped until 8 January 1957. The arbitrator and the English CA held that the charterers were in breach of Clause 21(A). Denning LJ in the CA noted the argument by counsel for the charterers that, although the charter party was on a printed form applicable to a time charter, the paramount feature of it was a voyage and so it was to be construed accordingly. However, Denning LJ held:

> The charterer must, of course, give his orders within the limits permitted by the contract … but still the ship is under his orders none the less … [T]he Eugenia was … under charterers' orders when she arrived off Port Said. Port Said and the Suez Canal were at that time zones which were dangerous within the war clause. So they were in breach of it. But even if they did not 'order' her to enter the Suez Canal, they allowed her to 'continue' when it was obviously dangerous, and were thus in breach of it (original emphasis).[168]

97. An 'ice clause' is commonly inserted in a charter party where ice hindrances may arise in the port of loading or discharge. For example, charterers may undertake to 'provide icebreaker assistance to enable the ship to reach, load at, and leave' the port of loading. Such a clause imposes an absolute obligation on the charterers to provide continuous icebreaker assistance[169] until the ship is able to proceed on her voyage from the loading port clear of all ice obstruction. This liability extends

---

168. *Ocean Tramp Tankers Corporation v. V/O Sovfracht (The Eugenia)* [1964] 2 QB 226 [[1964] 2 WLR 114; [1964] 1 All ER 161; [1963] 2 Lloyd's Rep 381] (CA), M.R. Lord Denning at 237.

169. *See* Uniform General Charter (1994 *Gencom*)(BIMCO 1994) Cl. 18; Association of Ship Brokers and Agents (USA) Inc *(NYPE 93) (*ASBA 1993) Cl. 33 (dealing with safely navigating ice hazards and following icebreakers) at http://www,bimco.org. *Ugleexport Charkow v. SS Anastasia* (1934) 39 Com Cas 238 (HL).

beyond port limits to as far out to sea as the ice obstruction extends.[170] The charterers are liable under such a clause, if they fail to provide icebreaker assistance, for damage that occurs to the ship while passing through the ice, unless they can prove that the damage would have occurred in any case.[171]

98. Penalty clauses purporting to stipulate a fixed penalty for non-performance of a charter party are of little practical effect. In early practice, it was common in charter parties to stipulate a fixed penalty for the non-performance of the charter party, usually in their terms 'penalty for non-performance of this agreement estimated amount of freight'.[172] In practice, such a clause does not, in its use of the word 'penalty', limit the amount of damages which may be claimed,[173] nor does it allow either party to claim the amount of the penalty for partial breach of the contract.[174] Since the clause has generally been considered inoperative and of having no effect on claims for damages under the charter party, it is difficult to justify its continued presence in standard form charter parties.[175]

II. Frustration of Charter Parties

99. Where a vessel becomes a total loss, is commercially destroyed, unduly detained, or if performance of the charter becomes illegal or impossible to perform, the charter may be said to have been frustrated.[176] The Iran-Iraq conflict gave rise to a series of cases in which the issues of frustration and consistency of maritime arbitrations were of fundamental importance. In *International Sea Tankers Incorporated of Liberia v. Hemisphere Shipping Co of Hong Kong (The Wenjang)* [1981] 2 Lloyd's Rep 308, Goff J in the Commercial Court regarded the basic issue as the assessment of warlike activities in the Shatt-al-Arab waterway, and when those activities rendered the performance of the contract a thing radically different from that which had been undertaken. Judicial concern at inconsistency of arbitral awards

---

170. *Russian Wood Agency v. Dampskibselskabet Heimdal (The Ask)* (1934) 39 Com Cas 238 (HL).
171. *Rendal A/S v. Arcos* [1937] 3 All ER 577 (HL), Lord Wright at 588.
172. S. Boyd, S. Berry, A. Burrows, B. Eder, D. Foxton & C. Smith, *Scrutton on Charterparties and Bills of Lading* [192] (21st ed., Sweet & Maxwell 2008).
173. *Harrison v. Wright* (1811) 13 East 343 [104 ER 402]; *Wall v. Rederiaktiebolaget Luggude* [1915] 3 KB 66; *Mitsui v. Watts* [1916] 2 KB 826 (CA).
174. *Leeds Shipping Co v. Societe Francaise Bunge* [1958] 2 Lloyd's Rep 127 (CA).
175. S. Boyd, S. Berry, A. Burrows, B. Eder, D. Foxton & C. Smith, *Scrutton on Charterparties and Bills of Lading* 348 (21st ed., Sweet & Maxwell 2008), observing that it is 'a mystery why the clause survives, except upon the supposition that chartering brokers regard it as a piece of sacred ritual'. *See also Lansa Shipping Co Ltd v. Glencore Grain BV (The Paragon)* [2010] 1 All ER (Comm) 459, [2009]EWCA Civ 855 (penalty clause concerning late delivery under a time charter party was inoperative).
176. *See Hong Kong Fir Shipping Co Ltd v. Kawasaki Kisen Kaisha Ltd* [1962] 2 QB 26 [[1961] 2 WLR 716; [1961] 2 All ER 257; [1961] 1 Lloyd's Rep 159] (CA); *Ocean Tramp Tankers Corporation v. V/O Sovfracht (The Eugenia)* [1963] 2 Lloyd's Rep 155 (QB) (applied in *Plaimar Ltd v. Waters Trading Co Ltd* (1945) 72 CLR 304). *See also Pioneer Shipping Ltd v. BTP Tioxide Ltd (The Nema)* [1981] 3 WLR 292 [[1981] 2 All ER 1030; [1981] 2 Lloyd's Rep 239] (HL).

can be particularly understood where arbitration produced totally different results for the date of frustration in virtually identical circumstances.[177]

100. In *Finelvet AG v. Vinava Shipping Co (The Chrysalis)* [1983] 1 WLR 1469 [[1983] 2 All ER 658; [1983] 1 Lloyd's Rep 309], the use of a declaration of war as the crucial determining date would have benefited the charterers as they would not have had to wait on delay or impossibility arising from actual hostilities in order to be discharged from the contract. The position was rejected by Mustill J, in the Commercial Court, on appeal from the decision of an arbitrator. A declaration of war did not prevent the performance of the contract. Mustill J distinguished between illegality, which was a question of law, and frustration, which was a question of mixed fact and law. It was the acts done in carrying out the war which might or might not prevent performance. Any presumption of frustration related to the duration of the state of war, and not the effect that the war might have on the performance of the contract. It followed that the charterers' argument that a declaration of war, without more, could frustrate a contract was wrong, and was, thus, rejected.[178]

101. Impracticability of performance is not generally recognized as grounds for discharge of a contracting party. In *Hyundai Merchant Marine Co Ltd v. Dartbrook Coal Sales Pty Ltd* [2006] 236 ALR 115, Dartbrook agreed to charter a vessel from Hyundai for the carriage of coal from Newcastle to Masinloc in the Philippines. Dartbrook was acting for other parties, Marumbeni Thermal Coal Pty Ltd and in connection with the charter party and the agreement for the sale of coal to the National Power Corporation. Anglo Coal (Dartbrook) Pty Ltd, Marubeni and Ssangyong Resources were joint venturers in a coal mining operation and Dartbrook Coal (Sales) was their agent for the sale of the coal.

102. Hyundai alleged Dartbrook (Sales) wrongfully repudiated the charter party on 14 April 2004 and sought damages from both Dartbrook and Marumbeni. Marumbeni held that the charter party was conditional on the sale of the coal being

177. *Golden Strait Corp v. Nippon Yusen Kubishika Kaisha (The Golden Victory)* [2007] 2 AC 353; [2007] 2 WLR 691 [2007] 3 AllER 1; [2007] UKHL 12. J. Bigham at [23] (dissenting) noting that '[t]he importance of certainty and predictability in commercial transactions has been a constant theme of English commercial law.'

178. *Finelvet AG v. Vinava Shipping Co (The Chrysalis)* [1983] 1 WLR 1469 [[1983] 2 All ER 658; [1983] 1 Lloyd's Rep 309] (QB). For a discussion of the effect of the Iran-Iraq war on charter party frustration *see* B. Hibbits, *The Impact of the Iran-Iraq Cases on the Law of Frustration of Charter Parties*, 16(441) JIMLC (1985); Institute of Maritime Law, *Problems of the Shatt-al-Arab* (Southampton: Institute of Maritime Law 1983). Maritime Law 1993) *See* M. Davies & A. Dickey, *Shipping Law* 398–399 (3d ed., Law Book Co 2004). 'The outbreak of [the Iran-Iraq War]. did not ipso facto frustrate time charterparties of the trapped ships, as it was possible that it might be of short duration only, The charterparties were frustrated only when it became clear that the conflict would continue for a sufficient period to bring to an end the contracts as commercial propositions'. For Australian legislation *see Frustrated Contracts Act* 1978 (NSW), s. 6(1)(c); *Frustrated Contracts Act 1988* (SA) s. 4(2)(c); *Fair Trading Act* 1999 (Vic) s. 32ZF (3), 9(a). Each Act is expressed to apply only to time and demise charterparties. In other Australian jurisdictions (or all in the case of voyage charterparties) the common law position will govern the allocation of losses (i.e., the recovery of monies is permitted under a frustrated charter party where there has been a total failure of consideration).

concluded and that no binding agreement was reached with National Power. The defendants put in issue whether it was ready, willing, and able to perform in accordance with the charter party. Each of the defendants held that Dartbrook's inability to ship the coal was for reasons beyond its control and constituted a force majeure event within the meaning of the charter party. At issue was whether Hyundai was obliged to use a vessel and seek a substituted cargo.

103. The Federal Court found for the plaintiff Hyundai holding that impracticability of performance was not generally recognized as grounds for discharge of a contracting party. Further, that what the courts recognize as constituting a force majeure was something irresistible, unforeseeable external to the person claiming discharge, making performance impossible not merely more difficult.[179]

§6. Bills of Lading

I. Principal Functions

104. A bill of lading[180] has three principal functions. These are:

(1) it is evidence of the previously concluded contract of carriage between the shipper and the carrier;
(2) it acts as a receipt by the carrier for the goods described in it; and
(3) it operates as a document of title to the goods, the property in which may be transferred by endorsement.

A bill of lading is normally issued once goods are shipped, or when received by the carrier for shipment. It is settled law that a bill of lading is not itself the contract of carriage but merely evidence of it.[181] The fact that a bill of lading has been issued

179. *See* S. Boyd, S. Berry, A. Burrows, B. Eder, D. Foxton & C. Smith, *Scrutton on Charterparties and Bills of Lading* [13] (21st ed., Sweet & Maxwell 2008).

180. *See* Department of Transport and Communications, *Draft Discussion Paper: Proposals for Reform of Australian Bills of Lading Legislation* (Canberra: A-G's Department 1993). A strict judicial interpretation in Australian courts as to what documents may be defined as a bill of lading is exemplified in *Carrington Slipways Pty Ltd v. Patrick Operations Pty Ltd* (1991) 24 NSWLR 745 (CA) and *Comalco Alumincan Ltd v. Mogal Freight Services Pty Ltd* (1993) 113 ALR 677 [[1993] ATPR (Digest) 53,472 (46–106)] (Fed Ct). However, the House of Lords in the *Raefaela S.* held that a non-negotiable or straight bill of lading was within the scope of Art. 1(b) of the Hague-Visby Rules and acted to transfer title; *see* fn. 286. On bills of lading generally, *see* F. Hannah & R. Grime, *Sea Carriage Documents* in *Australian Maritime Law* Ch. 4 (M. White ed., 2d ed., The Federation Press 2000); M. Davies & A. Dickey, *Shipping Law* Ch. 12 (3d ed., Lawbook Co 2004); G. Treitel & F. Reynolds, *Carver on Bills of Lading* (2d ed., Sweet & Maxwell 2005). Australian courts have on occasion applied a strict interpretation regarding what documents may be defined as a bill of lading: *see Carrington Slipways Pty Ltd v. Patrick Operations Pty Ltd* (1991) 24 NSWLR 745(CA); *Comalco Aluminium Ltd v. Mogul Freight Services Pty Ltd* (1993) 113 ALR 677(FCA). *Bills of Lading: Law and Contracts* N. Gaskell, R. Asariotis.Y. Baatz LLP 200.

181. *Sewell v. Burdick* (1884) 10 App Cas 74, Lord Bramwell at 104. *JL MacWilliam Co Inc v. Mediterranean Shipping Co SA (The Rafaela S)* [2005] 2 AC 423; [2005] 2 WLR 554; [2005] 2 All ER

does not mean that a contract has been concluded.[182] As Devlin J stated in *Pyrene Co Ltd v. Scindia Navigation Co Ltd* [1954] 2 QB 402 [[1954] 2 WLR 1005; [1954] 2 All ER 158; [1954] 1 Lloyd's Rep 321]:

> [W]hen parties enter into a contract of carriage in the expectation that a bill of lading will be issued to cover it, they enter into it upon those terms which they know or expect the bill of lading to contain. Those terms must be in force from the inception of the contract: if it were otherwise the bill of lading would not evidence the contract but would be a variation of it. Moreover, it would be absurd to suppose that the parties intend the terms of the contract to be changed when the bill of lading is issued.[183]

105. The bill of lading is in practice regarded as the source of the terms of the contract of carriage, even though the bill of lading issues after the contract is concluded. Where the terms of the contract and those in the bill of lading are at variance, the former governs the contract.[184] In *Owners of the Cargo of SS Ardennes v. SS Ardennes* [1951] 1 KB 55 [[1950] 2 All ER 517], the discrepancy was between an oral representation and a bill of lading.[185] The plaintiff shipped a cargo of oranges on the defendant's ship on the basis of the oral promise of the defendant's agent that the cargo would be shipped directly from Cartagena in Spain to London. A bill of lading issued after the loading gave the shipowners the freedom to carry the goods by any route direct or indirect to their port of destination. The carrying vessel stopped at Antwerp en route to London and the resultant delay caused loss to the plaintiff. C.J. Lord Goddard, finding for the plaintiff, held that although the bill of lading was not itself the contract of carriage, oral evidence was admissible to prove the existence of a previous bargain or promise, the terms of which were inconsistent with the terms contained in the bill of lading. Once a binding contract was concluded in terms not permitting deviation, nothing in the subsequently issued bill of lading could alter the terms of the previous contract.[186]

106. In *Australian Tallow & Agri-Commodities Pty Ltd v. Malaysia International Shipping Corporation* (2001) 50 New South Wales Law Reports (NSWLR) 579, a standard form bill of lading defined 'merchant' as including 'the shipper, holder, consignee, receiver of the goods, any person owing or entitled to the possession of the goods or this bill of lading and anyone acting on behalf of such person'.

86; [2005] UKHL 11, L.J. Steyn at [38]. *See also* G. McMeel, *'Straight' Bills of Lading in the House of Lords,* LMCLQ 273 (2005).

182. *Heskell v. Continental Express Ltd* [1950] 1 All ER 1033 (KB).
183. *Pyrene Co Ltd v. Scindia Navigation Co Ltd* [1954] 2 QB 402 [[1954] 2 WLR 1005; [1954] 2 All ER 158; [1954] 1 Lloyd's Rep 321], J. Devlin at 419.
184. *Pyrene Vo Ltd v. Scindia Navigation Co Ltd* [1954] 2 QB 402; [1954] @ WLR 1005; [1954] 2 All ER 158, J. Devlin at 419(QB).
185. *See also Smith v. Bedouin Steam Navigation Co Ltd* [1896] AC 70.
186. *Owners of the Cargo of SS Ardennes v. SS Ardennes* [1951] 1 KB 55 [[1950] 2 All ER 517], C.J. Lord Goddard at 60.

107. Further clauses in the bill of lading made the above persons jointly and severally liable for the payment of freight and gave the carrier a lien on the goods and any document relating to them.

108. The Court of Appeal of NSW held that a freight forwarder who arranges bills of lading for a shipper must be taken to know what are the terms of those bills of lading.

109. The freight forwarder was expressly covered by the definition of 'merchant' and was, therefore, jointly and severally liable for the payment of freight and to become a party to the contract of carriage with liability for such payment.

110. In *Spliethoff Transport BV v. Leisure Freight and Import Pty Ltd* [2013] FCCA 27 the applicant was a carrier of goods by sea incorporated in the Netherlands. It operated through an agent, Sevenstar Yacht Transport Australian Agencies Pty Ltd. The respondent company Leisure Freight specialized in the import of pleasure craft into Australia for private customers. Between 1 March 2011 and 1 March 2012 Sevenstar arranged for the import of sixteen pleasure craft or trailers for Leisure Freight. The port of loading (except for one craft) was Palm Beach, Florida and the destination or port of unloading was Newcastle/Brisbane/Fremantle.

111. The carrier was unable to ship on mid-April or March dates and the other times proposed by Sevenstar were not agreed between the parties. Leisure Craft claimed that Sevenstar failed to agree to a date of shipment and to ship the craft as required under the terms of the contractors and communicate that it was ready, willing, and able to complete the terms of the contract.[187] Leisure Freight accordingly claimed that Sevenstar had repudiated the contracts and so it terminated them. In the Federal Circuit Court of Appeal Raphael J found that there was no evidence that a vessel was considered to load the boats in question noting Lord Denning in *Mardelanto Compania Naviera SA v. Bergbau Handel GmbH (The Mihalis Angelos)* 1971 1 QB 164:

> If [the shipowner] or his agent breaks that [estimated loading] term by making the statement without any honest belief in its truth or without reasonable grounds for it, he must take the consequences. It is at lowest misrepresentation which entitles the other party to rescind: and highest a breach of contract which goes to the root of the matter[188]

Raphael J, finding for Leisure Freight, noted that the '*Mihalis Angelos* stands for the proposition that a purported termination will be valid if there was no valid reason for termination, even if that was not the reason given. Here the reason given for

187. The contact in this case resembled a simplified version of the Gencom charter party recommended by BIMCO and BIMCO's 'Conlinebooking 2000 Line Booking Note; *see* Gencom box 9' Expected ready to load (abt)'.

188. *The Mihalis Angelos* Lord Denning at, 194.

termination was delay, and I have found that to be the case, however it may be that misrepresentation could have more equally founded the notice of termination.'[189]

112. There are two exceptions to the general proposition that the bill of lading does not contain the contract of carriage between the carrier and the shipper but is only evidence of that contract. These exceptions are:

(1) Where a carrier issues a bill of lading to a charterer who is shipping its own goods on the chartered ship, the bill of lading acts, between those two parties, as a mere receipt of the goods.[190]
(2) When the bill of lading is passed to an endorsee by the shipper, irrespective of whether that shipper is a charterer, the contract between the shipowner and the endorsee is contained in the bill of lading.[191]

In *Leduc & Co v. Ward* (1888) 20 QBD 475, endorsees of a bill of lading sued the carrier for non-delivery of goods. The carrier pleaded that the goods had been lost through a peril of the sea, and this liability for loss was exempted by the bill of lading. The CA found for the endorsees on the basis that as the bill of lading was in the hands of the endorsees, the bill contained the contract as distinct from evidencing it.[192]

II. Evidence of Quantity Shipped

113. The bill of lading is prima facie evidence at common law that the quantity of goods claimed to have been shipped have, in fact, been shipped. A shipowner is entitled to show that the goods were never shipped.[193] If this is the case, the shipowner has no liability for the goods.[194] The rule was expressed in *Smith v. Bedouin Steam Navigation Co Ltd* [1896] AC 70, by Lord Watson as follows:

> The master of a ship has no authority to grant bills of lading for goods which were not put on board [the] vessel; but, when he signs a bill acknowledging the receipt of a specific quantity of goods, the shipowner is bound to deliver the full amount specified, unless he can show that the whole or some part of it was in fact not shipped. If the owner is able to satisfy that onus, by proving a

189. *Spliethoff Transport BV v. Leisure Freight and Import Pty Ltd* [2013] FCCA 27 J. Raphael at [77].
190. *Rodocanachi, Sons & Co v. Milburn Bros* (1886) 18 QBD 67 (CA).
191. *Leduc & Co v. Ward* (1888) 20 QBD 475 (CA); *Re The El Amira and The El Minia* [1982] 2 Lloyd's Rep 28 (CA). Where the endor*see* is a charterer, the charter party governs: *President of India v. Metcalfe Shipping Co Ltd* [1969] 2 QB 123.
192. *Leduc & Co v. Ward* (1888) 20 QBD 475 (CA), Lord Esher MR at 480, L.J. Fry at 483, L.J. Lopes at 485.
193. *Smith v. Bedouin Steam Navigation Co Ltd* [1896] AC 70.
194. *Grant v. Norway* (1851) 10 CB 665 [138 ER 263], followed by the HCA in *Rosenfeld Hillas & Co Pty Ltd v. The Fort Laramie* (1923) 32 CLR 25.

short shipment, he is, to that extent, relieved from the obligation which would otherwise attach to him under the bill of lading.[195]

114. In Rosenfeld *Hillas & Co Pty Ltd v. The Fort Laramie* (1923) 32 CLR 25, the High Court followed *Grant v. Norway* (1851) 10 CB 665 [138 ER 263], in holding that a bill of lading was not conclusive evidence of goods that were shipped. A bill of lading, which stated that a certain quantity of timber had been shipped on a vessel owned by several persons, was signed by the managing owner in his own name, describing himself as such. In an action in the High Court in Admiralty by an indorsee of the bill of lading against the ship for failure to deliver a certain part of the timber stated to have been shipped in the bill of lading, affirmative evidence was given by the defendant that supported the statement in the bill of lading. However, one of the defences relied on at the trial was that the timber in question had not been shipped. Reversing the decision of the High Court in Admiralty on the facts, the High Court[196] held that in relation to the execution and legal effect of a bill of lading there is no reason why the implied authority of a managing owner to bind the owners by an inaccurate statement as to the receipt of the goods should be greater than that of the master. Unless the holder of a bill of lading can prove an actual authority from the owners, greater than the apparent authority of the managing owner, such a holder cannot assert an authority larger than that of conducting the business in the usual manner. The 'usual manner' is to give a receipt for goods only after they are in fact shipped. If the goods have not been shipped, any receipt for them given by the managing owner is given beyond the scope of his or her implied authority, and in the absence of proof of actual authority, the co-owners (unless otherwise prevented from denying the managing owner's authority) are not bound.

115. Under the *Carriage of Goods by Sea Act* 1991 (Cth), there is provision for a bill of lading to constitute prima facie evidence of the receipt by the carrier of the goods described in the bill. Schedule 1 of this Act incorporates the Hague-Visby Rules. A shipper can demand that a bill of lading be issued to it showing '[e]ither the number of packages or pieces, or the quantity, or weight, as the case may be, as furnished in writing by the shipper'.[197] Where the shipper does so, the bill of lading is prima facie evidence of receipt. The shipper is 'deemed to have guaranteed to the carrier the accuracy at the time of shipment of the marks, number, quantity and weight, as furnished by him, and the shipper shall indemnify the carrier against all loss, damages, and expenses arising or resulting from inaccuracies in such particulars'.[198] Further, '[t]he right of the carrier to such indemnity shall in no way limit his responsibility and liability under the contract of carriage to any person other than the shipper'.[199]

---

195. *Smith v. Bedouin Steam Navigation Co Ltd* [1896] AC 70, Lord Watson at 77.
196. *Rosenfeld Hillas & Co Pty Ltd v. The Fort Laramie* (1923) 32 CLR 25, J. Starke at 29, J. Isaacs at 31, J. Higgins at 37.
197. Hague-Visby Rules, Art. 3 r. 3(b) (reproduced in *Carriage of Goods by Sea Act* 1991 (Cth)).
198. Hague-Visby Rules, Art. 3 r. 5.
199. Hague-Visby Rules, Art. 3 r. 5. Under Sch. III r. 4 of the *Carriage of Goods by Sea Act* 1971 (UK) as far as the statement as to quantity shipped, proof to the contrary is not admissible where the bill of lading has been transferred to a third party acting in good faith.

In *The Esmeralda 1* [1988]1 Lloyd's Rep 206, the NSW Supreme Court held that 'said to contained' clausing on a bill of in respect of a shipper-stuffed container did not conflict with the Hague Rules. It may be noted on the facts of the case the proviso to Article 3 Rule 3 would have entitled the carrier to refuse a demand by the shipper for an unqualified statement as to the content of the container.[200]

116. There is statutory provision for a bill of lading in the hands of its consignee or indorsee to be conclusive evidence as against the master or other person signing it that the goods represented to have been shipped were in fact shipped. This is provided by legislation.[201] However, the consignee or indorsee of a bill of lading may have no remedy against the shipowner. The statutory protection will not apply where the holder of the bill of lading knew when she or he took it that the goods had not been shipped or if the person signing can show that the misrepresentation was due to the fraud of the shipper, the holder of the bill of lading or some person under whom the holder claims.[202] The effect of this provision is to prevent the person who has actually signed the bill of lading, or the person in whose name and with whose authority it has been signed, in a proceeding between a consignee or indorsee for value and himself, from disputing the accuracy of the bill's statement as to kind and quantity of goods shipped. This will be the case unless the exception in the legislation applies.[203] It will not bind the shipowner when the bill of lading has been signed by its agents in their own names.

117. If a bill of lading contains the words 'weight and quantity unknown' this does not constitute prima facie evidence of shipment of the goods.[204] To succeed in an action for non-delivery a shipper has to show that the goods were in fact shipped.

In *New Chinese Antimony Co Ltd v. Ocean Steamship Co Ltd* [1917] 2 KB 664, a bill of lading stated that 937 tons of antimony oxide had been shipped on board. In the bill itself a printed clause stated 'weight, measurement, contents and value (except for the purposes of estimating freight) unknown'. It was held by the English

---

200. *See* S. Baughen, *Shipping Law* 74 (4th ed., Cavendish 2009).

201. But *see* F. Hannah & R. Grime, *Sea Carriage Documents* in *Australian Maritime Law* [4.2] (M. White ed., 2d ed., The Federation Press 2000). *Sea-Carriage Documents Act1997* (NSW) s. 12, *Sea-Carriage Documents Act 1998* (NT) s. 12, *Sea Carriage Documents Act 1995* (Qld) s. 10 (note that the term 'evidence' rather than 'prima facie evidence' is used in s. 10(2), *Sea Carriage Documents Act 1998*(SA) s. 11, *Sea Carriage Documents Act 1997* (Tas) s. 11, *Goods Act 1958* (Vic) s. 96, *Sea Carriage Documents Act 1997* (WA) s. 12. The Australian Capital Territory has no equivalent legislation.

202. *Sea Carriage Documents Act 1997* (NSW) s. 12(1), *Sea Carriage 1998* (NT) s. 12(1), *Sea Carriage Documents Act 1995* (Qld) s. 10(1), *Sea Carriage Documents Act 1998* (SA) s. 11(1), *Sea Carriage Documents Act 1997* (Tas) s. 11(1), *Goods Act 1958* (Vic) s. 96(1), *Sea Carriage Documents Act 1997* (WA) s. 12(1).

203. *Sale of Goods Act* 1923 (NSW), s. 50C; *Mercantile Act* 1867 (Qld), s. 7; *Mercantile Law Act* 1936 (SA), s. 15; *Bills of Lading Act* 1857 (Tas), s. 3; *Goods Act* 1958 (Vic), s. 74; *Bill of Lading Act* 1856 20 Vic 7 (WA). The ACT and the NT have no equivalent legislation. *See* A.P. Bell, *The Bills of Lading Act 1855 Today*, JBL 124 (1985). But *see* F. Hannah & R. Grime, *Sea Carriage Documents* in *Australian Maritime Law* [4.2] (M. White ed., 2d ed., The Federation Press 2000).

204. *See New Chinese Antimony Co Ltd v. Ocean Steamship Co Ltd* [1917] 2 KB 664 (CA). S. Boyd, S. Berry, A. Burrows, B. Eder, D. Foxon & C. Smith, *Scrutton on Charterparties and Bills of Lading* [A62] (21st ed., Sweet & Maxwell 2008).

CA that the bill of lading was not even prima facie evidence of the quantity of ore shipped. In an action against the shipowners for short delivery, the onus was on the plaintiffs to prove that the 937 tons had in fact been shipped.[205]

118. In *Ace Imports Pty Ltd v. Companhia de Navegacao Lloyd Brasileiro* (1987) 10 NSWLR 32, a 'shipped on board' bill of lading for a container shipment in respect of '437 cardboard boxes, containing cutlery and leaflets and posters' was endorsed by the carrier, who had no opportunity to inspect the contents prior to loading. The bill of lading also stated that the boxes were 'said to contain – packed by shippers'. Clause 9 of the bill of lading provided that it was 'prima facie evidence of the receipt by the carrier in apparent good order and condition, except as otherwise noted, of the total amount of the containers, packages or other units or weight of other cargoes specified on the face hereof'. In an action brought by the importer of the goods against the carrier, for damages for breach of carriage, breach of bailment and for negligence in respect of short delivery, the evidence established that the contents of the containers had been pillaged before the container was loaded on board. Yeldham J held that the carrier was not precluded by the terms of the bill of lading from denying that it had received for carriage the quantity of goods shipped. The endorsement in the bill of lading 'said to contain – packed by shipper' was a clear indication that the carrier made no representation as to the accuracy of the statement as to the contents of the container. Yeldham J stated that the carrier had no personal knowledge of the container's contents and relied on information supplied to him by the shipper.[206]

III. Good Order and Condition

119. Where goods in a bill of lading are described as being 'shipped in good order and condition', between a shipowner and a shipper other than the charterer, such admissions provide some evidence against the shipowner. The position between a shipowner and a shipper other than the charterer is that the relationship is governed by the charter party which cannot be varied by the bill of lading.[207] It must be shown by the shipper that the damage was due to the shipowner's fault, or that the goods were in fact shipped in good condition internally.[208] It is, however, open to both parties to agree by an express clause in the contractual document that the statements in the bill of lading shall be conclusive. Such a 'conclusive evidence clause' will bind the shipowner, unless fraud by the shipper can be proved.[209]

---

205. *New Chinese Antimony Co Ltd v. Ocean Steamship Co Ltd* [1917] 2 KB 664 (CA), C.J. Viscount Reading at 671 (L.J. Pickford agreeing), L.J. Scrutton at 673. *Carson v. Union Steamship Co* [1922] NZLR 778 (SC); *A-G (Ceylon) v. Scindia Steam Navigation Co Ltd* [1962] AC 60 (PC).
206. *Ace Imports Pty Ltd v. Companhia de Navegacao Lloyd Brasileiro* (1987) 10 NSWLR 32, J. Yeldham at 35–36.
207. *Rodocanachi, Sons & Co v. Milburn Bros* (1886) 18 QBD 67 (CA).
208. *Kaufman Ltd v. Cunard Steamship Co Ltd* [1965] 2 Lloyd's Rep 564 (Ex Ch Can).
209. *Grossfield v. Kyle Shipping Co Ltd* [1916] 2 KB 885 (CA). *See also Omega Tankers & Trailers Pty Ltd v. East-West Air Services Co Ltd* [2007] FCA 648.

120. In *The Peter de Grosse* (1876) 34 LT 749, the English CA held that the clause 'weight, content and value unknown' did not nullify the effect of the words 'in good order and condition'. Lord Justice James said:

> The bill of lading, taken together, must be considered to admit that the goods when shipped were, as far as they could be seen, in good order; and by adding the words above quoted, the master does no more than say that does not admit anything as to the contents of the packages, which he cannot see. He does admit, however, that the goods appear to be in good condition outside, and this throws upon the appellants the onus of proving that the damage did not arise whilst the goods were on board the ship or in their custody, or that it comes within the exceptions of the bills of lading.[210]

121. A general statement that goods have been shipped 'in good order and condition' amounts, if unqualified, to an undertaking by the shipowner that, on its own or its agent's judgment, the goods were shipped on this basis.[211] A clean bill of lading is one which has no clause or note in the bill of lading modifying or qualifying the statement that the goods were so shipped.[212] The shipowner is estopped from denying this statement as against an indorsee who, acting on that undertaking, has become an indorsee for value of the bill of lading. In *Canada & Dominion Sugar Co Ltd v. Canadian National (West Indies) Steamships Ltd* [1947] AC 46[213] it was stated in the bill of lading that a quantity of sugar was 'received in apparent good order and condition' but in the margin of the bill were stamped the words 'signed under guarantee to produce ship's clean receipt'. The sugar had been damaged prior to shipment and the ship's receipt stated 'many bags stained, torn and resewn'. The PC held that the statement as to condition was not unqualified. The stamped clause clearly indicated to any businessman that if the ship's receipt was not clean the statement in the bill of lading as to apparent order and condition could not be taken as unqualified. The defendants, therefore, were not estopped from proving that the sugar had been damaged before shipment.[214]

---

210. *The Peter de Grosse* (1876) 34 LT 749 (CA), L.J. James at 751.
211. *Compagnia Naviera Vascanzada v. Churchill* [1906] 1 KB 237; *The Tromp* [1921] P 337; *The Skarp* [1935] P 134; *Cremer v. General Carriers SA* [1974] 1 WLR 341 [[1974] 1 All ER 1; [1973] 2 Lloyd's Rep 366] (QB). *See also Bills of Lading Act* 1855 (UK). *See* S. Boyd, S. Berry, A. Burrows, B. Eder, D. Foxton & C. Smith, *Scrutton on Charterparties and Bills of Lading* [A 63] (21st ed., Sweet & Maxwell 2008).
212. *Canada & Dominion Sugar Co Ltd v. Canadian National (West Indies) Steamships Ltd* [1947] AC 46 (PC); *Silver v. Ocean Steamship Co Ltd* [1930] 1 KB 416 (CA); *Australian General Electricity v. AUSN Co* [1946] SASR 278; *NTI Ltd v. Queensland Insurance Co Ltd* [1962] SASR 51; *Associated Packaging Pty Ltd v. Sankyo Kaiun Kabushiki Kaisha* [1983] 3 NSWLR 293; *Westpac Banking Corporation v. South Carolina National Bank* [1986] 1 Lloyd's Rep 311 (PC); *Carrington Slipways Pty Ltd v. Pacific Austral Pty Ltd* (unrep, 2/2/1989, SC NSW J. Rogers, 13760 of 1984).
213. *Canada & Dominion Sugar Co Ltd v. Canadian National (West Indies) Steamships Ltd* [1947] AC 46 (PC), applied in *Tokyo Marine Fire Insurance v. Retla Steamship Co* [1970] 2 Lloyd's Rep 91 (9th Cir US).
214. *Canada & Dominion Sugar Co Ltd v. Canadian National (West Indies) Steamships Ltd* [1947] AC 46 (PC), the Court at 54–56.

122. The ambit of a policy of marine insurance[215] in the context of goods stated to be 'shipped in good order and condition' was considered in *NTI Ltd v. Queensland Insurance Co Ltd* [1962] SASR 51. Steel strip was sent from England to Port Adelaide insured against 'all risks of physical loss or damage from any external cause' other than 'loss damage or expense proximately caused by delay or inherent vice or nature of the property insured'. The Supreme Court of SA held that the bill of lading was merely prima facie evidence that the packages in which the goods were shipped were, as far as could be seen on reasonable examination, in good order and condition at the time of shipment. The consignee, on making out a prima facie case of a loss falling within the policy, the onus was on the insurer to prove that the loss was proximately caused by the inherent vice or nature of the shipment.[216]

123. Where a bill of lading expressly acknowledges receipt of goods 'in good order and condition', liability may depend on whether the bill of lading is a 'received on board' or a 'received on shipment' bill. In *Associated Packaging Pty Ltd v. Sankyo Kaiun Kabushiki Kaisha* [1983] 3 NSWLR 293, the plaintiff was the endorsee of two bills of lading issued on behalf of the first defendant, the carrier, evidencing a contract of carriage of a quantity of hessian bags from Chittagong in Bangladesh to Sydney. The first defendant admitted that the bills of lading were clean bills which expressly acknowledged receipt of the goods in apparent good order and condition. The plaintiff alleged that the goods when delivered had been damaged by water. The carrier argued that some water damage had occurred after the date of issue of the bills of lading and before the goods were taken on board the vessel and that such damage amounted to an act of God for which the carrier was not liable under the Hague Rules,[217] which were incorporated in the contract of carriage. The plaintiff's response was that the bills of lading were 'shipped on board bills' and their effect was to estop the carrier from alleging that the damage to the goods occurred before loading and in the manner claimed. It was common ground that the plaintiff had relied on the statements in the bills of lading in authorizing payment for the goods to be made, and that water damage was visible to the extent that the goods were not in apparent good order and condition. The bills of lading were 'received on board' as distinct from 'received for shipment' bills. Unlike a 'received for shipment' bill a 'shipped' bill of lading acknowledges that, at the date of the bill the goods have been received on board the vessel for carriage.[218] In the Supreme Court of NSW, Yeldham J held that the carrier was estopped as against the plaintiff from denying that as at the date of the respective bills of lading the goods were on board and then in apparent good order and condition.[219]

---

215. *See Laws of Australia* Thomson Reuters in *Insurance and Income Security, Marine Insurance* [22.1.4020]–[22.1.4430].
216. *NTI Ltd v. Queensland Insurance Co Ltd* [1962] SASR 51, J. Ross at 59.
217. By reason of Hague-Visby Rules, Art. 4 r. 2(d) (reproduced in Sch. 1 of the *Carriage of Goods by Sea Act* 1991 (Cth)).
218. *See Automatic Totalisators Ltd v. Oceanic Steamship Co* [1965] NSWR 702; Hague-Visby Rules, Art. 3 rr. 3, 7; G.J. Bonwick & E.C. Steer, *Ship's Business* 20 (4th ed., Maritime Press 1961).
219. *Associated Packaging Pty Ltd v. Sankyo Kaiun Kabushiki Kaisha* [1983] 3 NSWLR 293 (SC NSW), J. Yeldham at 294 citing *Silver v. Ocean Steamship Co Ltd* [1930] 1 KB 416 (CA), L.J.

124. In *Seafood Imports Pty Ltd v. ANL Singapore Pte Ltd* [2010] FCA 707 (2010) 272 ALR 149 Seafood Imports claimed damages arising from the deterioration of a consignment of frozen seafood which was carried from Yokohama in Japan to Melbourne. Under the bill of lading ANL Singapore acknowledged that the consignment had been received on board the ship in apparent good order and condition before carriage to Melbourne. The consignment was carried in a vessel owned by the China Shipping Container Lines (Hong Kong) Co Ltd.

125. According to a refrigeration expert giving evidence for Seafood Imports a rise in temperature in the refrigerated container of seafood was consistent with the power being off while the consignment was being stuffed at the cold store with the doors open On delivery of the container to Seafood's Melbourne premises the goods were found to have deteriorated. In the Federal Court Ryan J noted that under Article III Rule 2 of the *Hague-Visby Rules*[220] this imposed a condition that 'carrier shall properly and carefully load, handle, stow, carry, keep, care for and discharge the goods delivered'. Ryan J was satisfied that the goods were in good order and condition when stuffed into the container at the cold store and delivered to the ship at the terminal in Yokohama. However, that acknowledgement in the bill of lading only extended to the condition of the container and not to the condition of the cartons into which it was packed.[221]

126. The judge found ANL Singapore in breach of Article III Rule 2[222] and that the damage to the goods resulted from the container being stuck in defrost mode for at least three days during the voyage to Melbourne. ANL Singapore was found to have breached its obligations under Article III Rule 2 to properly and carefully to carry keep, care for, and discharge the goods.

IV. Transfer of Ownership

127. A bill of lading transfers ownership of goods, provided there is an intention to do so, where the bill of lading is delivered by a transferor to a transferee who gives valuable consideration for it. Possession of a bill of lading enables its holder to obtain delivery of goods at the destination port, or, when the goods are in transit, to pass the property in the goods by simply transferring the bill of lading.[223] In *Clements Horst Co v. Biddell Bros* [1912] AC 18, hops were shipped under a cif contract[224] from San Francisco to London. The buyer refused to pay for the goods

---

Scrutton at 425–427, L.J. Slesser at 441–442; *Canada & Dominion Sugar Co Ltd v. Canadian National (West Indies) Steamships Ltd* [1947] AC 46 (PC).

220. Subject to Art. IV r. 2 *Hague-Visby Rules*; *see* 181, 182, 102, 103.
221. J. Ryan at [27] citing *Marbig Rexel Pty Ltd v. ABC Containerline NV (TheTNT Express)* [1992] 2 Lloyd's Rep 536, Carruthers J at 641.
222. J. Ryan at [77].
223. *see Saunders v. Maclean* (1883) 11 QBD 327 (CA), L.J. Bowen at 341. *See* M. Davies & A. Dickey, *Shipping Law* (3d ed., Law Book Co 2004).
224. CIF contract: '[A] contract for the sale of goods which the price quoted by the seller includes *cost, insurance* and *freight* to the destination nominated.' *The CCH Macquarie Dictionary of Law* (rev

until actual delivery. The HL held that possession of the bill of lading was the legal equivalent of possession of the goods and under a cif contract the seller was entitled to payment on shipping the goods and tendering the bills of lading to the buyer. Although a bill of lading resembles a negotiable instrument it is not one because a transferee cannot ordinarily acquire a better title to the goods than that held by the transferor. The term 'negotiable' is used here in the common usage as meaning transferability.[225]

128. A bill of lading would not be regarded as a document of title if it provided that in the event of transshipment the shipowner accepted no responsibility beyond that of a forwarding agent. Such a document had been held to be good tender under a cif contract only where this was the usual or only available form in the trade. In *Plaimar Ltd v. Waters Trading Co Ltd* (1945) 72 CLR 304 [47 WALR 69], the High Court held that a contract for the sale of clove oil in 1941 to be dispatched from Zanzibar to Fremantle cif with a war risk insurance policy arranged by the seller charged to the buyer's account with terms net cash against delivery order or bill of lading to be, in its leading terms, a cif contract.[226] It was held that the reference to the delivery order gave the seller the option either to wait until the goods arrived and obtain a delivery order and tender that instead of the bill of lading, or tender a bill of lading with the invoice and an insurance policy.[227]

129. A shipowner who delivers goods to another without the production of the bill of lading does so at its own risk.[228] When a transferor delivers a bill of lading against a bill of exchange drawn by the transferee, it is implied, unless there is an express agreement to the contrary, that transfer of ownership of the goods to the transferee is conditional on the bill of exchange being accepted. In *British Imex Industries v. Midland Bank* [1958] 1 QB 542 [[1958] 2 WLR 103; [1958] 1 All ER 264], sellers sold the buyers a quantity of steel bars. The Midland Bank issued an irrevocable credit to the sellers under which it promised to pay them up to GBP 23,000 on presentation of the shipping documents, including the bill of lading. On the back of the bills of lading was a clause stating that the shipowners were not responsible for correct delivery unless every bar was marked with oil paint. The bills of lading presented to the bank described the goods but the shipowners did not acknowledge that the marking stipulation had been followed. The bank refused to pay on the ground that the bills of lading were not 'clean' and, therefore, not a good tender under the credit. In the QBD it was held that the bank was wrong in its claim as the bills were 'clean', even though they contained no acknowledgment that the

---

ed., CCH 1996), 30. Regarding standard international terms of trade (Incoterms) *see International 2010 Rules* at the International Chamber of Commerce *see* http://www.iccwbo.org/incotermsrules.

225. *See* 'non-negotiable document' in Art. 6 of the Hague-Visby Rules (reproduced in Sch. 1 of the *Carriage of Goods by Sea Act* 1991 (Cth)); *See also* S. Boyd, S. Berry, A. Burows, G. Eder, D. Foxton & C. Smith, *Scrutton on Charterparties and Bills of Lading* [B15] (21st ed., Sweet & Maxwell 2008).
226. *Plaimar Ltd v. Waters Trading Co Ltd* (1945) 72 CLR 304 [47 WALR 69], the Court at 312.
227. *Plaimar Ltd v. Waters Trading Co Ltd* (1945) 72 CLR 304 [47 WALR 69], the Court at 313.
228. *Sze Hai Tong Bank Ltd v. Rambler Cycle Co Ltd* [1959] AC 576 [[1959] 3 WLR 214; [1959] 3 All ER 182] (PC).

clause had been complied with. It was no concern of the bank to see that conditions on the back of a bill of lading had been complied with.[229]

130. Where transfer of ownership of goods is conditional on a bill of exchange being accepted, in the case of a transfer to a second transferee the latter acquires title to the goods if it had no notice at the time of transfer of the first transferee's conditional title to the goods. In *Cahn v. Pockett's Bristol Channel Steam Packet Co* [1899] 1 QB 643, A sold copper to B and sent B a bill of lading with a bank draft for the price. B was insolvent and did not accept the draft, but handed to a third party, C, the bill of lading in fulfilment of a sale of contract of the copper to C. C paid for the copper and took the bill of lading without notice of A's right as an unpaid seller. A stopped the copper in transit. The CA held that B was in possession of the bill of lading with A's consent so that C could obtain good title to the goods.[230] The general rule is that, where a bill of lading has been issued, the carrier at the discharge port must only part with the goods on presentation to him of one of the original bills of lading by the consignee or his agent.[231]

In *Mitsui Osk Lines (Thailand) Co Ltd v. Jack Fair Pty Ltd* [2015] FCCA 558 the issues raised the danger of a sea carrier delivering cargo without the presentation of the original bill of lading by the cargo interest. The case concerned a misdelivery of a consignment of two containers of bagged jasmine rice from Bangkok to Sydney. The unpaid Thai seller and shipper under the bill of lading commenced proceedings in Thailand against the issuer of the combined transport bill of lading and named carrier Mistsui Osk Lines (Mitsui).After proceedings in Thailand were settled Mitsui commenced proceedings in the Federal Circuit Court of Australia (the Court) against an Australian company Jack Fair Pty Ltd (Jack Fair) which was the 'notify party' named on the bill of lading. The bill of lading consignee was described as 'To the order of the shipper'. Mitsui took exception to the conduct of Jack Fair in inducing Mitsui to part with possession of the rice cargo on presentation of what the notify party represented to Mitsui was an original bill of lading duly endorsed by the notify party in accordance with the terms of the bill of lading. Mitsui argued that the notify party's conduct in presenting the endorsed bill of lading was misleading and deceptive conduct under section 18 of the *Australian Consumer Law*. In fact the document endorsed by the notify party was not an original bill of lading but in fact a non-negotiable copy bill of lading which the notify party had dressed up to look like an original bill of lading by placing its seal and a director's signature on the reverse side of the document. Mitsui claimed that Jack Fair was a party to the contract evidenced by the bill of lading. The Court found that as Jack Fair had

229. *British Imex Industries v. Midland Bank* [1958] 1 QB 542 [[1958] 2 WLR 103; [1958] 1 All ER 264], J. Salmon at 550–553. *See also Wunda Products Australia Pty Ltd v. Kyren Pty Ltd* [2010] SADC 96.

230. *Cahn v. Pockett's Bristol Channel Steam Packet Co* [1899] 1 QB 643 (CA), L.J. Romer at 666.

231. *See SA Sucre Export v. Northern River Shipping Ltd (The Sormovskiy 3068)* [1994] 2 Lloyd's Rep 226; *Kuwait Petroleum Corp. v. I & D Oil Carriers Ltd (The Houda)* [1994] 2 Lloyd's Rep 541; *MB Pyramid Sound NV v. Briese Schiffahrts GmbH & Co (The Ines)* [1995] 2 Lloyd's Rep 144. *See Motis Exports Ltd v. Dampskibsselskabet AF 1912 A/S* [1999] 1 Lloyd's Rep 837 for consideration of breach of shipowner's obligation by delivery against presentation of a forged bill of lading; *see* n. P. Todd, JBL [2000] 80.

failed to pay for the rice cargo, it was not entitled to endorse the bill of lading to obtain delivery of the goods, and that in doing so it had breached its contractual duties. The Court held that no fault could be attributed to the employees of Mitsui in Sydney who were deceived by the form of endorsement on the bill of lading represented by the notify party and that Mitsui's system for identifying genuine delivery documents was sound.

The Court also found for Mitsui against Jack Fair on the basis of conversion and breach an implied *Brandt v. Liverpool* agreement.[232] The Court (in the first application of section 18 of the *Australian Consumer Law* to a bill of lading case) found the notify party (the buyer of the rice),in breach of its contract with the Thai seller of the rice, had not paid for the cargo at the time it presented the purported endorsed original bill of lading in return for the delivery orders to enable it to obtain the cargo from Mitsui and that the notify party had deliberately altered the non-negotiable bill of lading to mislead Mitsui into believing it was a duly endorsed bill of lading. Mitsui, the Court found, had relied on the document to its detriment on the misrepresentation and so was entitled to damages from Jack Fair under the *Australian Consumer Law.229*

In *Ahmad v. Mitsui Osk Lines Ltd* (2005) 222 ALR 328, the plaintiff arranged for packages to be shipped from Mumbai to Sydney under a bill of lading. Most of the packages were released to a person other than the plaintiff. The rest of the packages were stored. The plaintiff claimed to have been entitled to the packages and sought to sue the defendant carrier on the bill of lading and conversion.

The Federal Court held, in dismissing the plaintiff's claim, that he was not a lawful holder or a holder in due course of the bill of lading to entitle him to sue for the non-delivery of the packages. If he had been so entitled the liability of the carrier would have been limited under the bill of lading to GBP 100 per package. Further, the defendant carrier was not guilty of conversion of the remaining packages but was entitled to payment for their storage.

131. Where a bill of lading is transferred to an indorsee, only the indorsee has the right to sue on it. In *Albacruz v. The Albazero* [1977] AC 774 [[1976] 3 WLR 419; [1976] 3 All ER 129], the plaintiff chartered a vessel from the defendant shipowners, on a five-year Shelltime B charter.[233] The carriage of a cargo of crude oil was covered under a bill of lading issued under the charter party naming the charterers as consignees.[234] In the course of the voyage, the vessel and its cargo became a total loss. At the time of the loss, the property in the cargo was with the cargo owners as indorsees of the bill of lading. The HL held, reversing the decision of the

---

232. J. Street at [73]; *Liverpool, Brazil & River Plate Steam Navigation Co* [1924] 1 KB 575(CA). 229 *See Competition and Consumer Act* 2010 (Cth*)* Sch. 2. *See* comment 'New Remedy for an Old Ailment: Australian Court Orders Bill of Lading Notify Party to Indemnify Ocean Carrier for Conversion of Cargo' (April 2015) Transport Trade and Energy E-bulletin. *See also Nikolaidiev v. The Queen* [208] FCA 1776 (false bill of lading); *Beluga Shipping GmbH v. Headway Shipping Ltd (No2)* [2008] FCA 1770 (fraudulent dating of bills).
233. For an explanation of Shelltime B charters *see* P. Gram, *Chartering Documents* (Lloyd's of London Press 1981). L. Gorton & R. Ihre, *A Practical Guide to Contracts of Affreightment and Hybrid Contracts* (New York: Lloy's of London Press, 1990).
234. *See* N.E. Palmer, *Bailment* 375–376 (2d ed., LBC 1991).

CA,[235] that the charterers were not entitled to recover damages for the loss of the goods. The judgment dealt with the principle in *Dunlop v. Lambert* (1839) 6 Cl & Fin 600 [7 ER 824] that where there is a delivery to a carrier to, in turn, deliver to a consignee, the latter is the proper person to sue the carrier if goods are lost; however, if the consignor has made a special contract with the carrier by which the goods are to be delivered to a particular person at any particular place, this special contract overcomes the necessity of proving ownership in the goods – so that the consignor can bring an action for damages against the carrier – although the goods may be the property of the consignee.[236] The HL was not prepared to extend the exception to a contract of carriage, as in the present case, which contemplated that the carrier would also enter into separate contracts of carriage with whoever became owner of the goods carried under the original contract.[237]

In *Albacruz v. The Albazero*, the seller and the buyer were in the same group of companies and property would have passed on shipment but for the lack of appropriation of the goods until the bills of lading were sent to the buyer.

132. The *Bills of Lading Acts* provide that transfer of rights and liabilities under a contract of carriage depend on the passing of property in the goods to the consignee or indorsee.[238] It is clear that the bills of lading legislation implies that the consignee or indorsee is a party to the contract. However, it is not clear how the property has to pass. There is a question on the wording 'upon or by reason of consignment or indorsement' whether property must pass at the same time as the consignment or indorsement of the bill of lading or not. There are two views in the interpretation of this provision. The narrow view takes a literal interpretation that the passing of property and the consignment must be synchronized[239] while the wide view considers the intention of the provision.[240] According to the wide view,

235. *Owners of the Cargo of The Albacruz v. The Albazero* [1975] 3 WLR 491 [[1975] 3 All ER 21] (CA).

236. *Dunlop v. Lambert* (1839) 6 Cl & Fin 600 [7 ER 824], the principle enunciated by Lord L.C. Cottenham at 626–627.

237. In *Albacruz v. The Albazero* [1977] AC 774 [[1976] 3 WLR 419; [1976] 3 All ER 129], Lord Diplock at 847 noted that the 'Bills of Lading Act 1855 [(UK)] and the subsequent development of the doctrine laid down in *Brandt v. Liverpool, Brazil & River Plate Steam Navigation Co* [1924] 1 KB 575 [(CA)] have [greatly] reduced the scope and utility of the rule in *Dunlop v. Lambert* [(1839)] 6 Cl & Fin 600 [[7 ER 824]] where goods are carried under a bill of lading'. *See also Quadro Shipping NV v. Bisley and Co Pty Ltd (The Protea Trader)* (1992) 113 FLR 280.

238. *Sale of Goods Act* 1923 (NSW), s. 50A; *Sale of Goods Act* 1972 (NT), s. 23; *Mercantile Act* 1867 (Qld), s. 5; *Mercantile Law Act* 1936 (SA), s. 14(1); *Bills of Lading Act* 1857 (Tas), s. 1; *Goods Act* 1958 (Vic), s. 73; *Bill of Lading Act* 1856 20 Vic 7 (WA), s. 1. The Act has no bills of lading legislation.

239. *See* S. Boyd, S. Berry, A. Burrows, B. Eder, D. Foxton & C. Smith, *Scrutton on Charterparties and Bills of Lading* [A14] (Sweet & Maxwell 2008).

240. *See also* P.N. Todd, *Contract with Consignees and Indorsees*, LIMCLQ 476 (1984); F.M.B. Reynolds, *The Significance of Tort in Claims in Respect of Carriage by Sea*, LIMCLQ 97 (1986); A.P. Bell, *The Bills of Lading Act 1855 Today*, JBL 124 (1985). *See* Davies M & Dickey A *Shipping Law* 247–251 (3d ed., Lawbook Co 2004).

the carrier and the buyer are bound provided only that property passes under the contract by virtue of which consignment or indorsement is made.[241]

133. English cases have favoured the wide view.[242] This view is preferred because it avoids the practical problems arising where the property passes to the consignees or indorsees at other times than the consignment or indorsement, frequent in international trade. If the wide view is applied, the consignees appear to have more protection from the terms of the provision. Roskill LJ stated a preference in *The San Nicholas* [1976] 1 Lloyd's Rep 8 for the wide view, 'because the narrow view would in some cases at least greatly lessen the security which those advancing money against shipping documents would acquire'.[243]

V. Authority to Sign Bill of Lading

134. At common law, a master has an ordinary or general authority to sign bills of lading on behalf of a shipowner. A shipowner will be bound by a bill of lading issued within the ordinary authority of the master even where the shipowner has limited this authority, unless this fact is known to the holder of the bill of lading.[244] A charterer's authority to bind a shipowner may vary according to the terms of the bill of lading and whether the charterer purports to sign for the master. Where the owners of time-chartered vessels leave the charterers or their agents to prepare and sign bills of lading for the master, the charterers, and their agents may have ostensible authority to bind the shipowners. In *The Nea Tyhi* [1982] 1 Lloyd's Rep 606, a vessel was time chartered on a NYPE form in which an additional clause gave the shipowners an express indemnity from charters in respect of liabilities arising from the charterers or their agents, including the master, signing bills of lading. The Commercial Court of the Queen's Bench held that although the charterers' agents had no actual authority to issue and sign 'under deck' bills of lading for cargo shipped on deck, they did have ostensible authority and so the shipowners were bound by the bills.

---

241. *See also Sewell v. Burdick* (1884) 10 App Cas 74, Lord Bramwell at 105; *Leigh & Sillavan Ltd v. Aliakmon Shipping Co Ltd (The Aliakmon)* [1986] AC 785 [[1986] 2 WLR 902; [1986] 2 All ER 145; [1986] 2 Lloyd's Rep 1].
242. *The San Nicholas* [1976] 1 Lloyd's Rep 8 (CA); *Karlshamns Oljefabriker v. Eastpoint Navigation Corporation (The Elafi)* [1982] All ER 208 [[1981] 2 Lloyd's Rep 679] (QB). But *see Enichemanic Spa v. Ampelos Shipping Co Ltd (The Delfini)* [1990] 1 Lloyd's Rep 252 (CA), L.J. Purchas at 261, L.J. Mustill at 274.
243. *The San Nicholas* [1976] 1 Lloyd's Rep 8 (CA), L.J. Roskill at 13. *See also* the solution provided by the *Carriage of Goods by Sea Act* 1991 (UK) and commentary in C. Debattista, *UK Carriage of Goods by Sea Act 1992: Goodbye to Title to Sue Problems – Or Is It?* 223 ff (Maritime Law Association of Australia and New Zealand Conference 1992).
244. *Manchester Trust v. Furness, Withy & Co Ltd* [1895] 2 QB 539 (CA); *The Berkshire* [1974] 1 Lloyd's Rep 185 (QB); *Fletcher Ltd v. Sigurd Haavik AS (The Vikfrost)* [1980] 1 Lloyd's Rep 560 (CA). *See also British Marine plc v. Wollongong Coal Co Ltd* [2015] FCA 347; *Hildebrand v. SAS Trustee Corporation* [2013] NSWLR 51; *Paharpur Cooling Towers Ltd v. Paramount (WA) No 2* [2009] WASC 73.

135. Charterers or their agents may also sign bills of lading without purporting to sign for the master. Although the wording of the bill of lading and the circumstances of its issue may provide otherwise, a court may hold that the contracts of carriage are with the charterers, and not the owners, particularly where the charterers are the owners or operators of vessels on a regular service, and the vessel at issue is to supplement that service.[245] Where the terms of a bill of lading, signed by the charterers or their agents 'or on behalf of the master', clearly indicate that the charterers are the carriers under the contract of carriage, evidenced by the bill of lading, the charterers will be bound by the bill, irrespective of the way in which it is signed.[246] In *Namchow Chemical Industrial Co Ltd v. Botany Bay Shipping Co (Aust) Pty Ltd* [1982] 2 NSWLR 532 the terms of the charter party directly relevant to the carriage of cargo were regarded as terms of the contract of affreightment,[247] to which an indorsee of a bill of lading was held to be a party. An exporter of beef tallow chartered a vessel on a tanker voyage charter party from the defendant for the carriage of cargo to various ports in Asia. The defendant was already the charterer under an earlier time charter party with the vessel's Korean owners. Two bills of lading were issued, both covering different parts of the cargo sold by the exporter to the plaintiff. The plaintiff, claiming under the bills of lading, brought an action in damages for short delivery. The New South Wales Court of Appeal (NSWCA) held that the terms of the voyage charter party, which were directly relevant to the shipment, carriage, or discharge of the cargo, should be regarded as terms of the contract of affreightment, to which the indorsee of the bill of lading was deemed to be a party. Whether the bills of lading were intended to be signed by the carrier personally, or as an agent for the master, and so binding on the owner, depended on the construction of the bills of lading with those terms of the voyage charter party which could be incorporated in it, under the circumstances of the transactions. On this basis, the carrier should be taken to have intended to issue the bills of lading on its own behalf, thus, making it a party to the contract of affreightment.[248]

136. Time charterers may determine, within wide limits, the form and content of the bills of lading a master may be required to sign.[249] The liability of the agent, where a contractual document[250] is signed as agent and not as principal, will depend on the intention of the parties as shown on the face of the document. In *Anderson's (Pacific) Trading Co Pty Ltd v. Karlander New Guinea Line Ltd* [1980] 2 NSWLR 870, frozen goods were loaded on to a vessel in Sydney for delivery to Rabaul, under bills of lading of which the plaintiff was a holder. On arrival the goods were found to be defrosted and were condemned by local health authorities. The vessel was chartered to the defendant under a document entitled 'Uniform Time-Charter'. The bills of lading were on the defendant's form of document which stated that they

245. *The Okehampton* (1913) 18 Com Cas 320 (CA).
246. *The Venezula* [1980] 1 Lloyd's Rep 393 (QB).
247. Contract of affreightment '[A] contract made by a shipowner to carry goods for payment.' The CCH Macuarie Dictionary of Law (rev ed., CCH 1996) p. 7.
248. *Namchow Chemical Industrial Co Ltd v. Botany Bay Shipping Co (Aust) Pty Ltd* [1982] 2 NSWLR 523 (CA), the Court at 529.
249. *Jones v. Hough* (1879) 5 Ex D 115 (CA).
250. *Kaleej International Pty Ltd v. Gulf Shipping Lines Ltd* (1986) 6 NSWLR 569 (CA).

were affirmed by the master, or duly authorized vessel's agents on signing. Neither the identity nor the existence of the owner was disclosed on the bills of lading, which were signed 'FOR KARLANDER NEW GUINEA LINE LTD ... As agents'.[251] The bills of lading included a standard form demise clause. In an action to determine whether the defendant was personally liable in the circumstances, Hunt J held that the 'Uniform Time-Charter', on its time construction, did not amount to a demise of the vessel to the defendants, as the owners had not wholly parted with possession or control of the vessel. To all intents and purposes, the master and crew were not employed by the defendant, who was at the time only the charterer of the vessel. In that the vessel had an identity of its own, the defendant may have signed as agent for the vessel, or for its owner. However, as the identity and existence of the defendant's principal was not disclosed, the defendant was liable on the bills of lading.[252] *In Mutual Export Corp v. Asia Australian Express Ltd (The Lakati Express)* (1990) 19 NSWLR 285; 103 Federal Law Reports (FLR) 32, a second subcharterer gave notice of default in payments due. The first subcharterer communicated to the second subcharterer that it accepted the conduct as repudiation of the charter party. The charter party between the two charterers had a clause giving the first subcharterer a lien on all cargoes and subfreights for any amounts due under the charter. The third subcharterer loaded goods under a bill of lading headed 'carrier/Asia Australian Express Ltd' and endorsed 'for the carrier' and' freight collect', and proceeded to deliver and unload the cargo. Unsure of its position under the next hire payment, the third subcharterer paid the money into a bank account. In proceedings by the first subcharterer for unpaid hire of the vessel and bill of lading freight, the third subcharterer was required to pay money into court. The Supreme Court of New South Wales held that, as a matter of construction, the bills of lading were charterers' bills.[253]

137. A master of a vessel under a time charter will not be entitled to object to signing bills of lading which impose greater liabilities on the owners than under the charter.[254] Any extra liability accordingly imposed on the owners can be recovered by them as an indemnity from the charterers.[255] However, the master is not required to sign bills of lading which either contains extraordinary terms or ones that are manifestly inconsistent with the charter party. In this situation, neither the charterers nor their agents can sign such a bill on behalf of the master, although in certain circumstances they might be regarded as having ostensible authority to do so.[256]

251. *Anderson's (Pacific) Trading Co Pty Ltd v. Karlander New Guinea Line Ltd* [1980] 2 NSWLR 870, J. Hunt at 870.
252. *Anderson's (Pacific) Trading Co Pty Ltd v. Karlander New Guinea Line Ltd* [1980] 2 NSWLR 870, J. Hunt at 873, 875.
253. *See Mutual Export Corp v. Asia Australian Express Ltd (The Lakati Express)*(1990) 19 NSWLR 285, J. Carruthers at 294 applying *Namchow Chemical Industrial Co Ltd v. Botany Bay Shipping Co (Aust) Pty Ltd* [1982] 2 NSWLR 523 (CA).
254. *Kruger v. Moel Tryvan Ship Co Ltd* [1907] AC 272, Lord Lindley at 279; *The Berkshire* [1974] 1 Lloyd's Rep 185 (QB), J. Brandon at 188; *Fletcher Ltd v. Sigurd Haavik AS (The Vikfrost)* [1980] 1 Lloyd's Rep 560 (CA), L.J. Browne at 567; *Tilmans v. Knutsford* [1908] AC 406, Lord Dunedin at 410.
255. *The Nea Tyhi* [1982] 1 Lloyd's Rep 606 (QB).
256. *Collen v. Wright* (1857) 8 El & Bl 647 [120 ER 241].

Where a principal, by his or her statements or conduct, leads the other party to reasonably understand that the agent has authority to act on its behalf, the principal will be bound. However, where the principal is not liable the agent may be sued by the other party in damages for breach of an implied warranty of authority. In *V/O Rasnoimport v. Guthrie & Co Ltd* [1966] 1 Lloyd's Rep 1, Mocatta J held that the defendants were liable for damage suffered by the plaintiff who had relied on the defendant's warranty of authority. The mere fact that neither a master nor an agent has ostensible authority from a shipowner to sign a bill of lading for goods not on board was not sufficient to exclude the implication of a warranty of such an authority from the signature of the bill of lading by the defendants and that, therefore, by issuing and signing the bill of lading as an agent of the shipowners, the defendants impliedly warranted that they had the authority to do so.[257]

138. A person who signs a bill of lading without the authority of the shipowner, stating that goods have been shipped when they have not, is liable to an indorsee of the bill of lading, who has relied on that statement, for damages for breach of warranty of authority.[258] The person who signed the bill of lading is not prevented[259] from showing that the goods shipped were marked other than as stated, unless the marks are material to the description of the goods.[260] As a general rule, a master does not bind the shipowners by a description in the bill of lading of the quality of the goods.[261]

VI. Cessation

139. A shipowner's liability for goods may cease once goods have been transshipped under a contract of carriage. In *The Berkshire* [1974] 1 Lloyd's Rep 185, a vessel left the loading port for the agreed discharge port, but on the charterer's instructions the goods were discharged at a different port and transhipped to the agreed port, where they were found to be damaged. While a 'liberty clause' in the bill of lading gave the shipowners a wide power to vary the performance of the contract, the Court held that the clause was not sufficiently clear to be given its literal effect. The clause stated that:

> Whenever the goods are consigned to a point where the ship does not expect to discharge, the carrier or the master may, without notice, forward the whole or any part of the goods before or after loading at the original port of shipment

257. *V/O Rasnoimport v. Guthrie & Co Ltd* [1966] 1 Lloyd's Rep 1 (QB), J. Mocatta at 11.
258. *V/O Rasnoimport v. Guthrie & Co Ltd* [1966] 1 Lloyd's Rep 1 (QB), J. Mocatta at 18 (assumed ships' agents who signed the bill of lading were 'other persons' for the purposes of s. 3 of the *Bills of Lading Act* 1855 (UK)).
259. *Sale of Goods Act* 1923 (NSW), s. 50C; *Mercantile Act* 1867 (Qld), s. 7; *Mercantile Law Act* 1936 (SA), s. 15; *Bills of Lading Act* 1857 (Tas), s. 3; *Goods Act* 1958 (Vic), s. 74; *Bill of Lading Act* 1856 20 Vic 7 (WA). The ACT and the NT have no equivalent legislation. *See* A.P. Bell, *The Bills of Lading Act 1855 Today*, JBL 124 (1985).
260. *Parsons v. New Zealand Shipping Co* [1900] 1 QB 714.
261. *Cox v. Bruce* (1886) 18 QBD 147 (CA).

> … by any vessel … whether operated by the carrier or by others and whether departing or arriving or scheduled to depart or arrive before or after the ship expected to be used for the transportation of the goods. This carrier, in making arrangements for any transhipments or forwarding vessel or means of transportation not operated by this carrier shall be considered solely the forwarding agent of the shipper and without any other responsibility whatsoever.[262]

The clause was narrowly construed as having only defined the basis on which the shipowners were entitled to forward the goods, by transshipment.[263]

140. In the case of liner and through bills[264] of lading there is usually an express provision that the shipowner shall have the liberty to trans-ship and forward the goods by any other line or vessel. In *Burns Philp & Co Ltd v. West Australian Steam Navigation Co Ltd* (1923) 33 CLR 135, wax matches were consigned to WA, shipped under deck from London on a vessel whose destination was Singapore. Under a transshipment provision in the bill of lading, the goods were trans-shipped at Singapore on another vessel for Fremantle, that vessel receiving them on the stipulation, usual for the carriage of dangerous goods, that they were to be stowed 'on deck at shipper's risk'. The matches had to be jettisoned to preserve the safety of the vessel between Singapore and Fremantle. The bill of lading included, *inter alia*, the following stipulations:

> Transhipment of cargo for ports where the ship does not call, or for [the] shipowner's purposes, to be at shipowners' expense, but at the risk of the owners of the goods from the time the goods leave the ship's deck, where the ship's responsibility shall cease … Goods forwarded by steamship or otherwise for shipment or after transhipment to be subject to the conditions and exceptions of the forwarding conveyance, and at the risk of the owners of the goods' (original emphasis).[265]

141. The High Court held that the effect of these stipulations was that the shipper, in the case of transshipment authorized by the bill, was bound by all clauses and conditions affecting carriage usually required by the forwarding vessel, and that the goods were rightly jettisoned and that, therefore, the shipowners were not liable.[266]

---

262. *See The Berkshire* [1974] 1 Lloyd's Rep 185 (QB), J. Brandon at 189.
263. *See also Captain v. Far Eastern Steamship Co* [1979] 1 Lloyd's Rep 595 (SC BC).
264. A 'liner' bill is issued by a shipping or conference line. A 'through' bill of lading is one that covers the entire carriage of goods consigned, including the land leg. In *Mayhew Foods Ltd v. Overseas Containers Ltd* [1984] 1 Lloyd's Rep 317 (QB), J. Bingham at 320 decided that the *Carriage of Goods by Sea Act* 1971 (UK) applied to the whole transit of goods, including the time when the goods were awaiting transshipment on land. There is no problem, therefore, with continuous documentary cover of goods by a bill of lading: *see* C. Debattista, *Sale of Goods Carried by Sea* 156–157 (Butterworths 1990), regarding a bill of lading giving 'through' cover.
265. *Burns Philp & Co Ltd v. West Australian Steam Navigation Co Ltd* (1923) 33 CLR 135, C.J. Knox & J. Starke at 139.
266. *Burns Philp & Co Ltd v. West Australian Steam Navigation Co Ltd* (1923) 33 CLR 135, C.J. Knox & J. Starke at 139–140.

142. Authority on the part of a bank in relation to indemnity and documentary credit was considered by the High Court of Australia in *Pacific Carriers Ltd v. BNP Paribas* (2004) 209 ALR 448 and it underlines a vital aspect of export financing and bank's liabilities.

143. New England Agricultural Traders Pty Ltd (NEAT) sold a cargo of legumes to the Royal Trading Company (Royal). The cargo was to be delivered to Calcutta. Patrick Carriers, the appellant was the time charterer of the vessel on which the cargo was carried. BNP was NEAT's Sydney banker and was financing the export transaction. Royal was financed by Singapore Overseas Enterprises (SSOE).

144. Problems were experienced with the discharge of the cargo in India in early 1990. SSOE made claims against Patrick. NEAT then became insolvent. Patrick then claimed to be indemnified by BNP. Two letters of indemnity were signed by the manager of the Documentary Credits Department of BNP which BNP subsequently argued had no authority to bind BNP.

145. The matter was appealed with leave to the HCA which held that there was nothing in the documents to indicate that BNP was merely verifying NEAT's execution of the documents. A reasonable person the Court held in the position of Patrick would have understood BNP was undertaking liability as an indemnifying party to support NEAT's liability. Patrick's assumption of the manager's authority to sign the letters of indemnity was assisted by BNP placing the manager in the position to deal with those documents.[267]

146. In *Cosco Container Lines Co Ltd v. Unity Int'l Cargo Pty Ltd* [2012] NSWDC 122 Cosco's containers were loaded with fibreglass and wool in Xingang, China for redelivery to Unity Int'l as consignee destination Brisbane and Sydney, Both Cosco and Unity Int'l had entered into an IMPORT Net Agreement (INA) for the delivery and loan of the containers. The INA expressly incorporated Cosco's standard bill of lading terms and conditions and conditions of its standard Equipment Handover Agreement (EHA). Where an INA has been signed, as it was by the defendant (being identified as the consignee on a seaway bill), electronic orders are sent to that party once they confirm, in this case to Cosco, that freight and local port charges have been paid.

147. Between Cosco and Unity Int'l, as a matter of practice, all charges invoiced by Cosco to the defendants were paid by Unity Int'l. Unity Int'l looked to the receiver of the goods, Global Fibreglass Pty Ltd, either to pay in funds or reimburse Unity Int'l for payments made to Cosco.

---

267. *See* E.P. Ellinger, *Documentary Letters of Credit* (Butterworths 1973); National Australia Bank *Finance of International Trade* 1985; J. Livermore, Ch. 17 in *Australian Law of Financial Institutions* S. Blay & E. Clark Harcourt Brace 1993. *See* E.P. Ellinger *Documentary Letters of Credit: A Comparative Study* (University of Singapore Press 1970).

148. The dispute arose when Global Fibreglass went into liquidation resulting in Unity Int'l not being paid by Global Fibreglass. Cosco sought to rely on the INA to recover the charges from Unity Int'l which on its part argued it was not a 'merchant' as defined in the INA. Rolfe J in the District Court (DC) of New South Wales (NSW) if this was accepted the terms of the INA would have no operation.[268]

149. In rejecting this Rolfe J held that the provisions of the INA constituted a distinct container use contract and should be accepted. The liability of Unity Int'l to pay 'detention' or 'demurrage' charges was held to be enforceable. These provision Rolfe J held not to constitute a penalty 6 as the parties had agreed that Unity Int'l would hire the containers until their return at the agreed contractual rate which was a separate obligation and not dependent on any breach of the contract.[269]

§7. The Hague-Visby Rules

I. Application of the Hague-Visby Rules

150. The *Carriage of Goods by Sea Act* 1991 (Cth) incorporates the Hague-Visby Rules and applies automatically to contracts contained in a bill of lading or other documents of title. The *Carriage of Goods by Sea Amendment Act* 1997 (Cth) has made important modifications to the Hague-Visby Rules as they apply in Australia under the *Carriage of Goods by Sea Act* 1991 (Cth). The purpose of the Hague-Visby Rules is to establish a balance between the shipper and the shipowner, the latter being obliged to accept certain listed liabilities in return for enumerated qualifications on its liability. In this sense, the Hague-Visby Rules represent a compromise between the positions under common law and under contract.[270] The *Carriage of Goods Sea Act* 1991 (Cth) repealed the *Sea – Carriage of Goods Act* 1924 (Cth), replacing the original Hague Rules with those amended by the 1968 Visby Protocol and 1979 SDR Protocols.[271] The amended Hague Rules, known as the

268. J. Rolfe at [27] referring to *Malaysia International Shipping Berhad v. VISA Australia Pty Ltd* (2003) VSCA 64 at [9] per J.A. Buchanan.

269. *See* J. Rolfe at [35] as to commercial parties to a commercial agreement *see RJ Bezinna Pty Limited and Ors v. Saxyby Mortgages Limited* (2004) NSW (CA) 211 J.A. Giles at [29].

270. *Gosse Millerd Ltd v. Canadian Government Merchant Marine Ltd (The Canadian Highlander)* [1929] AC 223, Viscount Sumner at 236.

271. The Hague-Visby Rules are reproduced in Sch. 1 of the *Carriage of Goods by Sea Act* 1991 (Cth). The Act came into effect on 31 Oct. 1991. The unamended Hague Rules as enacted under the *Sea – Carriage of Goods Act* 1924 (Cth) continue to apply to contracts of carriage entered into before 31 Oct. 1991: *Carriage of Goods by Sea Act* 1991 (Cth), s. 20(2). *See also* Explanatory Memorandum to the Carriage of Goods by Sea Bill 1991 (Cth). On the 1991 Act generally *see* On *the Carriage of Goods by Sea Act 1991*(Cth) *see* F. Hannah & A. Phillipides, *Carriage of Goods by Sea*, in *Australian Maritime Law* Ch. 3 (M. White ed., 2d ed., The Federation Press 2000). According to the *Carriage of Goods by Sea Act* 1991 (Cth) s. 18, the Act's provisions prevail over those of Pt V Divn 2 of the *Trade Practices Act* 1974 (Cth) to the extent of any inconsistency. According to s. 19 of the *Carriage of Goods by Sea Act* 1991 (Cth), nothing in the Act is to affect the operation of Pt IV Divn 10 or Pt VIII Divn 2 of the *Navigation Act* 1912 (Cth), or the *Limitation of Liability for Maritime Claims Act* 1989 (Cth). Section 2C of the *International Arbitration Act* 1974

Hague-Visby Rules, apply automatically to contracts contained in a bill of lading or other documents of title. This would not include, for example, a mate's receipt or a non-negotiable consignment note or sea waybill. The *Carriage of Goods by Sea Act* 1991 (Cth) provides that the Hague-Visby Rules apply, subject to section 10, to contracts of carriage by force of law independently of any contractual provision.[272] In addition, the Hague-Visby Rules apply to contracts entered into after 31 October 1991 which are contained in or evidenced by a non-negotiable document where the contract expressly provides that the Hague-Visby Rules are to govern as if it were a bill of lading.[273] This would cover a contract evidenced in a sea waybill. The Hague-Visby Rules apply to carriage between parties in two 'contracting States' (which includes Australia) where:

(1) the bill of lading is issued in a contracting State;
(2) the carriage is from a port in a contracting State; or
(3) the contract contained in, or evidenced by, the bill of lading provides that the Hague-Visby Rules or the legislation of any State giving effect to them are to govern the contract.

The Hague-Visby Rules apply irrespective of the nationality of the ship, carrier, shipper, consignee, or any other interested person.[274]

151. The *Carriage of Goods by Sea Act* expressly provides that the Hague-Visby Rules will not apply to sea-carriage between parties in any one State or Territory,[275] as intrastate shipping is governed by the States' legislation and the common law. The Act provides for the adaptation of an alternative regime of 'maritime cargo' liability, the Hamburg Rules (reproduced in Schedule 2 of the *Carriage of Goods by Sea Act*), in place of the Hague-Visby Rules at a future date, if such adaptation is deemed desirable. Australia has not adopted the Hamburg Rules; however, the Rules are in force as an international convention, the requisite number of States having adopted them.

(Cth) is repealed with a new s. 2C providing that the continued operation of s. 9 of the *Sea – Carriage of Goods Act* 1924 (Cth) under s. 20(2) of the *Carriage of Goods by Sea Act* 1991 (Cth) and ss 11, 16 of the *Sea-Carriage of Goods Act* 1924 (Cth) are not affected by the *Carriage of Goods by Sea Act* 1991 (Cth). For a discussion of the liability regimes of the Hague-Visby Rules and the Hamburg Rules and suggested amendments to the *Carriage of Goods by Sea Act* 1991 (Cth), *see* the Marine Cargo Liability Working Group, *Report to the Federal Minister of Transport* (Canberra: The Working Group, 1995).

272. *Carriage of Goods by Sea Act* 1991 (Cth), s. 8.
273. *Carriage of Goods by Sea Act* 1991 (Cth), s. 10(1)(b)(iii).
274. *Carriage of Goods by Sea Act* 1991 (Cth), s. 10; Hague-Visby Rules, Art. 10. That the reference to a bill of lading in s. 10(1)(a) of the *Carriage of Goods by Sea Act* 1991 (Cth) implies a reference to 'a contract' for the application of the Hague-Visby Rules: *see* D.A. Butler & W.D. Duncan, *Maritime Law in Australia* 79 (Legal Books 1992).
275. *See Carriage of Goods by Sea Act* 1991 (Cth), s. 10(2).

152. Any stipulation or agreement which ousts or seeks to lessen the jurisdiction of Commonwealth or State courts in respect of a bill of lading or similar document is made illegal.[276] All parties to a bill of lading (or similar document) relating to carriage of goods outward from Australia are deemed by the section to have intended to contract according to Australian law; that is, the law in force at the place of shipment.[277] The provision in the *Carriage of Goods by Sea Act* invalidates not only an attempt to confer jurisdiction on a foreign court, but also an attempt to refer disputes to overseas arbitration.[278]

153. In *Hi-Fert Pty Ltd and Another v. Kuikiang Maritime carriers Pty Ltd and Another* (1999) 173 ALR 142, Hi-Fert and Cargill were plaintiffs in proceedings against KMC and WBC in Admiralty proceedings. Cargill was the consignor and Hi-Fert was the consignee of a cargo of fertilizer carried under contract of affreightment between Hi-Fert and WBC on a ship owned by Kuikiang chartered by WBC. The cargo was contaminated by a quarantinable disease and could not be discharged. The appellants in its claim negligence and breach of contract against WBC. WBC and Kuikiang both applied for a stay of proceedings. The bills of lading issued by Kiukiang to Cargill, endorsed by Hi-Fert incorporated the arbitration clause providing for arbitration in London in accordance with the provisions of the *Arbitration Act* 1950(UK).

In *Dampskibsselskaber Norden A/Sv Beach Building and Civil Group Pty Ltd* (2012) FCA 696, Foster J noted that the form of words in section 11(1)(a) of the *Carriage of Goods by Sea Act* 1991(Cth) was inserted by Item 1 in Schedule 1 of

---

276. *Wilson v. Compagnie des Messageries Maritimes* [1954] 2 Lloyd's Rep 544 (HC); *see John Churcher Pty Ltd v. Mitsui & Co (Australia) Ltd* [1974] 2 NSWLR 179 [24 FLR 191] (arbitration clause in fob wool contract: contract held not to be a bill of lading for the purposes of s. 9 of the *Sea Carriage of Goods Act* 1924 (Cth); the Act did not oust the arbitration clause). *See also Kim Meller Imports Pty Ltd v. Eurolevant Spa* (1986) 7 NSWLR 269 where *Wilson v. Compagnie des Messageries Maritimes* case was followed. Fob contract: 'free on board contract; that is, a contract for the sale of goods under which the seller bears the cost of putting the goods on board ship for carriage to the buyer. Once the goods are on board, property and risk pass to the buyer': The CCH Dictionary of Law (rev. ed. 1996) 73. On the effect of the wording of the *Carriage of Goods by Sea Act* 1991 (Cth) s. 11(2)(b), (c) that an agreement in a bill of lading in or out of Australia 'has no effect so far as it purports to … preclude or limit the jurisdiction of a court of a State or Territory' *see Hi-Fert Pty Ltd v. Kiukang Maritime Carriers Inc.* (1996) 71 FCR where J. Tamberlin, of the Federal Court held that the wording of s. 11 (differing from s. 9 of the *Sea-Carriage of Goods Act* 1924 (Cth)) meant that the section had a different effect from its predecessors, and that a stay of proceedings in Australia could in some cases be granted on the basis of a foreign arbitration clause in a bill of lading; for a note on the *Hi-Fert* case *see* M. Davies, *A Chink (or two) in the Bill of Lading Plaintiff's Jurisdictional Armour? Good News for Australian Maritime Arbitration*, 26 ABLR 70 (1998). *See also Bulk Chartering & Consultants Aust Pty Ltd v. T&T Metal Trading Pty Ltd 'The Krasnogrask'* (1993) 31 NSWLR 18 where s. 9 of the *Carriage of Goods by Sea Act* 1991 (Cth) was held by the SC of NSW (Court of Appeal) (P. Kirby, dissenting) that s. 9 of the *Carriage of Goods by Sea Act* 1991 (Cth) did not operate to avoid or nullify an award made under an arbitration agreement.

277. *Carriage of Goods by Sea Act* 1991 (Cth), s. 11.

278. *See Sonmez Denizcilik ve Ticaret Anonim Sirketi v. MV Blooming Orchard [No. 2]* (1990) 22 NSWLR 273 [99 ALR 138] (clause in a voyage charter party providing for arbitration in London held to be invalid). For comment on the case *see* M. Davies, *Fruits of the Blooming Orchard*, ABLR 217 (1991).

the *Carriage of Goods by Sea Regulations 1998 (No2* (Cth*)*. Item 2 of Schedule 1 effected an identical change to section 11(2)(b). Foster J went on to state:

> In my view, these legislative changes indicate that, from 1997 onwards, the legislature was intending by the relevant amendments which it made to broaden the class of documents covered by s11(1)(b) of [the *Carriage of Goods by Sea Act* 1991] I see no warrant for doing this other than giving the words of the definition in Art 1(1)(g)(iv) a meaning reflective of ordinary English usage. Taking that approach, because the Charter party is a contract of carriage of goods by sea it contains or evidences such a contract. It is, therefore a 'sea carriage document' within the meaning of s 11(1)(a).The same result would be arrived at by simply constructing the phrase 'sea document' in sd11(1)(g)(iv) of the amended Hague Rules.[279]

154. On appeal from the primary judge, who ordered the staying of the whole proceedings and referring the matter to arbitration in London, the Federal Court held that claims against WBC for breach of the charter contract, negligence and breach of duty could be stayed under the *International Arbitration Act (Cth)* 1974 section 7. However, those claims would be only stayed on condition that the reference to arbitration would not proceed until after the final proceedings in the Federal Court. As to whether the claims against Kiukiang should be stayed as oppressive or vexatious the Federal Court applied the *Carriage by Sea Act* 1991 section 11(2) which provides that an agreement has no effect so far as it purports to preclude or limit the jurisdiction of a court of the Commonwealth in respect of a bill of lading relating to the carriage of goods from any place outside Australia to any place in Australia.[280]

In *TLC Air Conditioner (Zhongshan) Co Ltd v. Castel Electronics Pty Ltd* [2014] FCAFC 83 the Full Court of the Federal Court held that the phrase 'public policy' in the UNCITRAL *Model Law on International Commercial Arbitration* and the *International Arbitration Act* 1974 (Cth) section 19 is limited to the most basic, fundamental principles of justice and morality of the state, as limited by the international dimension of the context. The rules of natural justice fall within that conception, as they represent a fundamental principle of justice, namely fairness and the right to equal treatment of parties. The Court also held that natural justice will be denied when real unfairness or real practical injustice occurs in the conduct or resolution of the international litigation or dispute resolution process in question to be demonstrated by reference to established principles of natural justice or procedural fairness. Unless this is proven an international commercial arbitration award will not be set aside or denied recognition or enforcement under the UNCITRAL *Model Law*, Articles 34 and 36.[281]

279. J. Foster at [141].
280. Applying Compagnie des Messageries Maritimes v. Wilson (1954) 94 CLR 577. *See* L. Zhoa & Felix W.H. Chan, '*Incorporating the Charterparty's Applicable Law Clause into Bill of Lading*' LMCLQ 48 (2012).
281. Per Allsop CJ, Middelton, Foster JJ.

155. Under Article 1(a) of the Hague-Visby Rules (reproduced in Schedule 1 of the *Carriage of Goods by Sea Act* 1991 (Cth)), '[c]arrier' includes 'the owner or the charterer who enters into a contract of carriage with a shipper'. However, it has been held that the Rules apply only when the shipowner enters into a contract of carriage covered by a bill of lading or similar document of title with a shipper.[282] It appears that where the contract of carriage is between a shipper and a charterer, the shipowner will not be a party to that contract, subject to the obligations, or entitled to the protection under the Rules.[283] Also, a sea carrier who has subcontracted the sea leg of combined land/sea carriage for which a bill of lading has been issued, and the sea carrier's contract is not with either the consignor or consignee of goods, will not be regarded as the carrier under the Rules.[284]

156. Straight bills of lading are bills that name a consignee but do not have additional wording such as 'to order' which gives them negotiability of an ordinary bill of lading. A straight bill of lading is akin to a seaway bill in that neither is transferable like as an ordinary bill of lading. The HL in the *Rafaela S* [2005] AC 423[285] held that a straight bill of lading was a bill of lading for the purposes of the Article 1(b) of the Hague-Visby rules as, in the case before it, the consignee could not obtain delivery without presentation of the document and that the document was transferable but only once, from consignor to consignee.

II. The Carrier's Obligations

157. Under Article 3 Rule 1 of the Hague-Visby Rules (reproduced in Schedule 1 of the *Carriage of Goods by Sea Act* 1991 (Cth)), a carrier is obliged to exercise due diligence to make a ship seaworthy, cargo worthy, and to properly man, equip, and supply the ship. The *Carriage of Goods by Sea Act* 1991 (Cth) further provides that there is no obligation under the Act parallel to the absolute common law obligation to provide a seaworthy ship.[286] The statutory obligations begin before the commencement of the voyage, which appear to be from the period at the beginning of the loading until the vessel proceeds on its voyage,[287] but not at the time when

282. *J Gadsden Pty Ltd v. Australian Coastal Shipping Commission* [1977] 1 NSWLR 575 [31 FLR 157] (CA), P. Moffitt at 579, J.A. Samuels at 583.
283. *J Gadsden Pty Ltd v. Australian Coastal Shipping Commission* [1977] 1 NSWLR 575 [31 FLR 157] (CA), P. Moffitt at 579, J.A. Samuels at 583.
284. *Sidney Cooke Ltd v. Hapag-Lloyd AG* [1980] 2 NSWLR 587 [48 FLR 405]. *See* Hague-Visby Rules, Art. 10.
285. *See* the House of Lords in the *Rafaela s.* reported as *JI MacWilliam Co Inc. v. Mediterranean Shipping Co* [2005] UKHL 11; [2005] 1 Lloyd's Rep 347 holding that a non-negotiable or straight bill of lading is within Art. 1(b) of the Hague-Visby Rules and the *Carriage of Goods by Sea Act* 1971(UK). *See* S. Baughen, *Shipping Law* 24–25 (4th ed., Cavendish 2009), and G. McMeel, *Straight Bills of Lading in the House of Lords*, LMLQR 273 (2005).
286. *Carriage of Goods by Sea Act* 1991 (Cth), s. 17.
287. *Maxine Footwear Co Ltd v. Canadian Government Merchant Marine* [1959] AC 589 [[1959] 3 WLR 232; [1959] 2 All ER 740; [1959] 2 Lloyd's Rep 105] (PC), the Court at 603.

the voyage has commenced.[288] Due diligence approximates to the duty of care at common law and is a duty placed upon the carrier personally. It cannot be discharged by employment of competent contractors to carry out the work.[289]

158. A carrier is liable for the seaworthiness of a vessel only when it is within the carrier's control. As a result, the carrier incurs no liability for a new or used vessel which is unseaworthy due to existing defects the carrier or its authorized servants agents or independent contractors could not discover by the exercise of due diligence when the vessel came under its control.[290] Whether there has been an exercise of due diligence is a question of fact. In assessing whether a vessel was seaworthy, the court will take into account adherence to international safety provisions and similar maritime conventions as well as the equipment standards and crew competency of a vessel.[291]

159. If the obligation to exercise due diligence to make a ship seaworthy is not met, with consequent loss or damage to the cargo, the immunities given under Article 4 Rule 1 of the Hague-Visby Rules do not apply.[292] However, limitations on time in Article 3 Rule 6 and the amount of compensation in Article 4 Rule 5 still apply. Under Article 4 Rule 1, on a cargo owner's establishing unseaworthiness, the burden of proof is on the carrier to prove due diligence so as to avoid liability.

160. In *Great Metal Industries Co Ltd v. Malaysian International Shipping Corporation Berhad* (1998) 72 ALJR 1592, the respondent carrier's container ship encountered severe but predicted weather while crossing the Great Australian Bight. Exceptionally heavy waves caused loss of and damage to the appellant's cargo. At first instance, the judge held that the carrier had not breached the obligations under the Hague Rules and was immune from liability because the damage to the cargo resulted from 'perils of the sea'. Following an unsuccessful appeal to the NSWCA the appellant was given special leave to appeal to the High Court.

161. The High Court held that Malaysian International had discharged its obligations under the Hague rules Article 3 Rule 1 and Article 3 Rule 2 'properly and carefully load, handle, stow, carry, keep, care for and discharge the goods carried'. There was no question of damage to the goods resulting from the unseaworthiness

288. *Leesh River Tea Co Ltd v. British India Steam Navigation Co Ltd* [1967] 2 QB 250 [[1966] 3 WLR 642; [1966] 3 All ER 593].

289. *W Angliss & Co (Aust) Pty Ltd v. Peninsular & Oriental Steam Navigation Co* [1927] 2 KB 456.

290. *Union of India v. NV Reederij Amsterdam* [1963] 2 Lloyd's Rep 223 (HL) *Delaware North Marine Experience v The Ship Eye-Spy* [2017] FCA 708.

291. *Minnesota Mining & Manufacturing (Australia) Pty Ltd v. The Novoaltaisk* [1972] 2 NSWLR 476 (identical pipes clearly labelled as to different functions held to be due diligence in proper equipment of a ship).

292. *Maxine Footwear Co Ltd v. Canadian Government Merchant Marine* [1959] AC 589 [[1959] 3 WLR 232; [1959] 2 All ER 740; [1959] 2 Lloyd's Rep 105] (PC), the Court at 602–603.

of the ship and no question arising under Article 4 Rule 1 whether such loss or damage having occurred that it had been caused by want of diligence on the part of the carrier to make the ship seaworthy.[293]

In *Westrac Equipment Pty Ltd v. Assets Venture* (2002) 192 ALR 27 Westrac Equipment Pty Ltd (Westrac) were distributors of heavy earth moving equipment. It had contracted to deliver a bulldozer to a purchaser in the Cocos Islands (with property to pass on delivery). Westrac contracted with the second defendant to transport the bulldozer who then contracted with the owners of the *Assets Venture* to ship the bulldozer from a port in Malaysia to the Cocos Islands. The second defendant had supplied the bolster and chains for the bulldozer for it to be ready for transportation. The vessel carried the bulldozer from Port Kelang in Malaysia to Christmas Island. There the bolster and the bulldozer were removed from the No. 1 hold and placed on deck to make way for a cargo of superphosphate. Ten days out from Christmas Island bound for the Cocos Islands the crew nod the bolster and bulldozer were not on board. Westrac sued both the owners of the *Assets Venture* and the second defendant for the loss.

Westrac claimed against the *Asset Venture* in bailment and in negligence and for damages for loss suffered. It also claimed against the second defendant for breach of contract and damages in bailment and in negligence for the loss.

It was held that the *Assets Venture* owed a duty of care to Westrac arising from a 'bare bailment'[294] and were liable to Westrac unless it could establish it had taken reasonable care of the bulldozer. As sub-bailee the *Assets Venture* was under the same duty as a bailee as it had not taken necessary care in securing the bulldozer as deck cargo according to the accepted practices for storing such cargo, or according to good seamanship[295]. The second defendant was under the same duty which it breached by failing to deliver the bulldozer as directed by the *Assets Venture*. It was held that the sub-bailee cannot claim default by the bailee to excuse the sub-bailee's duty to Westrac (the bailor) unless the circumstances show that the act of sub-bailment is contemplated to be a termination of the bailment. These did not indicate this to be so and accordingly the second defendant was liable to Westrac.[296]

In *Anglo Irish Beef Processors International v. Federated Stevedores Geelong* [1997] 2 VR 676 the Victorian CA held that where the *Hague Rules* apply,[297] there seems to be no reason why the shipper should not choose to sue the carrier in tort

293. Following *Shipping Corporation of India Ltd v. Gamlen Chemical Co (A/Asia) Pty Ltd* (1980) 147 CLR 142 at 164–166. 'No single criterion standing alone, will identify whether what occurred is properly to be called a peril of the sea'.

294. J. Lee at [20] On the ruling that the second defendant was a sub-bailee of the plaintiff's machine J. Lee cited N.E. Palmer, *Bailment* 34 (2d ed., Law Book Co 1991). *See* S. Baughen, *Bailments Continuing Role in Cargo Claims,* LMCLQ 393–405 (1999). *See* B. Davenbport, *Misdelivery: A Fundamental Breach,* LMCLQ 386 (2000).

295. J. Lee at [24] On the duties and liabilities of bailees, negligence and duty of care *see Nudrill Pty Ltd v. La Rosa (No3)* [2011] WADC 178 (clause in bill of lading protecting stevedores).

296. J. Lee at [45]–[46] citing *York Products Pty ltd v. Watt & Sanderson Pty Ltd* [1968] 3 NSWLR 551; *York Products v. Gilchrist, E.A. Marr (Contracting) Pty Ltd v. Broken Hill Pty Ltd* [1970] 3.

297. J. Bergin at [60]–[61].

or in contract., even when the carrier may have the advantage of any of the *Hague-Visby Rules* provisions limiting the carrier's liability.[298] Article 5 Rule 6 requiring a suit to be brought within a year covers both an Action in contract and tort.

162. Under Article 3 Rule 1 of the Hague-Visby Rules (reproduced in Schedule 1 of the *Carriage of Goods by Sea Act* 1991 (Cth)),[299] a carrier is bound to properly and carefully load, handle, stow, keep, care for, and discharge the goods carried.[300] This provision, subject to the protection of Article 4 Rule 1, exempts the carrier and the vessel from liability for loss or damage arising or resulting from unseaworthiness unless caused by a lack of due diligence on the part of the carrier to make the vessel seaworthy[301] and the further exemptions provided to a carrier by the seventeen exceptions under Article 4 Rule 2. The duty of due diligence on the part of the carrier extends to agents the carrier employs to fit the vessel.[302] Under Article 3 Rule 1 of the Hague-Visby Rules, a carrier undertakes to load the cargo and to proceed upon and complete the voyage with all reasonable dispatch. A breach of this undertaking, if sufficient to deprive the shipper of the whole benefit of the contract, may entitle the shipper to refuse to perform its part of the contract.[303] If the breach is not so serious the carrier will be liable for damages if the loss incurred could be reasonably anticipated as the result of delay.[304]

163. According to Article 3 Rule 1, the carrier must properly man, equip, and supply the ship and make the holds, refrigerating, and cool chambers and all other parts of the ship in which goods are carried fit and for their reception, carriage, and preservation.[305] The carrier is also obliged under Article 3 Rule 2, subject to the immunities contained in Article 4, to properly and carefully load, handle, stow, carry, keep, care for, and discharge the goods carried.[306] Where goods are lost or damaged, the carrier or other person claiming immunity, will be liable unless she or he satisfies the burden of proving the exercise of due diligence.[307]

---

298. J. Bergin at [72], [75] finding that Smith Bros did rely on misleading or deceptive statements in the notice, applying the *Trade Practices Act* 1974(Cth) s. 52 (now *see Competition and Consumer Act* 2010 (Cth) s. 18).
299. Brooking, Phillips & J.J. Charles at 691 citing *Cia Portorafi Commerciale SA v. Ultramar Panama Inc (The Captain Gregos) (No[1])* [1990] 3 All ER 967, L.J. Binham at 973–974.
300. *See Merchant Shipping Act* 1979 (UK); A.A. Mocatta, M.J. Mustill & S.C. Boyd, *Scrutton on Charterparties* 422–463 (19th ed., Sweet & Maxwell 1984).
301. *Commonwealth v. Burns Philp & Co Ltd* (1946) 46 SR (NSW) 307.
302. *Riverstone Meat Co v. Lancashire Shipping Co (The Muncaster Castle)* [1961] AC 807 [[1961] 2 WLR 269; [1961] 1 All ER 495; [1961] 1 Lloyd's Rep 57] (obligation not discharged by evidence of due diligence in the selection of an independent contractor where damage was caused by negligence of that person or his or her employee).
303. *Universal Cargo Carriers Corporation v. Citati* [1957] 2 QB 401 [[1957] 2 WLR 713; [1957] 2 All ER 70].
304. *Monarch Steamship Co Ltd v. Karlshamns Oljefabriker (A/B)* [1949] AC 196 [[1949] 1 All ER 1].
305. *See McGregor v. Huddart Parker Ltd* (1919) 26 CLR 336.
306. But *see*, *McEwan & Co v. Brabender* (1895) 1 LR (NSW) 200 (FC); *Dimond v. William Collin & Sons Ltd* [1912] QWN 1 [5 QJPR 187].
307. Hague-Visby Rules, Art. 4 r. 1. But *see Colonial Sugar Refining Co Ltd v. British India Steam Navigation Co Ltd* (1931) 32 SR (NSW) 245 [49 WN 55]. *See* J. Wong, *Container Transportation and*

In *Woolworth Ltd v. APL Co Pty Ltd* [2001] NSWC 662 two containers of frozen prawns were shipped from Sydney by Woolworths to the original supplier in Bangkok. At Freemantle the cargo was unloaded at Woolworth's direction and shipped back to Sydney. On arrival one of the containers of prawns was stored at Woolworth's agent's storage depot without refrigeration and the cargo suffered thaw damage. Woolwoths claimed that the defendant APL Pte Ltd (APL) as the carrier of the goods owed a duty of care to Woolwoths to provide Woolworths' agent Smith Bros Trade and Transport Terminal Pty Ltd (Smith Bros) with sufficient instructions to ensure that the prawns were properly cared for after delivery to Smith Bros. Woolworths also claimed under section 52 of the *Trade Practices Act* 1974 (Cth) that Woolworth's agent, Smith Bros, relied on APL's inaccurate description of the goods and as a result the container was stored without refrigeration and the cargo damaged.

In the Supreme Court of New South Wales Bergin J noted that Woolworths claimed that APL owed it a duty of care to ensure that the contents of the container were accurately identified. Woolworths claimed that the duty of care was based on a long term relationship with Smith Bros which set up a system describing the contents of the containers in a coded form and knew that Smith Bros would rely on that code. The only documents that Smith Bros received in relation to this matter for the identification of the contents of the container did not have any information about the temperature for storage of the container. This information was only available in the Export Received Advice and Bill of Lading and the bill of lading (or express bill).

The judge noted that the duty to describe the contents of the container accurately arose from the relationship between Woolworths and Smith Bros since 1994. It was clear that Smith Bros relied on the description to create its delivery orders. The delivery order generated by Smith Bros from APL's notice was presented for collection of the container. The judge was satisfied that Smith Bros was relying on the notice which identified the contents of the container. It was reasonably foreseeable that Smith Bros and Woolworths would freely on the description of the contents of the container used in the notice. In the circumstances of the system in place between APL, Woolworths, and Smith Bros APL owed a duty of care to provide Smith Bros with an accurate description of the contents of the container. Their duty was breached by an inaccurate description of the container which led to it being placed in storage without power resulting in damage to the container's contents. APL was found to have made a misleading or deceptive statement on which Woolworths relied and as a result of which damage was caused to the cargo.

III. Exemptions from Liability

164. A carrier is permitted certain immunities from the time goods are loaded to when they are discharged from the ship in return for fulfilling its obligations under the Hague-Visby Rules (reproduced in Schedule 1 of the *Carriage of Goods by Sea*

Anomolies in the Law, 340 ABLR 21 (1995); M. Davies, *Two Views on Free In and Out Stowed Clauses in Bills of Lading*, 22 ABLR 198 (1994).

Act 1991 (Cth)).[308] Article 4 Rule 2 of the Hague-Visby Rules provide that neither the carrier nor the ship shall be responsible for loss or damage arising or resulting from a list of excepted perils, including act, neglect, or default of the master, mariner, pilot, or servants of the carrier in the navigation or management of the ship.[309] If the loss or damage is caused partly by the unseaworthiness of the ship and partly by negligent management and the shipowner fails to show the extent of the damage caused by negligent management then the shipowner will not have the benefit of Article 4 Rule 2.[310] The carrier and the ship are further exempted from liability for loss or damage caused by fire, unless caused by the actual fault or privity of the carrier, perils, dangers, and accidents of the sea and other navigable waters.[311]

165. The other exemptions are: act of God; act of war; act of public enemies; arrest or restraint of princes, rulers or people, or seizure under legal process; quarantine restrictions; acts or omissions of the shipper or owner of the goods, its agent, or representative; strikes or lock-outs or stoppage or restraint of labour from whatever cause, whether partial or general; riots and civil commotions; saving or attempting to save life or property at sea; wastage in bulk or weight or any other loss or damage arising from inherent defect, quality, or vice of the goods; insufficiency of packing; insufficiency or inadequacy of marks; latent defects not discoverable by due diligence; any other cause arising without the actual fault or privity of the carrier, or without the fault or neglect of the agents or servants of the carrier.[312] In *Great China Metal Industries Co Ltd v. Malaysian International Shipping Corporation Berhad*,[313] the NSW Supreme Court (CA) held that where a loss falls within the perils of the sea exception under Article 4 Rule 2(c), the burden of proving that the shipowner is not entitled to the benefit of the exception on the grounds of the shipowner's negligence, or that of its servants and agents, is on the person contending. The term 'perils of the sea' does not apply to damage or wear and tear resulting from the natural and inevitable action of the wind and waves, but, by loss by peril of the sea is not limited to loss resulting from extreme and unexpectedly violent weather. Nor does the reasonable expectation of violent weather preclude fortuitous damage to cargo from being regarded as loss resulting from a peril of the sea. In each case, the question is whether the accident should reasonably have been foreseen and, if so, whether steps should reasonably have been taken to prevent it. Following the successful appeal to the Court of Appeal, the appellant was given special leave to appeal to the High Court. The High Court held that the carrier had discharged its obligations under Article 3 Rule 6 to 'properly and carefully load,

---

308. Hague-Visby Rules, Art. 1(e) (reproduced in Sch. 1 of the *Carriage of Goods by Sea Act* 1991 (Cth)).
309. *Chubu Asahi Cotton Spinning Co Ltd v. The Tenos* (1968) 12 FLR 291 [88 WN (Pt 1) (NSW) 395] (SC); *Minnesota Mining & Manufacturing (Australia) Pty Ltd v. The Novoaltaisk* [1972] 2 NSWLR 476.
310. *Commonwealth v. Burns Philp & Co Ltd* (1946) 46 SR (NSW) 307.
311. *Vacuum Oil Co Pty Ltd v. Commonwealth & Dominion Line Ltd* [1922] VLR 693 [44 ALT 46].
312. Hague-Visby Rules, Art. 4 r. 2.
313. [1996] 39 NSWLR 683 following *Shipping Corporation of India Ltd v. Gamlen Chemical (A/Asia) Pty Ltd* (1980) 147 CLR 142; comparison made with the different approach by the US and Canadian courts to the concept of a 'peril of the sea' 697–698.

handle, stow, carry, keep, and discharge the goods carried'. There was no question of damage to the goods resulting from the unseaworthiness of the ship and no question arising under Article 4 Rule 1 whether such loss or damage having occurred that it had been caused by want of diligence on the part of the carrier to make the ship seaworthy.[314]

In *Hilditch Pty Ltd v. Dorval Kaiun KK (No2)* [2007[FCA 2014, Hilditch imported refined oil products from SK Corporation (SK), a Korean company. A cargo of refined oil products was ordered from SK, which chartered the *M/T Golden Lucy 1* from Darval. The vessel carried refined oil and caustic soda. The vessel discharged the oil at Botany Bay. The surveyor there was concerned at the possibility of cross contamination between the cargoes of oil and caustic soda. After 12,000 litres had been discharged the oil was found to be contaminated by caustic soda and so was not to specification and commercially unsaleable. Darval argued in the Federal Court that it was entitled to the benefit of Article 4 Rule 2(i) of the *Hague Visby Rules* which provide that 'Neither the carrier nor the ship shall be responsible for the loss or damage resulting from (i) Act or omission of the shipper or owner of the goods, his agent or representative'.

Rares J found that the damage did not arise from any act or omission on the part of Hilditch to stop the discharge of the oil within the meaning of Article 4 Rule 2(i).Whether a carrier can rely on an immunity under Article 4 Rule 2 will depend on the circumstances of the case. Where the facts disclose that a loss was caused by not concurrent effects of excepted or non-excepted circumstances, the carrier remains liable. Despite Hilditch not applying some common sense and halting the discharge of the oil, the damage did not arise from any act or omission of Hilditch so as to activate the exception of Darval's liability within the meaning of Article 4 Rule 2(i).[315]

166. A bill of lading will be construed in the event it is claimed to cover the land leg of a multimodal carriage. In *Parlux SPA v. M&U Imports Pty Ltd* (2009) 250 ALR 340, an importer M&U Imports agreed to purchase a consignment of 10,000 electrical hair dryers and parts from Parlux. The terms of the sale were 'FOB Italian Port'. The goods were sent by container and taken by road by Gava International Freight to La Spezia. It was then loaded on to a ship to Melbourne. When the container was opened at M&U importer's warehouse in Melbourne only 6,188 hairdryers and parts had been dispatched. M&U sued Parlux for its failure to deliver the goods as agreed and the trial judge awarded M&U damages against Parlux. M&U claimed that if the missing goods were removed from the container it was during the land leg; that the bill of lading covered the land leg and in the absence of fault or neglect by Gava it was liable to M&U under that bill of lading. It was common ground that the goods did not arrive at M&U's warehouse and could not have gone missing on the ship.

---

314. Following *Shipping Corp of India Ltd v. Gamlen Chemical Co (A/ Asia) Pty Ltd* (1980) 147 CLR 142.

315. J. Rares at [93]–[94] noting that the carrier will only escape liability if it proves the loss or damage was caused by an excepted circumstance alone: *see Aktieselskabet de Danske Sukkerfabrikker v. Bajamar Compania Naviera SA (The Torenia)* [1983] 2 Lloyd's Rep 210 (QBD), J. Hobhouse at 218.

Following the successful appeal to the Court of Appeal, the appellant was given special leave to appeal to the High Court. The High Court held that the carrier had discharged its obligations under Article 3 Rule 6 to 'properly and carefully load, handle, stow, carry, keep, and discharge the goods carried'. There was no question of damage to the goods resulting from the unseaworthiness of the ship and no question arising under Article 4 Rule 1 whether such loss or damage having occurred had been caused by want of diligence.

167. However, the trial judge dismissed the claim against Gava which had two separate contacts with Parlux; one for the sea and another for the land leg. M&U also argued that the bill of lading in this case was a bill of lading for the purposes of the *Sea Carriage Documents Act* 1998 (Vic)[316] as 'a multimodal bill of lading' as covering both carriage by land and sea.

168. On appeal to the Victorian Court of Appeal, it held that in construing the bill of lading the most important part of the bill was the front in its printed terms and corresponding details inserted by the parties. Even though terms of carriage printed on the back of the bill may contemplate multimodal carriage, the preferred interpretation is evidenced by the terms and details entered by the parties. Where a bill of lading had spaces for place of receipt and delivery in the absence of such details as this case the document should be regarded as a port-to-port bill only.[317]

169. An exception to a carrier's liability for loss and damage in the case of fire is provided by Article 4 Rule 2(b) of the Hague-Visby Rules (reproduced in Schedule 1 of the *Carriage of Goods by Sea Act* 1991 (Cth)) unless caused by the actual fault or privity of the carrier. This part of the Rules has to be considered with Pt 3 of the *Navigation Act* 2012 (Cth) sections 108–110. Article 4 Rule 2(b) of the Hague-Visby Rules extends to shipowners and carriers generally where the Rules apply. The burden of proof is on the person claiming the benefit of this exception to show that neither the actual fault or privity of the carrier nor the fault or neglect of the agents or servants of the carrier contributed to the loss or damage. The carrier's reliance is subject to its exercising the duty of due diligence under Article 3 Rule 1 of the Rules where breach of that duty causes the loss or damage, and the carrier not making an unpermitted deviation.[318] If the deviation is voluntary for the benefit of the shipowners and the consequent delay was to the detriment of the cargo, the deviation will not be excused by the Rules.[319] The carrier will not escape liability

316. *See* Reform of Bills of Lading Legislation
317. *Pacific Carriers Ltd v. Paribas* (2004) 218 CLR 451 applied.
318. Hague-Visby Rules, Art. 4 r. 4.
319. *Thiess Bros (Queensland) Pty Ltd v. Australian Steamships Pty Ltd* [1955] 1 Lloyd's Rep 459 (SC NSW) where a claim for freight that was due before the deviation occurred was successful (following *Hain SS Co Ltd v. Tate & Lyle Ltd* (1936) 41 Com Cas 350); *F Kanematsu & Co Ltd v. The Shahzada* (1956) 96 CLR 477 [30 ALJ 478]; *see Danae Shipping Corporation v. Tao & Guven Turkish Insurance Co Ltd (The Daffodil B)* [1983] 1 Lloyd's Rep 498 (QB); *Kenya Railways v. Antares Co Pty Ltd* [1987] 1 Lloyd's Rep 424 (CA); *Cia Portorafti Commerciale SA v. Ultramar Panama Incorporated (The Captain Gregos)* [1989] 2 All ER 54 [[1989] 2 Lloyd's Rep 63] (QB); reversed by the English Court of Appeal in *Cia Portorafti Commerciale SA v. Ultramar Panama*

unless it can show that loss or damage was occasioned either by an act of God, or by the Queen's enemies, or as the result of inherent vice in the goods and also that such loss or damage would have occurred if there had been no deviation.[320]

IV. Duty Not to Deviate

170. Under Article 4 Rule 4 of the Hague-Visby Rules (reproduced in Schedule 1 of the *Carriage of Goods by Sea Act* 1991 (Cth)) a carrier is not liable for any loss or damage resulting from any deviation to the agreed route to save life or property at sea, or any reasonable deviation. Shipowners have attempted, in response to the courts' consideration of what may or may not amount to a reasonable deviation, to extend their right to call at ports and to deviate by use of 'liberty clauses' in their agreement with shippers which purport to give the vessel express liberty to deviate. In practice, these clauses are so worded to include almost every possible deviation.[321] The courts generally construe such clauses narrowly so that the main object of the contract at issue is not defeated.[322] However, the High Court has noted that an appropriately worded exemption clause may operate to exclude even a breach which defeats the main object of the contract.[323] Additionally, the Hague-Visby Rules apply to contracts of carriage by force of law so that even if wrongful deviation were to have its traditional effect at common law,[324] the discharge of a contract

Inc. (The Captain Gregos No. 2) [1990] 2 Lloyd's Rep 395. *See* T. Carver, *Carriage of Goods by Sea* paras 1161–1208 (13th ed., Stevens 1982); W. Tetley, *Marine Cargo Claims* Chs 5, 31 (3d ed., Blais 1988); C.M. Mills, *The Future of Deviation in the Law of Carriage of Goods*, 4 LMCLQ 587 (1983); C. Debattista, *Fundamental Breach and Deviation in the Carriage of Goods by Sea*, JBL 22 (1989); J. Livermore, *Deviation, Deck Cargo and Fundamental Breach*, 2 JCL 241 (1990); S. Baughen, *Does Deviation Still Matter?*, LMCLQ 70.

320. *F Kanematsu & Co Ltd v. The Shahzada* (1956) 96 CLR 477 [30 ALJ 478].

321. *See* the examples given in J. Livermore, *Deviation, Deck Cargo and Fundamental Breach*, 2 JCL 241, 249 (1990).

322. *Leduc & Co v. Ward* (1888) 20 QBD 475 (CA); *Thiess Bros (Queensland) Pty Ltd v. Australian Steamships Pty Ltd* [1955] 1 Lloyd's Rep 459 (SC NSW), J. Kinsella at 463; but *see Nissho Iwai Australia Ltd v. Malaysian International Shipping Corporation, Berhad* (1989) 167 CLR 219 [63] ALJR 468; 86 ALR 375.

323. *Darlington Futures Ltd v. Delco Australia Pty Ltd* (1986) 161 CLR 500 [61] ALJR 76; 68 ALR 385; 5 ACLC [132]; *Nissho Iwai Australia Ltd v. Malaysian International Shipping Corporation, Berhad* (1989) 167 CLR 219 [63] ALJR 468; 86 ALR 375; *See also J I Case (Australia) Pty Ltd v. Tasman Express Line Ltd (The Canterbury Express)* (1990) 102 FLR 59 (SC NSW).

324. The carrier is under a common law obligation not to deviate from the agreed route of the voyage, which is, prima facie, the direct geographical route (*see* para. 51). Such presumption may be overcome by evidence showing that the route taken was the usual and reasonable route for the ship and that the contract did not expressly provide otherwise: *Reardon Smith Line Ltd v. Black Sea & General Insurance Co Ltd* [1939] AC 562 [[1939] 3 All ER 444], Lord Porter at 584. The route will not necessarily be the usual commercial route if the ship is not engaged in that type of voyage. Unintentional departure from the agreed route due to navigational instrument failure is not a relevant deviation: *Dunne v. Australasian Steam Navigation Co* (1876) 14 SCR (NSW) 131 (FC), C.J. Martin at 144. *See also Evans v. Quenbeyan City Council* [2011] NSWCA 230.

due to that deviation would have no effect on the immunities enjoyed by the carrier under Article 4.[325]

171. In *Nikolay Malakhov Shipping Co Ltd v. Sea Saffor Ltd and Another* (1998) 44 NSWLR 379, under a bill of lading incorporating the Hague Rules and making the law of Malaysia the proper law of the contract of carriage goods were shipped from Malaysia. Due to deviation caused an industrial dispute the goods were unloaded at a different port in NSW from that nominated in the bill. The carrier arranged for bond storage and road transport. The goods were damaged by rain while being held in open storage before transport by road.

172. The consignee, intending to sue the carrier, mistakenly named an unrelated shipping company as defendant. More than a year had elapsed since the delivery on the goods when the consignee applied to amend the statement of claim.[326] At first instance, leave to amend was granted, judgment being given to the consignee.

173. On appeal to the NSWCA held a defence grounded on the time bar provision of the Hague Rule, Article 3 Rule 6, would be rejected. Article 3 Rule 2 of the Hague Rules to discharge goods properly and carefully ceases unless contractually extended with the delivery of the goods across the ship's rail or from its tackle.[327]

In *Tasman Express Line Ltd v. JI Case (Aust) Pty Ltd* (1992) 11 FLR 108.a harvester that had been transported from New Zealand (NZ) to Australia was damaged during unloading in Sydney. The cargo had been shipped on deck by agreement and the bill of lading contained an exclusion clause relating to deck cargo. The trial judge held that the carrier could not rely on the exclusion clause for the reason that there had been a deviation or fundamental departure from the main purpose of the contract by negligence in the course of unloading the cargo. The New South Wales Court of Appeal held that the question involved the true construction of the bill of lading and, in particular, whether the conduct of the carrier or the stevedores was outside the scope of the exclusion clause.[328] On the facts the negligent conduct involved was not outside the scope of the exclusion clause and the appellant could rely on it to defeat the respondent's claim. The respondent's argument that, when

---

325. *See* J. Livermore, *Deviation, Deck Cargo and Fundamental Breach*, 2 JCL 241, 263–264 (1990); *Kenya Railways v. Antares Co Pty Ltd* [1987] 1 Lloyd's Rep 424 (CA), L.J. Lloyd at 429–430; *The Hollandia* [1983] AC 565 [[1982] 3 WLR 1111; [1982] 3 [1991[LMCLQ 70All ER 1141; [1983] 1 Lloyd's Rep 1]; *see* S. Baughen, *Shipping Law* 98–102 (4th ed., Cavendish 2009). S. Boyd, S. Berry, A. Burrows, B. Eder, D. Foxton & C. Smith, *Scrutton on Charterparties and Bills of Lading* [B12] (21st ed., Sweet & Maxwell 2008) especially 404–406 (citing *Stag Line Ltd v. Foscolo Mango & Co Ltd* [1932] AC 328. *See* S. Baughen, *Does Deviation Still Matter?*, LMCLQ 70 (1991).

326. *Supreme Court Rules* 1970 (NSW) Pt 2, r. 4.

327. *Lloyd Steel Co (Aust) Pty Ltd v. Jade Shipping SA* [1985] 1 NSWLR 212 and *Bridge Futures Shipping Pty Ltd v. Grand Shipping SA* [1991] 1 VR 258 followed. *See also Tutt Bryant Group Ltd v. Japan Vanlines Co Ltd* [2010] NSWSC 1464 (Art. 3 r. 2).

328. Applying *Sydney City Council v. West* (1965) 114 CLR 481; *Darlington Futures Ltd v. Delco Australia Pty Ltd (1986) 161 CLR 500; Nissho Iwai Australia Ltd v. Malaysian International Shipping Corp Berhad* (1980) 167 CLR 219; *Photo Production Ltd v. Securicor Transport Ltd* [1980] AC 827.

the exclusion clause had that effect, there was no contract between the parties, failed. The clause was not contrary to public policy nor was the conduct of the carrier in such a contractual provision misleading or deceptive within the ambit of fair trading legislation.

Additionally, the *Hague-Visby Rules* apply to contracts of carriage by force of law so that even if wrongful deviation were to have its traditional effect at common law,[329] the discharge of a contract due to that deviation would have no effect on the immunities enjoyed by the carrier under Article 4.

V. Dangerous Goods

174. Under Article 4 Rule 6 of the Hague-Visby Rules (reproduced in Schedule 1 of the *Carriage of Goods by Sea Act* 1991 (Cth)) where goods of an inflammable, explosive, or dangerous nature are shipped without the knowledge and consent of the carrier or its agent and become a danger to the ship or cargo they may be landed at any place or destroyed or made harmless by the carrier.[330] Article 4 Rule 6 envisages two situations:

(1) Where goods of an inflammable, explosive, or dangerous nature are shipped on an interstate or international voyage without the consent of the carrier, master, or agent of the carrier, those goods may be landed or destroyed before discharge by the carrier without compensation, the shipper being liable for all damages and expenses, directly or indirectly connected with the shipment.
(2) Where goods are shipped on a similar voyage but with the consent and knowledge of the relevant parties as to the nature and character of the goods, but these become a danger to the ship or cargo, these goods may be landed or destroyed or rendered harmless by the carrier, with the latter being liable only for general average.[331]

Article 4 Rule 3 provides that a shipper is not responsible for any loss or damage arising without some fault or neglect on the part of the shipper or its agent or servants.

329. *See Reardon Smith Line Ltd v. Black Sea & General Insurance Co Ltd* [1939] AC 562,Porter LJ at 584.

330. *Navigation Act* 2012 (Cth) s. 4. *See Paul Equipment Leasing Pty Ltd v. Scheepvaartonder Emmagracht* [2008] NSWSC 850 (damage to locomotives in transit); *see also Hilditch Pty Ltd v David Kaiun KK* (No 2) [2007] FCA 2014. *See* S. Baughen, *Dangerous Cargo and the Claimant's Dilemma*, 5(1) Shipping and Transport International 7–9 (2005); S. Baughen & S.J. Campbell, *Apportionment of Risk and the Carriage of Dangerous Cargo*, 8(1) International Maritime Law (2001).

331. For the principle of general average *see* Insurance and Income Security 'Loss' Laws of Australia, Thomson Reuters [22.1.4360]–[22.1.4420].For an example of liability for damage and loss of cargo involving dangerous goods *see McKay Massey & Harris v. Chemical Industries of Australia and New Zealand [No2]* [1960] Lloyd's Rep (VSC).

175. The *Navigation Act* 2012 (Cth) prohibits the shipping of dangerous goods, defined as those listed in the *International Maritime Dangerous Goods Code (IMDG)* issued by the International Maritime Association, unless a description of the goods is distinctly marked on the outside of the package and the owner or master of the ship is provided with a written description of the goods at or when the goods are placed on board. The owner or master of a ship may refuse to carry dangerous goods, may open any package suspected of containing such goods, and throw overboard any that have been shipped without the master's knowledge.[332] An offence is committed under the *Navigation Act* 2012 (Cth) by persons on any package or in any document relating to the carriage of such goods.[333]

The requirements to properly label dangerous goods, to give a description of such goods to the master or owner of the ship, and not to carry dangerous goods under a false description, apply to foreign vessels if at the time the goods are carried or placed on the vessel, the vessel is in, or entering or leaving in an Australian port or in the internal waters or the territorial sea of Australia, other than in the course of innocent passage.[334]

VI. Limitation of Actions

176. Under Article 3 Rule 6 of the Hague-Visby Rules (reproduced in Schedule 1 of the *Carriage of Goods by Sea Act* 1991 (Cth)), an action must be brought by the owner of goods within one year from when the goods were or should have been delivered, otherwise the carrier and the ship are discharged from all liability in respect of those goods.[335] Delivery is judged as completed either when the goods are loaded on the wharf or freed from the ship's tackles or, at the very latest as soon as the consignee has a reasonable opportunity to take possession of the goods,[336] as in the instance where goods are to be collected from a warehouse. In *Automatic Tube Co Pty Ltd v. Adelaide Steamship (Operations) Ltd* [1966] WAR 103 [9 FLR 130], the court found that delivery had taken place when the goods were landed at the wharf, not later upon delivery to other premises to await collection by the plaintiff.

332. *Navigation Act* 2012 (Cth) s. 116.
333. *Navigation Act* 2012 (Cth) s. 118.
334. *Navigation Act* 2012 (Cth) ss 115(1)(c); s. 116(1)(d); s. 117(1)(b); s. 14(1) for definition of 'Australian port' and 'internal waters of Australia'. *See* S. Baughen, *The 'Clause Paramount' and the One Year Time Bar the Mariner* LMCLQ 173–175(1996).
335. *Colonial Sugar Refining Co Ltd v. British India Steam Navigation Co Ltd* (1931) 32 SR (NSW) 245 [49 WN 55]. In *Nikolay Malakhov Shipping Co Ltd v. Seas Sapfor Ltd* (1998) 44 NSWLR 371, a consignee in suing the carrier for negligence mistakenly named an unrelated shipping company as defendant. When the consignee applied to amend the statement of claim more than a year had expired since delivery of the goods and judgment at first instance was given to the applicant. The SC of NSW (Court of Appeal) held (J. Handley, dissenting) that given the mistake in the statement of claim was amenable to correction under the *Supreme Court Rules* 1979 (NSW) (Pt 20, r. 43) a defence grounded on the time bar provision in the Hague Rules Art. 3, r. 6 should be rejected; *see* IV (193).
336. *Australasian United Steamship Navigation Co Ltd v. Hiskens* (1914) 18 CLR 646 [[1914] VLR 684]; *Keane v. Australian Steamships Pty Ltd* (1929) 41 CLR 484 [2 ALJ 367; [1929] VLR 116].

177. An action[337] includes the commencement of arbitration.[338] Under State and Territory legislation, a court has a discretion to extend the time, in the case of arbitration proceedings,[339] beyond the limit under Article 3 Rule 6*bis* of the Hague-Visby Rules.[340] Where an order is made by a court to extend the time limit in which arbitration proceedings may be commenced a cause of action barred by Article 3 Rule 6 is accordingly revived. In *Australian Shipping Commission v. Kooragang Cement Pty Ltd* [1988] VR 29, a time charter party in the Baltime 1939 form between the appellant shipowner and the respondent charterer contained the provisions of the Hague-Visby Rules, including the requirement to bring proceedings within one year of delivery. The respondent successfully obtained an extension of time to commence arbitration, the Full Court noting that the relevant provision of the *Commercial Arbitration Act* 1984 (Vic) 'avowedly. contemplates the variation of a contract [which] seeks to deprive a party of an entrenched right'.[341]

178. The time limit refers to the issue of proceedings and not to service of notice of proceedings on the defendant.[342] The carrier may be estopped from relying on Article 3 Rule 6 or any other limitation provision in the contract of carriage if the carrier leads the cargo owner to believe that time will not run for the purposes of the limitation provision.[343] Claims for loss or damage occurring outside the limit of the Rules, that is, before loading or after the goods have been discharged, must be brought within the limitation period fixed by State or Territory legislation (three or six years),[344] or within the time specified in the contract.

179. In *Pacific Resources International Pty Ltd v. UTI (Aust) Pty Ltd* [2012] NSWSC 1274 a warehouse at Botany, Sydney and its contents were destroyed by fire. The defendant UTI (Aust) Pty Ltd (UTI) was the leasee of the warehouse. The plaintiffs, Pacific Resources (PCI) stored fish oil and Brackley Industries Pty Ltd

337. The term used in Hague-Visby Rules, Art. 3 r. 6 is 'suit'.
338. *Australian Shipping Commission v. Kooragang Cement Pty Ltd* [1988] VR 29 (FC). *Commercial Arbitration Act 2010* (NSW) s. 21; *Commercial Arbitration Act 2011*(Tas) s. 19; *Commercial Arbitration Act* (SA) s. 19; *Commercial Arbitration Act* (WA) s. 19; *Commercial Arbitration Act 2011*(Vic) s. 19.
339. *See Commercial Arbitration Act* 1986 (ACT), s. 48; *Commercial Arbitration Act* 1984 (NSW), s. 48; *Commercial Arbitration Act* 1985 (NT), s. 48; *Commercial Arbitration Act* 1990 (Qld), s. 48; *Commercial Arbitration Act* 1986 (SA), s. 48; *Commercial Arbitration Act* 1986 (Tas), s. 48; *Commercial Arbitration Act* 1984 (Vic), s. 48; *Commercial Arbitration Act* 1985 (WA), s. 48.
340. *Bis*: renumbered for convenience to avoid renumbering of succeeding articles.
341. *Australian Shipping Commission v. Kooragang Cement Pty Ltd* [1988] VR 29 (FC), J. Tadgell at 38.
342. *Van Leer Australia Pty Ltd v. Palace Shipping KK* (1981) 180 CLR 337 [55 ALJR 243; 34 ALR 3], J. Stephen at 340–341.
343. *Commonwealth v. Verwayen* (1990) 170 CLR 394 [64 ALJR 540; 95 ALR 321; but *see P s. Chellaram & Co Ltd v. China Ocean Shipping Co* (1991) 65 ALJR 642 [102 ALR 321; 5 ACSR 633; 9 ACLC 1,603] (HC) (where this defence was unsuccessful).
344. *See Limitation Act* 1985 (ACT), s. 11; *Limitation Act* 1969 (NSW), s. 14; *Limitation Act* 1981 (NT), s. 12; *Limitations of Actions Act* 1974 (Qld), s. 10; *Limitation of Actions Act* 1936 (SA), s. 35; *Limitation Act* 1974 (Tas), s. 4; *Limitation of Actions Act* 1958 (Vic), s. 5; *Limitation Act* 1935 (WA), s. 38.

(Brackley) stored CD's and DVD's PRI and Brackley sued UTI for the damage caused by the loss of their goods.

180. UTI leased the warehouse from GTA Industrial Custodian Pty Ltd (GTA) and by the terms of the lease UTI was prohibited from using the premises for the storage of fish oil and thermoplastic materials including polypropylene. UTI's standard terms and conditions (STC's) included a clause that provided that UTI would not be liable in tort or contract or otherwise for loss or damage to or deterioration of the goods or misdelivery or failure to deliver for any reason whatsoever, including without limitation negligence, breach of contract, or wilful act or default by UTI for any loss or damage.[345]

181. Stevenson J in the Supreme Court of NSW found that the fire was caused by negligence on UTI's part and that UTI's STC's were effective to exclude liability to PRI and Brackley. However, it was held that UTI made misleading representations to PRI and Brackley[346] concerning the storage of goods and that both these parties relied on these misrepresentations to their detriment. The issue according to Stevenson J was whether GTA as lessor of the warehouse to UTI owed a duty of care to take reasonable care to its customers PRI and Brackley. It was held that GTA owed no such duty.[347]

182. UTI was found liable to both PRI and Brackley on the basis of misleading and deceptive representations[348] which did not indicate that the storage was subject to GTA's restrictions which included the goods of PRI and Brackley

VII. Limitation of Liability

183. The liability of a carrier for loss or damage as to the actual amount recoverable by a cargo owner is limited under Article 4 Rule 5 of the Hague-Visby Rules (reproduced in Schedule 1 of the *Carriage of Goods by Sea Act* 1991 (Cth)).[349] Article 4 Rule 5 provides that unless the nature and value of the goods have been declared by a shipper before shipment and inserted in the bill of lading,[350] or where the nature or value of the goods had been knowingly misstated by a shipper in the

345. *See* J. Stevenson at [77] where Cl. 15 was stated to be 'drawn in very broad terms' and at [88] 'the clause is effective to exclude UTI's liability to the extent that the clause states'; citing *Jireh International Pty Ltd t/as Gloria Jean's Coffee v. Western Exports Services Inc* [2011] NSWCA 137 J. Macfarlan at [55] distinguishing *MacRobertson Miller Airline Services v. Commissioner of State Taxation* [1975] HCA 55.
346. On the basis of the *Trade Practices Act* 1974 (Cth) s. 52 at [268].
347. At [331].
348. At [250]–[254].
349. For limitation of liability for maritime claims under the *Limitation of Liability for Maritime Clauses Act* 1989 (Cth), *see* Ch. 6, limitation of liability [211]–[216].
350. On the operation of the unamended Hague Rules in this regard, *see Parke, Lacey, Hardie Ltd v. The Clan MacFadyen* (1930) 30 SR (NSW) 438 [47 WN 160]; but *see Australasian United Steamship Navigation Co Ltd v. Hiskens* (1914) 18 CLR 646 [[1914] VLR 684].

bill of lading,[351] the liability of a carrier or a ship is limited to 666.67 units of account (SDRs) per package or unit or two units of account (SDRs) per kilogram of gross weight of the goods lost or damaged, whichever is higher.[352] The alternative measure of gross weight of the goods overcomes problems concerning the appropriate measure for bulk cargo, but is applicable to any cargo.[353]

184. 'Package or unit' means the unit in which the shipper packed the goods so that where goods are carried in or on a container, pallet, or similar article of transport used to consolidate goods, the number of packages or units enumerated in the bill of lading as packed in such an article of transport are deemed to be the number of packages or units for the purpose of Article 4 Rule 5 of the Hague-Visby Rules in the bill of lading. Where there is no such enumeration the container is regarded as the sole package or unit to which the limitation applies.[354]

In *William Holyman & Sons Ltd v. Foy& Gibson Pty Ltd* (1945) 73 CLR 622 goods were shipped by a bill of lading under Clause 14 of which it was agreed that the value of each package did not exceed L5, and that the shipowner was not to be accountable beyond that value in the absence of a declaration as to the true character and value and payment of extra freight. The goods were not delivered.

The High Court held that Clause 4 was not a declaration of the nature and value of the goods with the *Hague Rules* Article 4 Rule 5 and was void as an attempt to fix a maximum amount of liability other than that permitted by the rule. Therefore, the shipowner was liable for the actual value of the goods by way of damage.[355]

185. In *El Greco(Australia) Pty Ltd v. Mediterranean Shipping Co SA* (2004) 200 ALR 449, the parties entered into agreement for the carriage of posters and prints by sea from Australia to Greece. These were placed in 2000 packages in a single container although described as 200,945 pieces in the bill of lading. The prints and posters were damaged by seawater during the voyage. The primary judge held that the carrier was liable for the damage. The liability was limited to a certain amount per package or unit under Article 4 Rule 5(a) of the amended Hague Rules/ Art 4 Rule 5(c) deemed the number of packages or units to be the number set out in the bill of lading as packed in the shipping container. Without such an enumeration the container itself became the only package or unit. The liability of the respondent carrier was calculated by the primary judge on the description of 200,945 pieces as an enumeration for the purposes of Article 4 Rule 5(c).

---

351. On the operation of the unamended Hague Rules in this regard, *see Frank Hammond Pty Ltd v. Huddart Parker Ltd* [1956] VLR 496, J. Garvan-Duffy at 501–502.
352. Hague-Visby Rules, Art. 4 r. 5(a). The Special Drawing Right (SDR) in the International Monetary Fund is calculated daily and its value obtained from the Reserve Bank under Art. 4 r. 5(d). The relevant day for conversion of the limitation amount in the Australian dollar is at the discretion of the court hearing the issue.
353. Considering *Riverstone Meat Co Pty Ltd v. Lancashire Shipping Co Ltd The Muncaster Castle* (1961) AC 807; *Shipping Corp of India Ltd v. Gamlen Chemical Co (A/ Asia) Pty Ltd* (1980) CLR 142.
354. Hague-Visby Rules, Art. 4 r. 5(c).
355. Affirmed *William Holyman & Sons Pty Ltd v. Foy & Gibson Pty Ltd* [1946] VLR 26.

186. The Federal Court, in dismissing the carrier's appeal, held that an enumeration for the purposes of Article 4 Rule 5(c) consists of a setting out of the numbers on the face of a sea-carriage document. It need not be contractually agreed to constitute an enumeration for the purposes of Article 4 Rule 5(c).

187. Article 4 Rule 5 provides that the limitation will not apply where the damage is a result of an intentional or reckless act or omission by the carrier.[356] It appears that Article 4 Rule 5 requires a high standard of proof and that 'reckless' involves either a high degree of subjective realization that damage will probably occur or a deliberate avoiding of obtaining information which would have led to the same realization.[357]

188. A carrier can increase (but not decrease) its liability by agreeing to a higher maximum with a shipper.[358] A shipowner and its insurers may agree that liability will be accepted for a higher amount. The new Article 4*bis* applies the limits of liability under Article 4 Rule 5 to actions brought against a carrier whether based on contract or tort.[359] Where an action is brought against a servant or agent of a carrier (not being an independent contractor), the servant or agent is entitled to the limits of liability under the Hague-Visby Rules unless the damage resulted from the intentional or reckless misconduct of the servant or agent.[360] The total recoverable from the carrier, in aggregate, and its servants or agents is not to exceed the limits under the Hague-Visby Rules.[361]

VIII. Third Party Liability on a Bill of Lading

189. A 'Himalaya' clause may extend the benefit of an exemption from liability to a carrier's independent contractors.[362] The drafting of what is commonly known

356. Hague-Visby Rules, Art. 4 r. 5(e). *See Commonwealth v. Shenzhen Energy Transport Co Ltd* [2015] FCA 757.
357. *See* A. Diamond, *The Hague-Visby Rules*, 2 LIMCLQ 225, 246 (1978).
358. Hague-Visby Rules, Art. 4 r. 5(g).
359. Hague-Visby Rules, Art. 4 *bis* r. 1. *Bis*: renumbered for convenience to avoid renumbering of succeeding articles.
360. Hague-Visby Rules, Art. 4*bis* rr. 2, 4.
361. Hague-Visby Rules, Art. 4*bis* r. 3.
362. *See* N.E. Palmer, '*The Stevedore's Dilemma: Exemption Clauses and Third Parties*', JBL 101, 220 (1974); A.J. Duggan, *Offloading the Eurymedon*, 753 MULR 9 (1974). *See* generally on the issue of third party liability on bills of lading J. Livermore, *Exemption Clauses and Implied Obligations in Contract* 183–207 (LBC 1986). For the issue of privity of contract in the English Court of Appeal and House of Lords decisions *see The Pioneer Container* [1994] AC 324 and *The Mahkutai* [1996] AC 630; [1996] 2 Lloyd's Rep 1. For a comment on *The Mahkutai see* C. Macmillan, '*Elder, Dempster Sails On: Privity of Contract and Bailment on Terms*' LMCLQ 1 (1998). In *WMC Engineering Services Pty Ltd v. Brambles Holdings Ltd* (1997) Unreported (Western Australia Supreme Court) the court did not find it necessary to decide whether the principles stated in *The Pioneer Container* should be followed in Australia but *obiter* expressed the view that if that were the case it should be narrowly interpreted. *See* M. Davies, *Australian Maritime Law Decisions*, LIMCLQ 394, 397–399 (1998). *See* N.E. Palmer, *Subailment on Terms*, LMCLQ 177 (1988); A.P. Bell, *Sub-bailment on*

as a 'Himalaya'[363] clause had the intended effect of granting the benefit of an exemption clause on all servants or agents (including independent contractors) of a carrier and asserting that the carrier was contracting as agent or trustee for such servants or agents, who were, accordingly, to be considered as contracting parties. In *Scruttons Ltd v. Midland Silicones Ltd* [1962] AC 446 [[1962] 2 WLR 186; [1962] 1 All ER 1], the HL held that stevedores were not parties to a bill of lading which limited the liability of the carriers for damage to goods. The agency argument put forward on the stevedores' behalf in that case was regarded by Lord Reid as having validity in specific circumstances only:

> I can see a possibility of success of the agency argument if (first) the bill of lading makes it clear that the stevedore is intended to be protected by the provisions in it which limit liability, (secondly) the bill of lading makes it clear that the carrier, in addition to contracting for these provisions on [its] own behalf, is also contracting as agent for the stevedore, (thirdly) the carrier has authority from the stevedore to do that, or perhaps later ratification by the stevedore would suffice, and (fourthly) that any difficulties about consideration moving from the stevedore were overcome.[364]

190. These tests laid down by Lord Reid were applied by the PC in *New Zealand Shipping Co Ltd v. AM Satterthwaite & Co Ltd (The Eurymedon)* [1975] AC 154 [[1974] 2 WLR 865; [1974] 1 All ER 1015; [1974] 1 Lloyd's Rep 534] where it was held:

(1) The bill of lading entered into between the shipper and the carrier exempted the carrier, its servants, and independent contractors from liability in respect of the performance of the contract; the exemption was designed to cover the whole carriage by whoever performed it.
(2) The contract was between the shipper and the stevedore, made through the carrier as agent, and by unloading the vessel for the shipper, the stevedore provided the consideration necessary for the benefit of the exemptions in his favour in the contract.[365]

Terms: a New Landmark, LMCLQ 177 (1995). The *Pioneer Container* has had favourable treatment recently in Australian case law and academic discussion: *see* K. Lewins, '*Sub-bailment on Terms and the Australian Consumer*', 9 Murdoch Electronic L. J. (2002) at http://www.murdoch.edu.au/elaw/v93/lewins93.html.

363. *See Adler v. Dickson* [1955] 1 QB 158 [[1954] 3 WLR 696; [1954] 3 All ER 397; [1954] 2 Lloyd's Rep 267] (CA).

364. *Scruttons Ltd v. Midland Silicones Ltd* [1962] AC 446 [[1962] 2 WLR 186; [1962] 1 All ER 1], Lord Reid at 474.

365. *New Zealand Shipping Co Ltd v. AM Satterthwaite & Co Ltd (The Eurymedon)* [1975] AC 154 [[1974] 2 WLR 865; [1974] 1 All ER 1015; [1974] 1 Lloyd's Rep 534] (PC), Lords Wilberforce, Hodson, Simon & Salmon at 166. For a discussion of the Commonwealth decisions subsequent to *The Eurymedon* decision *see* P. Clarke, *The Reception of the Eurymedon Decision in Australia, Canada and New Zealand*, 29(132) ICLQ (1980); P.J. Davies & N.E. Palmer, *The Eurymedon Five Years On*, JBL 337 (1979). *The Eurymedon* was apparently ignored by J. Nettlefold in *Philip Morris (Aust) Ltd v. Transport Commission* [1975] Tas SR 128.

191. In *Port Jackson Stevedoring Pty Ltd v. Salmond & Spraggon (Australia) Pty Ltd (The New York Star)* (1980) 144 CLR 300 [54 ALJR 552; 30 ALR 588], the PC, reversing a majority decision of the High Court[366] unanimously reaffirmed the correctness of the decision in *The Eurymedon*. The Committee felt that any stevedores employed by the carrier would normally come within the phrase 'servant or agent of the carrier' used in the bill of lading. The Committee regarded it as unreal to suggest that the carrier's obligations ended at the ship's rail since the bill of lading further provided that as soon as the goods left the ship's tackle the carrier's liability was that of an ordinary bailee. The bill of lading accordingly envisaged a continuing responsibility for the goods and the carrier's operating in accordance with those terms and the Committee recognized the usual commercial practice by which the stevedores take delivery of the goods, sorting them and storing them until the consignee arrives to take them. If the carrier acted as stevedore itself, its liability would be determined by the terms of the bill of lading.[367]

192. In *Nissho Iwai Australia Ltd v. Malaysian International Shipping Corporation, Berhad* (1989) 167 CLR 219 [63 ALJR 468; 86 ALR 375 the High Court held that a carrier of a container holding cartons of frozen prawns (which was stolen from Glebe Island terminal after the container was stacked by stevedores) was, on construction of the relevant terms of the bill of lading, not guilty of any negligence and was exempted from liability even though one of its employees or subcontractors could have avoided the loss. The fact that the main object had been defeated provided no ground for concluding that non-delivery of the goods was outside the protection of the exemption clause.[368] The decision of the PC in *The New York Star* has been favourably adopted in three cases in NSW[369] and indeed these have arguably extended it. It would appear that these three cases significantly extend Lord Reid's four conditions in *The Eurymedon* for third-party protection under a

366. *Port Jackson Stevedoring Pty Ltd v. Salmond & Spraggon (Australia) Pty Ltd* (1978) 139 CLR 231 [52 ALJR 337; 18 ALR 333; [1979] 1 Lloyd's Rep 298], C.J. Barwick dissenting at 243. For comment on *Port Jackson Stevedoring Pty Ltd v. Salmond & Spraggon (Australia) Pty Ltd (The New York Star)* (1980) 144 CLR 300 [54 ALJR 552; 30 ALR 588] (PC) *see* N.E. Palmer & P. Davies, *The Eurymedon; Aground or Afloat?,* Mod LR 41, 74 (1978)*; R. Reynolds, Again the Negligent Stevedore,* 183 LQR 95 (1979); C. Ying, *The Himalayan Clause Revisited,* 22 Mal LR 212 (1980); M. Tedeschi, *Consideration, Privity and Exemption Clauses: Port Jackson Stevedoring Pty Ltd v. Salmond and Spraggon (Australia) Pty Ltd,* 55 ALJ 876 (1981).

367. Essentially approving C.J. Barwick's, *Analysis Regarding Consideration: Port Jackson Stevedoring Pty Ltd v. Salmond & Spraggon (Australia) Pty Ltd* (1978), 139 CLR 231 [52 ALJR 337; 18 ALR 333; [1979] 1 Lloyd's Rep 298], C.J. Barwick at 245–247.

368. *Nissho Iwai Australia Ltd v. Malaysian International Shipping Corporation, Berhad* (1989) 167 CLR 219 [63] ALJR 468; 86 ALR 375; [1989] Aust Torts Reports 68,711 (*see* paras 309–312)], the Court at 229–230.

369. *BHP Ltd v. Hapag-Lloyd AG* [1980] 2 NSWLR 572; *Sidney Cooke Ltd v. Hapag-Lloyd AG* [1980] 2 NSWLR 587 [48 FLR 405]; *Celthene Pty Ltd v. WKJ Hauliers Pty Ltd* [1981] 1 NSWLR 606. *See also Life Savers (Australasia) Ltd v. Frigmobile Pty Ltd* [1983] 1 NSWLR 431 (CA), approving *Mercedes Benz Pty Ltd v. Scan Carriers AS (The Celthene)* (unrep, 25/11/1981, SC NSW J. Rogers, 10138 of 1980); *Continental Seagram Pty Ltd v. ABC Container Line NV Pty Ltd* (unrep, 2/2/1989, SC NSW J. Rogers, 13760 of 1984). *See also* S.W. Hetherington, *Liability and Entitlement to Indemnity, (The Antwerpen),* LMCLQ 16 (1994) (on *Glebe Island Terminals Pty Ltd v. Continental Seagram Pty Ltd (The Antwerpen)* [1994] 1 Lloyd's Rep 213 (CA NSW).

contract of carriage to subcontractors undertaking the land transportation leg in a contract involving sea-carriage. It also appears possible for the carrier and agents to obtain a promise by means of a suitably worded clause that the cargo owner will not make a claim against the subcontractor or subcontractors.[370] The 'Himalaya' clause need not refer solely to subcontractors, but to any persons performing services covered in the definition of 'carriage'. Such a clause has been described as 'the ultimate Himalaya clause'.[371] Although none of the NSW decisions cited, nor that of the Privy Council in *The New York Star*, are binding on the High Court, it has been argued that they should be followed by the court.[372]

§8. Reform of Bills of Lading Legislation

193. The *Carriage of Goods by Sea Amendment Act* 1997 (Cth) repealed provision in the *Sea Carriage of Goods Act* 1991 (Cth) to bring in the Hamburg Rules.[373] This means that the Hamburg Rules will not automatically come into force in Australia on a given date provided by the *Carriage of Goods by Sea Act* 1991 (Cth). However, the Rules will commence only if the Minister decides that the amended Hague Rules should be replaced by the Hamburg Rules.[374] As a result, the Hamburg Rules are kept under review by the Federal Government for another ten years and Hague Rules as amended will continue to apply to Australia's maritime liability regime.

194. The *Carriage of Goods by Sea Amendment Act* 1997 (Cth) provides for regulations to modify Schedule 1 (the amended Hague Rules) in order to update the amended Hague Rules for the following purposes:

370. *See* Cl. 4(2) of the bill of lading in *BHP Ltd v. Hapag-Lloyd AG* [1980] 2 NSWLR 572.
371. S.W. Cavanagh, *The Ultimate Exclusion Clause*, ALJ 59, 67 (1985).
372. *See* J. Livermore, *Exemption Clauses and Implied Obligations in Contract* 205–207 (LBC 1986). For discussion of the issues arising from *New Zealand Shipping Co Ltd v. AM Satterthwaite & Co Ltd (The Eurymedon)* [1975] AC 154 [[1974] 2 WLR 865; [1974] 1 All ER 1015; [1974] 1 Lloyd's Rep 534] (PC) and *Port Jackson Stevedoring Pty Ltd v. Salmond & Spraggon (Australia) Pty Ltd (The New York Star)* (1980) 144 CLR 300 [54 ALJR 552; 30 ALR 588] (PC) and related cases *see* J.O. Malcolm, *The Negligent Pilot and the Himalaya Clause: A Saga of Disagreement*, ALJ 67, 14 (1993). *See* now *Contracts (Rights of Third Parties) Act* 1999 (UK) which although not providing for third parties to become subject to obligations under a contract does not prevent a clause in a contract subject to the *Carriage of Goods by Sea Act* 1992 (UK) from giving a third party the right to rely on exclusion and limitation clauses in the contract; *see* S. Baughen, *Shipping Law* 37 (4th ed., Cavendish 2009). *See* on the Rotterdam Rules intended to replace the Hague, Hague-Visby and Hamburg Rules S. Baughen, *Shipping Law* 150–178 and T. Nikaki, *The Statutory Himalaya-Type Protection Under the Rotterdam Rules: Capable of Filling the Gaps?*, JBL 4, 403 (2009); M. Sturley, T. Fujita & J. van der Ziel, *The Rotterdam Rules; The UN Convention on Contracts for the International Carriage of Goods Wholly or Partly by Sea*, 27(1) ANZ Mar LJ 42–45 (2013).
373. *Carriage of Goods by Sea Amendment Act* 1997 (Cth) Sch. 1 repealing ss 2(2), (3), (4), (5) and (6) of the *Carriage of Goods by Sea Act* 1991 (Cth).
374. *Carriage of Goods by Sea Amendment Act* 1997 (Cth) Sch. 1 inserting s. 2A in the *Carriage of Goods by Sea Act* 1991 (Cth).

(a) to provide for the coverage of a wider range of sea carriage documents (including documents in electronic form);
(b) to provide for the coverage of contract for the carriage of goods by sea from places in countries outside Australia to places in Australia in situations where the contracts do not incorporate, or do not otherwise have effect subject to, a relevant international convention;
(c) to provide for increased coverage of deck cargo;
(d) to extend the period during which carriage may incur liability;
(e) to provide for carriers to be liable for loss due to delay in circumstances identified as being inexcusable.[375]

195. The *Carriage of Goods by Sea Amendment Act* 1997 (Cth) improves the Australian marine cargo regime in respect of coverage of a wider range of sea-carriage documents, of importers, deck cargo, and liability for loss due to delay.[376] The amended Act covers all relevant shipping documents, both negotiable and non-negotiable and provides for the coverage of a wider range of contracts of carriage, including the various types of non-negotiable documents (sea waybills, ship's delivery orders) as well as bills of lading. The amended Act applies where the contract of carriage does not incorporate any international convention. As a result, importers' contracts of carriage are covered by the international convention in force in the Act. The Act was specifically amended by the introduction of a provision applying the Hague-Visby Rules to a contract of carriage by sea from any place outside Australia to any place in Australia which does not incorporate in its terms a standard of carrier liability at least equivalent to the Hague Rules.

196. Deck cargo is covered by the liability regime under the amended Act provided that, no later than at the time of booking, the specific stowage requirements of the shipper have been notified to and agreed by the carrier. Under the Hague-Visby rules deck cargo is specifically excluded from the definition of goods.[377] The amended Act recognizes that excluding deck cargo from the liability regime is inappropriate in modern shipping, especially in the context of containerization.

197. The amended Act extends carrier liability to the period during which the cargo is in the carrier's care within the limits of the wharf or terminal at the ports of loading and discharge under the original terms of the Hague-Visby Rules, the period of the carrier's responsibility was restricted to 'tackle to tackle', from the time when the goods were loaded on, to the time when they were discharged from the ship.[378] The modified Rules now provide for the period of the carrier's responsibility to cover the period during which the carrier is in charge of the goods at the

375. *Carriage of Goods by Sea Amendment Act* 1997 (Cth) s. 7 repealing *Carriage of Goods by Sea Act 1991* (Cth) s. 7. The modifications of the Hague-Visby Rules are contained in the *Carriage of Goods by Sea Act* 1991 (Cth) Sch. 1A, Schedule of Modifications (amendment by the *Carriage of Goods by Sea Regulations* 1998 (Cth)).
376. *Carriage of Goods by Sea Regulations* 1998 (Cth); *Carriage of Goods by Sea Regulations* (No. 2) (SR 1998 No and SR 1998 No. 324); in force from 1 Jul. 1998.
377. *See* the Hague-Visby Rules, Art. 1(c).
378. *See* the Hague-Visby Rules, Art. 1(e).

port of loading, during the carriage and at the port of discharge, 'port-to-port'. The carrier is deemed to be in charge of the goods from the time it takes over the goods from the shipper until it delivers the goods by handing them over to the consignee.

198. The amended Act extends carrier's liability to cover loss due to delay. Under the unamended Hague-Visby Rules, shippers can sue for loss due to unreasonable deviation. The amended Rules specifically provide that the carrier is liable for loss resulting from delay in delivery (as well as from loss of or damage to the goods) if the occurrence which caused the delay took place while the goods were in the carrier's charge unless the carrier proves that it took all measures that could be reasonably required to avoid that occurrence and its consequences.[379] The delay will be excusable where:

(a) deviation was authorized by the shipper;
(b) circumstances beyond the control of the carrier or its servants or agents;
(c) reasonable necessity for compliance with an express or implied warranty;
(d) reasonable necessity to save the ship or its cargo;
(e) saving human life or aiding a ship in distress;
(f) reasonable necessity for obtaining medical or surgical aid for a person on board;
(g) barratous conduct[380] of master or crew; and
(h) industrial action if it was not substantially caused or contributed to by the carrier's unreasonable conduct.

199. The *Sea-Carriage Documents Bill* 1996 (Cth) was introduced by the Federal Government to serve as a model for States and Territories to reform their bills of lading legislation. As a result, all States have enacted uniform bills of lading legislation[381] (the Acts). The Acts introduce the term 'sea-carriage document' to cover bills of lading, sea waybills, and ship delivery orders. 'Lawful holder' is defined as a person coming into possession of the bill of lading in good faith as the consignee of the goods or as a result of any endorsement or other transfer of the bill.[382] The Acts take a similar approach as the *Carriage of Goods by Sea Act* 1991 (UK) by linking the contract of carriage to the lawful holder of the bill of lading

379. The carriers bear the liability for loss due to delay as the Hamburg Rules limit of 2.5 times the freight payable on the goods delayed, except where the delay is an 'excusable delay'; *see Marine Insurance Act* 1909 (Cth) s. 55.

380. 'Barratous conduct' is any wrongful act wilfully committed by the master and crew to the prejudice of the owner – for example, scuttling of a vessel; *see Piermay Shipping Co SA and Brandt's Ltd v. Chester* [1979] 1 Lloyd's Rep 1.

381. *Sea-Carriage Documents Act* 1996 (Qld); *Sea-Carriage Documents Act* 1997 (NSW); (Tas) (WA); *Sea-Carriage Documents Act* 1998 (Vic); 1998 (SA). *See* M. Davies, *Australian Maritime Law Decisions*, LIMCLQ 394, 397 (1998) where the point is made that even when bills of lading legislation is uniform (as it now is) conflictive questions regarding which Act applies will arise in every case concerning title to sue. For a review of varying international approaches to reform of bills of lading law *see* A.N. Yiannapoulos (ed.), *Ocean Bills of Lading: Traditional Forms, Substitutes and EDI Systems* (Kluwer Law International 1995) and see J. Livermore, at 57 ff.

382. *See Sea-Carriage Documents Act* 1997 (NSW) s. 5.

and so reducing the uncertainty as to the rights and liabilities under contracts of carriage. All rights under the contract of carriage are given and transferred to the lawful holder of a sea-carriage document.[383] As a result, when a person passes over the bill of lading, the rights are transferred to and vested in the recipient even if the passing of the bill of lading occurs later than the transfer of the property in the goods.

200. The Acts provide that the transfer of the bill of lading extinguishes any entitlement to rights which derive from a person having been an original party to the contract. The Acts use the term 'data message' and define its meaning according to the UNCITRAL Model Law on Electronic Commerce. This Model Law is further followed by the Acts providing necessary provisions on 'electronic and computerized sea-carriage documents' so that they apply to sea-carriage documents in the form of a data message in the same way that they apply to written sea documents.[384]

§9. Cargo Owner's Rights in Tort to Sue a Carrier

201. In Australia, the question of recovery by buyers whose goods suffer loss or damage due to a carrier's negligence where the goods are still at the buyer's risk, is still open. A buyer whose goods suffer loss or damage due to negligence of a carrier where the goods are at the buyer's risk before any property has passed, and any rights over the contract of carriage transferred, provides a continuing problem for the courts. These cases have involved cargo owners suing shipowners in tort where, generally, the former have purchased the goods under cif or c & f contracts,[385] and at the time of damage to the goods have not had any title to them, either because they have not been holders of the bill of lading, or because there existed a title reservation clause.

---

383. *Sea-Carriage Documents Act* 1997 (NSW) s. 8.

384. *Sea-Carriage Documents Act* 1997 (NSW) ss 6 and 7. On electronically transmitted sea-carriage documents *see* G. Chandler III, *The Electronic Transmission of Bills of Lading*, J. Mar L. & Com 571 (1989); D. Faber, *Electronic Bills of Lading*, 232 LMCLQ 2 (1996); K.M. Kindred, *Trading Internationally by Electronic Bills of Lading*, 7 Banking & Finance L. Rev. 265 (1992); J. Livermore & K. Eurjai, *Electronic Bills of Lading: A Progress Report*, J. Mar L. & Com 55 (1997); J. Livermore & K. Eurjai, *Electronic Bills of Lading and Functional Equivalence*, J. Information L. & Technology 2 (1998), http://elj.warwick.ac.uk/jilt/ecomm/ 98_2liv/fdefault.htm. M. Clarke, *Transport Documents: Their Transferability as Documents of Title: Electronic Documents*, LMCLQ 359 (2002). *See* [2012] LMCLQ 184 casenote on '*CWS Tankship v. Kwangju Bank* 'Digital signature and the statutory signature requirement'. N Gaskell, *Bills of Lading in an Electronic Age* LMCLQ 233. *See Mediterranean Shipping Company SA v. Glencore International AG* [2017] EWCA Civ 365 where the UK Court of Appeal held that an electronic release note was not a document or a delivery order under the *Carriage of Goods by Sea Act* 1992 (UK) s 1(4). *See* discussion of the legal status of electronic pin codes at [55][60] Lewison, Henderson LJJ and Sir Christopher Clarke.

385. Cif contract: 'a contract for the sale of goods under which the price quoted by the seller includes *cost, insurance and freight* to the destination nominated' (original emphasis): *The CCH Macquarie Dictionary of Law (Sydney CCH (rev ed.1996)*, 73.C & F contract, *Term in Sales Contract Means that the Price so Includes Cost and Freight to the Named Destination*, in *Black's Law Dictionary* (6th ed., West 1990).

202. The HL in *Leigh & Sillavan Ltd v. Aliakmon Shipping Co Ltd (The Aliakmon)* [1986] AC 785 [[1986] 2 WLR 902; [1986] 2 All ER 145; [1986] 2 Lloyd's Rep 1],[386] and the PC in *Candlewood Navigation Corporation Ltd v. Mitsui OSK Lines Ltd (The Mineral Transporter)* [1986] AC 1 [[1985] 3 WLR 381; [1985] 2 All ER 935],[387] both denied recovery to c & f buyers and time charterers respectively since it was held that they had no proprietary interest in the property in question when it was damaged by the negligent defendants. These two decisions reaffirm the rule in *Cattle v. Stockton Waterworks Co* (1875) LR 10 QB 453 that only those with a proprietary interest in the damaged ship or cargo can recover economic losses in negligence. The principle laid down in *The Aliakmon* leaves without protection parties who accept risk in the goods without legal ownership or possession which amounts to bailment or custody. At risk are buyers who accept a delivery order in lieu of a bill of lading, a common practice in respect of unascertained goods, where damage occurs before the delivery order is passed on to them.[388] However, in Australia the question of recovery by such plaintiffs is still open.[389] Notwithstanding the decision of the PC in *The Mineral Transporter*, purely economic loss is recoverable in Australian courts.[390]

§10. International Liner and Cargo Shipping Legislation

203. Part X of the *Competition and Consumer Act* 2010 (Cth) restricts the use of anticompetitive agreements between ocean carriers.[391] The principal objects of

386. Overruling *Schiffahart & Kohlen GmbH v. Chelsea Maritime Ltd* (The Irene's Success) [1982] QB 481 [[1982] 2 WLR 422; [1982] 1 All ER 218; [1981] 2 Lloyd's Rep 635]. *See Margarine Union v. Cambray Prince Steamship Co Ltd* (The Wear Breeze) [1969] 1 QB 219; J. Powles, *Title to Sue, Problems of Consignees and Others*, JBL 313 (1987); A.M. Tettenborn, *The Carrier and the Non-owning Consignee – An Inconsequential Immunity*, JBL 12 (1987).
387. *See also The Aramis* [1987] 2 Lloyd's Rep 58 where consignees were held by the Commercial Court of Queen's Bench to have an implied contract entitling them to sue the carriers.
388. *See* J. Powles, *Title to Sue, Problems of Consignees and Others*, JBL 313, 317 (1987).
389. Note in *J Gadsden Pty Ltd v. Australian Coastal Shipping Commission* [1977] 1 NSWLR 575 [31 FLR 157] consignees suing on bailment and in negligence were successful, the Court of Appeal of NSW affirming that the defendants, not being parties to the bill of lading, were not entitled to the one-year time bar for actions for loss or damage to goods under the Hague-Visby Rules, Art. 3 r. 6 (reproduced in Sch. 1 of the *Carriage of Goods by Sea Act* 1991 (Cth)).
390. *See Caltex Oil (Australia) Pty Ltd v. The Dredge Willemstad* (1976) 136 CLR 529 [51 ALJR 270; 11 ALR 227]; *San Sebastian Pty Ltd v. Minister Administering Environmental Planning & Assessment Act* 1979 (NSW) (1986) 162 CLR 340 [61 ALJR 41; 60 LGRA 405; 68 ALR 161; 3 BCL 24]. *See* M. Davies & G. Lawson, *Limiting Shipowner's Liability for Economic Loss*, 271 ABLR 16 (1988); M. Davies, *The Elusive Carrier: Whom Do I Sue and How?*, 230 ABLR 19 (1991).
391. *Competition and Consumer Act* 2010 (Cth).Pt X (formerly entitled the *Trade Practices Act* 1974 (Cth) was introduced by the *Trade Practices (International Liner Cargo Shipping) Amendment Act* 1989(Cth): *see* W. Pengilley, *A Summary of the Provisions of the Trade Practices (International Liner Cargo Shipping) Amendment Bill 1989*, 6 MLAANZJ. 25 (1989). On 5 Oct. 2005 a Productivity Commission report was released that recommended the repeal of Part X (replacing the current industry specific exemption scheme with an obligation for shipping conferences to seek authorization from the Australian Competition and Consumer Commission under Part VII, in view of the declining importance of shipping conferences) although no substantive legislative amendments have since followed: *see* Productivity Commission, Review of Part X of the Trade Practices

Part X include ensuring that Australian exporters have access to reliable international sea carriage on competitive and stable terms.[392] Section 10.01(2) outlines a range of measures to achieve these objects, mostly by permitting shipping conference agreements (if meeting defined standards[393]) and attempting to prevent abuses of conference power.

204. A shipping conference (broadly defined as an unincorporated body of two or more ocean carriers, carrying on separate businesses of scheduled international carriage[394]) may register a 'conference agreement'[395] to receive limited exemption from some of the Act's competition provisions.[396] However, the exemption only applies to the 'blue water' (sea transport) component of the service and to activities which take place outside Australia.[397] Parties to a registered conference agreement (and designated ocean carriers exercising substantial market power[398]) are also required to negotiate freight rates and service agreements with representative shipper bodies. These representative bodies[399] are associations that have been specifically nominated by the Minister for Infrastructure, Transport, and Regional Development.[400]

Additionally, all ocean carriers are required to nominate an Australian agent, who must be registered under the Act.[401] All registered conference arrangements are open to public inspection, together with details of ocean carrier agents, designated shipper bodies, and designated ocean carriers exercising substantial market power.[402]

Act 1974: International Liner Cargo Shipping (Productivity Commission 2005) pp. xlvi,li-liv at http://www.pc.gov.au/projects/inquiry/partx/docs/final report.

392. *See Competition and Consumer Act* 2010 (Cth) s. 10.01.10.
393. *See Competition and Consumer Act* 2010 (Cth) ss 10.06–10.08.
394. *Competition and Consumer Act* 2010 (Cth) s. 10.02.
395. *Competition and Consumer Act* 2010 (Cth) s. 10.2.
396. *See Competition and Consumer Act* 2010 s. 10.15, s. 10.17.
397. *Competition and Consumer Act* 2010 (Cth) s. 10.14.
398. *Competition and Consumer Act* 2010 (Cth) ss 10.50–10.53.
399. *Competition and Consumer Act* 2010 (Cth) ss 10.41, 10.52.
400. *Competition and Consumer Act* 2010 (Cth) ss 10.02, 10.03, 10.41.
401. *Competition and Consumer Act* 2010 (Cth) ss 10.69–10.72.
402. *Competition and Consumer Act* 2010 (Cth) ss 10.10–10.13. For further information *see* the Registrar of Liner Shippings at http://www.infrastructure.gov.au/maritime/ports/liner/index.aspx.

Chapter 2. Shipping Law

§1. Introduction

205. Shipping law concerns the statutory and common law regarding the operation of maritime vessels. The body of law is given here in outline only and reference should be made to more detailed specialist sources.[403] This chapter also includes a brief summary of admiralty jurisdiction in Australia under which a claimant may be entitled to bring an action against a ship.[404]

206. The Constitution does not give the Federal Parliament an express concurrent power over navigation and shipping. The Commonwealth's power is dependent on section 98 of the Constitution. Section 11(i) gives the Commonwealth power to regulate international and interstate shipping. It is generally accepted that section 98 gives power to the Federal Parliament to legislate directly with respect to shipping and navigation, if this is sufficiently linked to the trade and commerce power.[405] It should be noted that although the *Navigation Act* 1912 (Cth) was based on the power of the Commonwealth to make laws in respect of navigation and shipping (section 51(i) and section 98) there have been problems with demarcation between State and Commonwealth regulation of the coasting trade.[406] In 1976, the Commission of Inquiry into the Maritime Industry noted that the Commonwealth Government had proposed to pass legislation seeking enactment by the United Kingdom Government to remove restrictions placed on the powers of State Parliaments to legislate on shipping matters. The issue was resolved by the operation of the *Australia Act* 1986 (Cth) section 4 which repealed sections 735 and 736 of the *Merchant Shipping Act* 1894 (Imp) in so far as they formed part of the laws of an Australian State.

207. The current legal position of the Commonwealth is that it can, in contrast to the earlier position, impose tighter controls on coastal and interstate shipping. This can be attributed partly to the constitutional dominance of the Commonwealth being upheld in relation to offshore resources and territorial waters as a result of the High Court decision in *New South Wales v. The Commonwealth* (1975) 135 CLR 337.[407] The States followed this decision with the 'Offshore Constitutional

---

403. *See* M.W.D. White & A.I. Philipides, *Shipping: Laws of Australia 34.3*, in *Transport: Laws of Australia* (J. Livermore ed., LBC 1999). *Laws of Australia* Chs 1–13 (Thomson Lawbook). R.S.T. Chorley, & O.C. Giles. *Shipping Law*, (N.J. Gaskell & Debattista ed., 9th edn, Pearson Higher Education 2013).

404. *See Admiralty Act* 1988 (Cth); *see* J. Crawford, *Admiralty: Laws of Australia* 34.4.

405. *See Australia Steamships Ltd v. Malcolm* (1914) 19 CLR 298 at 335.

406. *See Western Transport v. Knopp* (1964) 38 ALJR 237. *See* now *Navigation Act* 2012 (Cth).

407. All six States brought an action in the HC seeking declarations that the *Seas and Submerged Lands Act* 1973 (Cth) was wholly or partly invalid. The 1973 Act gave effect to two Geneva Conventions of 1958 (the Convention on the Territorial Sea and the Contiguous Zone and the Convention on the Continental Shelf) and included provision that sovereignty in the internal waters of Australia (any waters on the landward side of the territorial sea) vested in the Crown. The States argued that they had, before Federation and afterwards, sovereignty and legislative power over the territorial sea adjacent to their coasts up to a three-mile limit and over the seabed of the territorial sea. The HC rejected the argument and held that the 1973 Act was a valid exercise by the Commonwealth of the

Settlement' which included agreement (given legislative effect) that the States could exercise jurisdiction from low-water mark out to the three-mile limit.[408]

§2. REGISTRATION OF SHIPS

208. Registration of ships in Australia is regulated by the *Shipping Registration Act* 1981 (Cth) and legislation in all States and the NT covers registration and licensing of vessels.[409] Under the Act ships were given Australian nationality as defined.[410] A ship is, for the purposes of the *Shipping Registration Act* 1981 (Cth), any kind of vessel capable of navigating the high seas.[411] The definition of a 'ship' in the Act includes:

(a) barge, lighter, or other floating vessel;
(b) a structure that is able to float or be floated and is able to move from one place to the other; and
(c) an air cushion vehicle or similar craft, used wholly or primarily in navigation by water, but does not include a vessel, structure, vehicle, or craft declared by the regulations not to be a ship for the purposes of this definition.

The *Shipping Registration Act* 1981 (Cth) defines a ship in terms of a vessel 'capable of navigating' the high seas.[412]

---

external affairs power under s. 51(xxix) of the Constitution. The HC also held that the low-water mark constituted the relevant seaward boundary of the States' territory for the exercise of sovereignty and legislative power. *See* M. Davies & A. Dickey, *Shipping Law* 32–35 (LBC 1990). The *Maritime Legislation Amendment Act* 1994 (Cth) amended the *Sea and Submerged Lands Act* 1973 (Cth) inserting reference in the title to the Exclusive Economic Zone; *see* Division 1A, sovereign rights regarding the Exclusive Economic Zone (EEZ). *See* e.g. M. Davies & A. Dickey, *Shipping Law* (3d ed., Law Book Co 2004); D.A. Butler & W.D. Duncan, *Maritime Law in Australia* [1.15.3] (1st ed., Legal Books 1992). *See also* M. White, *Australia's Offshore Legal Jurisdiction Part 1-History and Development*, 25 Austl & NZ Mar LJ 3 (2011).

408. *See Coastal Waters (State Powers) Act* 1980 (Cth); *Coastal Waters (State Title) Act* 1980 (Cth); *Coastal Waters (Northern Territory Powers) Act* 1980 (Cth); *Constitutional Powers (Coastal Waters) Act* 1979 (NSW); 1980 (QLD); 1979 (SA); 1979 (Tas); 1979 (WA).

409. *See Uniform Shipping Laws Code* 1989; *Commercial Vessels Act* 1979 (NSW); *Marine Act* 1981 (NT); *Queensland Marine Act* 1958 (Qld); *Boating Act* 1974 (SA); *See Shipping* 34.3.18 *Laws of Australia* Thomson Lawbook at 34.3.18.

410. *See Shipping Registration Act* 1981 (Cth) s. 3(1); all vessels registered before the 1981 Act under the *Merchant Shipping Act* 1894 (Imp) were deemed to be British ships with British nationality; *see Oteri v. The Queen* (1976) 51 ALJR 122.

411. *See Shipping Registration Act* 1981 (Cth) s. 3(1); other similar but not identical definitions *see* the *Admiralty Act* 1988 (Cth), s. 3(1), *Navigation Act 2012* s. 14(1). The term 'high seas' has been held, in relation to its use in the *Merchant Shipping Act* 1894 (Imp), to be used in its admiralty law context that is, to include '[A]ll oceans, seas, bays, channels, rivers, creeks, and waters below the low-water mark, and where great ships could go, with the exception only of such parts of such oceans, etc. as were within the body of some county'; 'high seas' is used in the same context in the *Shipping Registration Act* 1981 (Cth). *See General Credits (Finance) Pty Ltd v. Registrar of Ships* (1982) 61 FLR 329, J. McPherson at 334.

412. *See Shipping Registration Act* 1981 (Cth) s. 3(1). The *Admiralty Act* 1988 (Cth) s. 3(1) and the *Navigation Act 2012*(Cth) s. 14(1), s. 15 (regulated Australian vessel) s. 22 'taken to sea-goes to

209. The Registration of ships in Australia is governed by the *Shipping Registration Act* 1981(Cth). This Act repealed Part 1 of the *Merchant Shipping Act* 1894 (Imp)[413] which had previously regulated the registration of Australian ships. All ships registered under the Imperial Act were deemed to be British ships and possess British nationality. Section 29(1) of the *Shipping Registration Act* 1981 (Cth) introduced a new registration regime whereby ships were conferred with Australian nationality

210. The *Shipping Registration Amendment (Australian International Shipping Register) Act* 2012 (Cth) amended shipping law by differentiating between registration in the Australian General Shipping Register and the International Shipping Register under the *Shipping Registration Act* 1981 (Cth) section 56(2). The International Shipping Register seeks to facilitate Australian participation in international trade, provides an opportunity in an internationally competitive register to facilitate the long-term growth of the Australian shipping industry and promote the enhancement and viability of the Australian maritime skills base and the Australian shipping industry.

The *Maritime Powers Act 2013* (Cth) provides for administration and enforcement of Australian law in maritime areas. The Act seeks to give greater certainty to maritime officers working in difficult conditions powers to give effect to Australian laws and international agreements and decisions.[414]

The *Coastal Shipping (Revitalising Australian Shipping) Act 2012* (Cth) by 3(1) provides a framework for coastal trading in Australia which promotes a viable shipping industry that contributes to the Australian economy, facilitates the long-term growth of the Australian shipping industry, enhances the efficiency and reliability of Australian shipping, as part of the national transport system, maximizes the use of vessels registered in the Australian General Shipping Register in coastal trading,

---

sea, plies, runs or proceeds on a voyage or has been got underway for the purpose of running or proceeding on a voyage. [A]vessel is not taken to sea merely because the vessel has got underway to move it from one berth to another or place in a port to another berth or place in a port'. *See also* 'seagoing' 'discussed in *Smith v. Peres* [2006] NSWSC 299[159]–[180] where it was decided that "seagoing" meant that the vessel goes to sea or is capable of going to sea. The Court also commented that the definitions of "seagoing" were found in legislation, cases and even dictionary definitions are broad. *See also Salt Union v. Wood* [1893] QB 370,370 per Lord Coleridge that' its capacity to go to sea was not the point, no doubt she could go to sea, but she does not go'. *See* discussion of this issue at J. Allen, *To Limit or Not to Limit: Limitation of Liability in West Australian Waters-A Call for Reform*, 24 A & NZ Mar LJ 93, 97 (2010) both define 'ship' in terms of a vessel 'used in navigation' by water. *See* definition of offshore facility under ss 4 and 5 *Navigation Act* 1912(Cth) as amended by the *Maritime Transport and Offshore Facilities Act* 2005 (Cth).

413. The *Shipping Registration Act 1981* (Cth) adopts many of the provisions of the *Merchant Shipping Act 1894* (Imp). Therefore, decisions concerning the Imperial Act remain important when construing similar provisions in the *Shipping Registration Act* 1981 (Cth); *see General Credits (Finance) Pty Ltd v. Registrar of Ships* (1982) 61 FLR 329 (QSC) J. MacPherson at 334. For the issuing of temporary licences to use foreign vessels on Australian coastal voyages *see* the *Coastal Trading (Revitalizing Australian Shipping) Act* 2012 (Cth).

414. *See Maritime Powers Act* 2013 (Cth) ss 8, 12. For amendments made to other legislation, *see Maritime Powers (Consequential Amendments) Act* 2013 (Cth).For definition of 'maritime officers' *see Maritime Powers Act* 2013 (Cth) s 104(1).

promotes competition in coastal trading, and ensures efficient movement of passengers and cargo between Australian ports. These objects are aimed to be achieved by ensuring that a vessel used to engage in coastal trading under a general licence has unrestricted access to Australian water, one that is time limited to a voyage authorized has similar access and one on an emergency has the requisite licence.[415]

§3. LIMITATION OF LIABILITY

211. Shipowners, charterers, managers, operators, and salvors have historically been entitled to limit their liability to persons suffering loss or damage through the operation, management, or salvage of a ship.[416] Shipowners and other operators are entitled to limit their liability in applications made before 1991 only in the absence of fault or privity on their part. This entitlement is provided by the *International Convention Relating to the Limitation of Liability of Owners of Sea-Going Ships* Brussels 10 October 1957 (1957 Convention) [1981] Australia Treaty Series (ATS) 2 which was enacted in Australia by the *Navigation Amendment Act* 1979 (Cth).[417] The 1957 Convention provisions were replaced by the *Convention on Limitation of Liability for Maritime Claims* London 19 November 1976 (1976 Convention) on 1 June 1991. The 1976 Convention Article 1, as was the case with the 1957 *Convention*, gives the right to limit liability in respect of claims to an owner, charterer, manager, and operator of a sea-going ship, and insurers and salvors, the liability of the owner, including the liability of the vessel. It also extends the right to limitation to any person for whose act, neglect, or default the shipowner or salvor is responsible,

415. *See* ss (2); the three types of licence are listed in Part 4. *See* now *Shipping Legislation Bill* 2015 and *Coastal Shipping Reforms Discussion Paper* Canberra, March 2017. For a licensing decision case under the *Coastal Shipping (Revitalising Australian Shipping) Act* 2012 (Cth) *see CSL Australia Pty Ltd v. Minister for Infrastructure and Transport* [2014] FCA 1160.; *see also Mentink v. Registrar of the Australian Register of Ships (No 2)* (2015) FCR 234. *See* J. Porter (case note) ANZMarLJ (2015) 29(1) 8–7.

416. *See* M. Davies & A. Dickey, *Shipping* Ch. 16 (3d ed., Lawbook Co 2004); *see*, J. Livermore, *Laws of Australia* Ch. 8 (Thomson Lawbook) for detailed coverage of limitation of liability, including its historical origins; *see* J. Livermore, *Limitation of Liability* in *Laws of Australia: Shipping*, Ch. 8, 34.3 (LBC 1999). N. Gaskell, *In Limitation of Liability and Division of Loss in Operation,* in *Marsden & Gault on Collisions at Sea* (S. Gault, S. Hazelwood, A. Tettenborn, E. Cole & T. Macey eds, (14th ed., Sweet & Maxwell 2016).

417. British law under the *Merchant Shipping (Liability of Shipowners and Others) Act* 1958 (UK) s. 2(4) was ruled by the HC not to apply to NSW in *Bistricic v. Rokov* (1976) 135 CLR 552. In *China Ocean Shipping Co v. South Australia* (1979) 145 CLR 172, the HC held that the *Merchant Shipping Act* 1894 (Imp) applied in Australia after federation but the beneficial amendments to it, including an international convention, did not. To remedy the effect of the *Bistricic* and *China Shipping* cases the Commonwealth enacted the *Navigation Amendment Act 1979* (Cth) which repealed Part VIII of the *Navigation Act 1912* (Cth) and replaced it with new provisions limiting the liability of the shipowners by inserting s. 333 that the 1957 Convention provisions had the force of law as part of the law of the Commonwealth. For a discussion of *Bistricic see Amarantos Shipping Co Ltd v. South Australia* [2004] SASC 57, J. Debelle at [19]–[22]; *see* J. Livermore, *Shipping: Laws of Australia*, Ch. 8, paras 106–108. *See International Maritime Conventions Act* 2001 (Cth) adding Sch. 1A to Sch. 1 of the *Limitation of Liability for Maritime Claims Act* 1989 (Cth).

which may include servants and agents and, probably, independent contractors.[418] However, as distinct from the position under the *Navigation Act* 2012 (Cth) there is no equivalent section deeming certain non-seagoing ships to be sea-going ships. The better view is that the Commonwealth has not retreated from this minor legislative area, but reserved its position for later review.[419]

212. Where a claim is made or likely to be made against a person with entitlement to limit their liability, that person may apply to the court to determine the limit of liability. The claims that are subject to limitation set out by the *1976 Convention*, Article 2(1), reflect those of the *1957 Convention* and are as follows:

(a) loss of life or personal injury or loss of or damage to property, occurring on board or in direct connection with the operation of the ship or with salvage operations;
(b) loss resulting from delay in the carriage by sea of cargo, passengers, or their cargo;
(c) loss from infringement of non-contractual rights; for example, fishing rights; and
(d) claims with respect to attempts by third parties to minimize loss caused by the defendant.

213. However, the *Limitation of Liability for Maritime Claims Act* 1989 (Cth), section 6, excludes from operation in Australia the following claims for which provision had been made in the *1976 Convention*:

(a) claims in respect of the raising, removal, destruction, or rendering harmless of the cargo of a ship that is sunk, wrecked, stranded, or abandoned; and
(b) claims in respect of the removal, destruction, or rendering harmless of the cargo of the ship.

214. Claims exempted from limitation are set out in the *1976 Convention*, Article 3, as follows:

(a) salvage or contribution in general average;
(b) oil pollution damage;

---

418. *See* the shipowner's defence that the occurrence was not the result of its fault and privity now replaced by the more stringent provisions under the *1976 Convention* Art. 4 (*see* below); *see Arthur Guinness & Son (Dublin) Ltd v. The Freshfield (Owners) (The Lady Gwendolen) (Limitation)* [1965] 2 All ER 283; *Rederij Erven H Groen v. The England (The England)* [1973] 1 Lloyd's Rep 373; Bowbelle, The [1990] 3 All ER 476; *Grand Champion Tankers Ltd v. Norpipe A/S (The Marion)* [1984] 2 All ER 343 followed in the SC of Queensland in *Barameda Enterprises Pty Ltd v. Connor* [1988] 1 Qd R 359, [1987] 2 Lloyd's Rep 666; *Arthur Guinness* and *The Marion* were followed in the Federal Court in *Alstergren v. Owners of the Ship 'Territory Pearl'* (1992) 112 ALR 133. *See* C.N. Cheka, *Conduct Barring Limitation,* 18 J Mar L & Com 487 (1987) and B. Sheen, *Limitation of Liability: The Law Gave and the Lords have Taken Away,* 18 J Mar L & Com 473 (1987).

419. But *see* now *Navigation Act 2012* (Cth) s. 22 above at 246 n. 4.

(c) nuclear damage;
(d) specifically nuclear damage from a nuclear ship; and
(e) those arising out of contracts of service.[420]

215. The provisions of the *1976 Convention* do not apply to a ship that belongs to the naval, military, or air forces of a foreign country. Claims in respect of damage to harbour works, basins and waterways and aids to navigation have priority over other claims, including personal claims.

216. The shipowner is given the right to limit liability by the *Limitation of Liability for Maritime Claims Act* 1989 (Cth), section 9. The *1976 Convention* does not attach to the cause of action or claim which is the subject of the right to limit, but by reason of the procedural step seeking to limit liability. Shipowners and others are barred by certain reckless or intentional personal conduct from limiting liability. Under Article 4 of the *1976 Convention* certain conduct will bar the right of limitation of liability:

> A person shall not be entitled to limit his liability if it is proved that the loss resulted from his personal act or omission, committed with the intent to cause such loss, or recklessly and with knowledge that such loss would probably result.

The test under Article 4 imposes a heavy burden on those seeking to defeat the limitation provision as it requires a high degree of personal fault in the owner.[421]

In *Bahamas Oil Refining Company International LTD v. The Owners of the Cape Bari Tankschiffahrts GMBH & Co KG ('The Cape Bari')* [2016] UKPC the Privy Council allowed an appeal from the Court of Appeal of the Commonwealth of Bahamas. This decision provided clarification on whether a shipowner can waive its right to limit liability under the *Convention on Limitation of Liability for Maritime Claims 1976* and how a contract purporting to exclude the right to limit should be construed. The convention had set the limit at a much higher level than before its implementation. However, in exchange for the limitation fund claimants had to accept that there were extremely limited opportunities to break the right to limit. The availability of affordable marine insurance was also a public policy consideration in the framing of the Convention.[422]

---

420. *See Navigation Amendment Act* 2011 (Cth) Sch. 1 amending s. 6(1) of the *Navigation Act* 1912 (Cth) regarding the definition of 'agreement' to mean: (a) in relation to the ship-the agreement between the owner of the ship, or a representative of the owner of the ship and the crew of the ship; (b) in relation to a seaman belonging to the ship the agreement between the owner of the ship, or a representative of the owner, and the seaman. *See also* the *Navigation Act* 2012(Cth) s. 93(a),(b) by which an owner of a regulated vessel or foreign vessel (*see* s. 14(1) is not entitled to limit their liability in respect of any claim described in 1(a) Art. 2 of the Limitation of Liability for Maritime Claims Convention.

421. M. Davies & A. Dickey, *Shipping Law* Ch. 16 (3d ed., Lawbook Co 2004).

422. *See* N. Meeson & J.R.K. Kimbell, *Admiralty Jurisdiction and Practice* (4th ed., Informa) and P. Griggs, R. Williams & J. Farr, *Limitation of Liability for Maritime Claims* (4th ed., Informa 2004).

This compromise was recognized by the PC which noted that under the Convention: 'shipowners agreed to a higher limit of liability in exchange for an almost indisputable right to limit their liability, The effect of articles 2 and 4 {in the Convention is that the claims in article 2 are subject to limitation of liability unless the person making the claim proves that the loss resulted from the personal act or omission of the shipowner committed with intent to cause such loss, or recklessly and with knowledge that such a loss would probably result. This imposes upon the claimant a heavy burden'.

It was a misunderstanding of the broader application of this high threshold for establishing 'conduct barring limitation' under Article 3 of the Convention that led the Bahamas Court of Appeal into error. Prior to its decision both case law and leading texts indicated it was possible to exclude limitation of liability by contract.[423]

217. General limits of liability and limits for passenger claims are calculated in accordance with the *1976 Convention* formulas (Article 6)[424] based on tonnage[425] and units of account. Claims in respect of a single occurrence are aggregated and valued in terms of the International Monetary Fund's valuation of a country's (SDRs).[426] The amount recoverable on a particular claim may be further reduced by the application of the Hague Rules under the *Carriage of Goods by Sea Act* 1991 (Cth).[427] The Hague Rules limitation applies to a particular claim, and the right to limit under the *Limitation of Liability for Maritime Claims Act* 1989 (Cth) applies to all claims governed by the *1976 Convention.* Therefore, limitation under the Hague Rules is applied first, the amount recoverable as a result may then be further reduced if the total overall limitation amount is insufficient to meet all claims.

The 1996 Protocol to the 1976 Limitation Convention has substantially increased the limitation figures under the 1976 Convention.[428]

The revised limitation figures are as follows:

FUND A claims arising out of death and personal injury

Tonnage not exceeding 2,000 tons: flat rate of 2 million SDRs. Tonnage in excess of 2,001 tons: 2 million SDRs plus additional amounts on the following sliding scale:

See also 'Back on Course-Excluding the Right to Limit Liability under the 1976 Convention a discussion of the *Cape Bari* case (2016) 30 ANZMarLJ 12 S. Walpole & L. Rees-Murphy. The authors take the view that the *Cape Bari* decision is that which Australian courts have adopted; *see* (2016) 30 ANZMarLJ 12 at 19.

423. The *Cape Bari* [2016] UKPC 20 citing *The Leerort* [2001] 2 Lloyd's Rep 391, 293–294 [9] (Lord Phillips MR) *The Satinita* [1897] AC 59; *Virginia Carolina Chemical Co v. Norfolk American Steam Shipping Co* (1912) 1KB 229 ('Virginia'). *See Codelfa Constructions* (1982) 149 CLR 332 approving *Reardon Smith Line Ltd v. Yngar Hansen Tangen* [1976] 1WLR 989,995–996.

424. *See Limitation of Liability for Maritime Claims Act* 1989 (Cth), Sch. 1. *See* M. Davies & A. Dickey, *Shipping Law* Ch. 16 (3d ed., Lawbook Co 2004).

425. Navigation Act 2012 (Cth) s. 14(1). *Navigation Act 2012* (Cth) s. 14(1) for definition of 'tonnage' under the *1976 Convention,* Art. 6.

426. *See also Limitation of Liability for Maritime Claims Act* 1989 (Cth), Sch. 1.

427. *See also Carriage of Goods by Sea Act* 1991 (Cth), Sch. 1.

428. *See* Sch. 1A *Limitation of Liability for Maritime Claims Act* 1989 (Cth).

2,001–30,000 tons	an extra 800 SDRs per ton
30,001–70,000 tons	an extra 600 SDRs per ton
70,001–and above	an extra 400 SDRs per ton

Fund B-all other claims
Tonnage not exceeding 2,000 tons: flat rate figure of 1 million SDRs:

2,001–30,000 tons	an extra 400 SDRs per ton
30,001–70,000 tons	an extra 300 SDRs per ton
70,001 tons and above	an extra 200 SDRs per ton

Other amendments under the 1996 Protocol are as follows:

(a) The global limits for passenger claims under Article 7 are to be calculated by multiplying 175,000 SDRs by the number of passengers that the ship is authorized to carry. The overall cap of 25 million SDRs in respect of such claims is removed.
(b) Article 3 of the 1976 Limitation Convention is amended as to exclude the right to limit in respect of any claim for 'special compensation' under Article 14 of the 1989 Salvage Convention.
(c) Article 18 of the 1976 Limitation Convention is amended so as to allow a State Party to exclude any claims covered by the 1996 Hazardous and Noxious Substances Convention from the 1998 Protocol.[429]

§4. MARINE POLLUTION

218. There are a range of conventions governing marine pollution and safety; these include:

(a) MARPOL.
(b) Sea Dumping.
(c) Intervention.
(d) Civil Liability.
(e) Fund – The Protocol and The National Plan and.

429. For details and comment on the 1996 Protocol *see* S. Baughen, *Shipping Law* 427–428, Ch. 20 (4th ed., Cavendish 2009), on limitation of liability generally. Australia is not a signatory to the *Athens Convention on the Carriage of Passengers and Their Luggage by Sea, 1974.* For a commentary on the disadvantageous provisions of the *Athens Convention* impacting on passengers subject to the 1974 rates of liability *see* K. Lewins *Australian Cruise Passengers Travel in Legal Equivalent of Steerage-Considering the Merits of a Passenger Liability Regime for Australia*, 38 ABLR 127 (2010); K. Lewins, *Cruise Ship Operators, Australian Consumer Law and Civil Liability Acts,* Pt 2, 30(1) ANZMarLJ n. 93–110 (2016); *See also* K. Lewins *International Carriage of Passengers by Sea* Sweet & Maxwell (2016).

(f) Preparedness and Response.

I. MARPOL

219. The *International Convention for the Prevention of Pollution from Ships* (MARPOL) set up a new regime to deal with marine pollution and now provides a stringent control of pollution by oil and noxious substances. The provisions of MARPOL are enacted in Australia in the *Protection of the Sea (Prevention of Pollution from Ships) Act* 1983 (Cth) and the *Navigation (Protection of the Sea) Amendment Act* 1983 (Cth).[430] There are five annexes to MARPOL. Annex 1 deals with oil and related substances. Oil is defined as 'petroleum in any form'. An International Oil Prevention Certificate is to be issued to any oil tanker of 150 gross tonnage or more and to other ships of 400 gross tonnage or more. The Regulations provide for separation of oily mixtures into clean seawater (for discharge) and oil (to be retained on board in a 'slop tank' and then discharged to shore facilities).[431] Ships in the latter category are required to have a sludge tank to receive oily residues that cannot otherwise be dealt with. Discharge into the sea of oily mixtures are totally prohibited[432] in special areas.

220. Annex II deals with noxious liquid substances[433] and Annex III with harmful packaged substances defined as:[434]

> any substances which if introduced into the sea [are] liable to create hazards to human health, to harm living resources and marine life, to damage amenities or to interfere with legitimate uses of the sea.

Together with Annex I, these Two Annexes are mandatory. Annex IV, which is optional, deals with sewage[435] and provides that ships over 200 tons gross tonnage or carrying more than ten persons are prohibited from discharging sewage into the sea except upon certain conditions.[436] Sewage that has been treated by an approved

430. For the 1978 Protocol to MARPOL *see* ATS 29; *see Protection of the Sea (Prevention of Pollution from Ships)* Act 1983 (Cth) Sch. 10-5. *See* generally *Shipping: Laws of Australia* 34.3, Ch. 10 paras 145–151. *See also Protection of the Sea (Powers of Intervention) Act* 1981 (Cth) Schs 1 and 2; *see International Maritime Conventions Legislation Amendment Act* 2001 (Cth) s. 3(1) amending the *Protection of the Sea (Powers of Intervention) Act* 1981 (Cth) repealing the Protocol in relation to Intervention as affected by the Marine Environment Protection Committee of the International Maritime Organization resolution in Sch. 4 revising the annex (list of substances) to the Protocol.
431. Annex I regs 13–16.
432. These include the Antarctic (areas 60 degrees South) Torres Strait and the Great Barrier Reef, the latter brought into the definition of 'nearest land' for the purposes of discharging (reg 1(2)).
433. Annex II, Appendix II listing chemicals categorized according to their likely pollution effect if released into the sea.
434. *See* Australian Government Australian Maritime Safety Authority 'Fact Sheet' particularly Sensitive Areas http://amsa.gov.au.
435. *See Protection of the Sea (Prevention of Pollution from Ships) Act* 1983 (Cth) Pt IIIB (Division I) covers the Antarctic.
436. Annex IV reg 8.

treatment plant has no restrictions except that its discharge should not produce discolouration or visible solids. Disinfected and comminuted sewage should not be discharged closer than 4 miles from 'nearest land' and sewage which is not dealt with by such a plant mentioned above should not be discharged less than 12 miles away from nearest land and, if a holding tank is used, when the ship is under way.

221. Annex V, also optional, deals with disposal of garbage,[437] the disposal into the sea of plastics, including synthetic ropes. Fishing nets and plastic garbage is prohibited absolutely. Garbage is defined as:

> All kinds of victual, domestic and operational waste excluding fresh fish and parts thereof, generated during the normal operations of the ship and liable to be disposed of continuously or periodically.[438]

However, Annex V does apply to special areas as defined.

222. There are certain exceptions to the provisions listed above. In respect of harmful substances these may not be jettisoned unless necessary for the security of the ship or saving of life at sea. A similar exception is made in respect of discharge of oil or oily wastes, including discharge resulting from damage to a ship after all reasonable precautions were taken to minimize it, or the owner or master of the ship did not act with intent to cause damage or did not act recklessly or the discharge was approved of and done to combat specific pollution incidents.[439]

II. Sea Dumping

223. Under the *International Convention on the Prevention of Marine Pollution by Dumping of Wastes and other Matters 1972*, known as the London Dumping Convention, ships and aircraft subject to the Convention are not permitted to freely dump or incinerate wastes at sea. The London Dumping Convention defines dumping as 'deliberate disposal at sea of wastes or other matter' from vessels, aircraft, platforms, and other man-made structures at sea.[440] The London Dumping Convention is given effect in Australia by the *Environment Protection (Sea Dumping) Act* 1981 (Cth).[441]

437. Disposal is to be as far as practicable from the nearest land, not less than 25 nautical miles for dunnage, lining, and packaging materials which will float and not less than 12 nautical miles for food wastes and all other garbage. Nearest land is defined in the same terms as for provisions regarding sewage in Annex IV so that the Great Barrier Reef is protected.
438. Annex V reg 1(1).
439. Annex 1, reg 11.
440. *London Dumping Convention*, Art. III.
441. *See also Environmental Protection (Sea Dumping) Amendment Act* 1986 (Cth) controlling dumping of radioactive waste material.

III. Intervention

224. The *International Convention relating to Intervention on the High Seas in cases of Marine Pollution 1969*[442] permits States, other than the flag State of the vessel, to the Convention to take action beyond their territorial seas to prevent, mitigate, or eliminate imminent danger to their coastline against escape of oil from a vessel. The Convention was extended to substances other than oil by a 1973 Protocol.[443] The 1969 Convention and the 1973 Protocol were given effect to in Australia by the *Protection of the Sea (Powers of Intervention) Act* 1981 (Cth).[444]

IV. Civil Liability

225. The *International Convention on Civil Liability for Oil Pollution Damage 1969*[445] applies to damage caused by tankers of over 2,000 tonnes spilling persistent oil. This is defined under the Convention, essentially as heavy petroleum products, such as crude oil, fuel oil, heavy diesel oil, and lubricating oil, carried on board as bunkers. The Convention is given force in Australia by the *Protection of the Sea (Civil Liability) Act* 1981 (Cth).

The Convention introduced compulsory insurance by a levy on tanker owners. The owner of a ship carrying more than 2,000 tonnes oil cargo registered with a State that is party to the Convention has to maintain insurance or other financial security enough to cover its maximum liability for pollution damage under the Convention. The present maximum limitation calculated on the tonnage of the ship is approximately USD 25 million. Parties to the Convention can require ships to hold a certificate evidencing insurance liability before they can use their ports. The 1992 Protocol to the Convention, now in force, raises the maximum limit to approximately USD 106 million. Voluntary insurance schemes have been set up by tanker owners (*see* below). Defences under the Convention include damage resulting from war or an act of God, caused wholly by a third party intentionally, or negligence or other wrongful act by government or other authority responsible for maintenance of lights or other navigational aids.

V. Fund: The 1992 Protocol and the National Plan

226. The *International Convention on the Establishment of an International Fund for the Compensation for Oil Pollution Damage 1971*[446] is a supplementary

442. *See* ATS 4.
443. *See* ATS 5.
444. *See* Schs 1 and 2 to the Act; *see* now amended by the *International Maritime Conventions Legislation Amendment Act* 2001 (Cth) repealing by s. 3(1) definition of 1973 Protocol as affected by the Marine Environment Protection Committee of the International Maritime Organization resolution revising annex (list of substances) to the Protocol; *see* Sch. 4.
445. *See* ATS 3.
446. *See Protection of the Sea (Oil Pollution Compensation Fund) Act* 1993 (Cth), Sch. 1.

convention to deal with a situation where there is inadequate compensation to victims of oil pollution under the *Civil Liability Convention.* The *Fund Convention*, as it is generally known, provides further insurance cover by a compulsory levy on the owners of persistent oil carried in tankers. The levy is applied to any oil company receiving more than 150,000 tonnes of contributing oil (i.e., heavy oil) annually. The compensation regime is administered by the International Oil Pollution Compensation Fund (IOPC Fund). Claims under the Fund convention are not accepted for environmental damage, but only for the costs of clean-up and quantifiable economic loss. The *Fund Convention* has been denounced by Australia[447] and superseded by the 1992 Protocol. The 1992 Protocol amending the *Fund Convention* provided a mechanism for compulsory denunciation of the *Fund Convention* when at least eight States became parties to the 1992 Protocol and when the total quantity of contributing oil received by importers of oil reached 750 million tonnes (which occurred in November 1996). The *Protection of the Sea (Oil Pollution Compensation Fund) Act* 1993 (Cth) came into force in May 1998 and repealed the *Fund Convention.*[448] The upper limit of liability of the Fund to a shipowner is about USD 90 million. The 1992 Protocol raised this to about USD 240 million when certain membership requirements are met.

227. The essence of the *Fund Convention* is contained in the *National Plan to Combat Pollution of the Sea by Oil 1973* (the National Plan) which coordinates the resources of the Commonwealth, States, and the oil industry in the event of oil pollution incidents. The National Plan follows the Fund Convention in that the 'polluter pays' principle applies. This is implemented by a levy similar to that applied to commercial ships using Australian ports and related services for the maintenance of lighthouses and other navigational aids. The levy, as did the National Plan, came into force on 1 October 1989. The relevant legislation is contained in the *Protection of the Sea (Shipping Levy) Act* 1981 (Cth), the *Protection of the Sea (Shipping Levy Collection) Act* 1981 (Cth), and the *Protection of the Sea (Shipping Levy) Amendment Act* 1984 (Cth).[449]

---

447. Had Australia failed to denounce the *Fund Convention* by 15 May 1997 the result would have been that Australia would remain a party to the original *OILPOL Convention* with its lower compensation levels and more limited scope of application. Additionally, Australia would belong to a scheme whose ability to meet large claims would be in serious doubt, with major oil importers no longer contributing. The decision to denounce the *Fund Convention* by Australia was based on the low Australian risk compared with the cost of membership and concern that Australia would be cross-subsidizing high risk in the international arena; *see* Department of Trade and Communications, *Status of Conventions – Australian Position* (Canberra, 1 May 1989).

448. From 16 May 1998, members of the 1992 Fund Convention ceased membership and on 24 May 2002 the Fund Convention ceased to be in force; *see* S. Baughen, *Shipping Law* 345–347 (4th ed., Cavendish 2009). For the replacement regime for the *Fund Convention, see Protection of the Sea (Oil Pollution Compensation Fund) Act* 1993 (Cth); *Protection of the Sea (Impositions of Contributions to Oil Pollution Compensation Fund – Customs) Act* 1993 (Cth).

449. All these Acts came into effect on 18 Dec. 1986. *See also* Protection of the Sea (Shipping Levy) Regulations (SR No. 227 of 1982); Protection of the Sea (Shipping Levy Collection) Regulations (SR No. 225 of 1982); Protection of the Sea (Shipping Levy) Regulations (Amendment) (SR No. 257 of Protection of the Sea (Imposition of Contributions to Oil Pollution Compensation Funds – Excise Act 1993 (Cth); Protection of the Sea (Imposition of Contributions to Oil Pollution Compensation Funds-General) Act 1993 (Cth) – General.

VI. Preparedness and Response

228. The International Convention on Oil Pollution Preparedness, Response, and Cooperation 1990, came into force in May 1995 and was implemented in Australia in the *Protection of the Sea (Prevention of Pollution from Ships) Act 1983 (Cth)*. The Convention seeks to deal with catastrophic oil spills such as the Exxon Valdez in Alaska. The Convention aims at facilitating international cooperation in preparation for and response to major oil pollution incidents. The Convention includes provision for ships to carry oil spill emergency plans for setting up national and regional systems for preparedness and response; oil pollution emergency plans for ships; offshore platforms and sea ports; technical cooperation, and training; facilitation of international cooperation and mutual assistance.

VII. The 2001 Bunker Oil Pollution Convention

229. The Bunker Oil Convention which came into force on 21 November 2008 was put into effect in Australia by the *Protection of the Sea (Civil Liability for Bunker Oil Pollution Damage) Act* (Cth) 2008. The Convention covers oil spills outside a vessel wherever occurring causing damage within the territory, in this case, of Australia, including the territorial sea and EEZ.[450]

230. Strict liability applies to the shipowner as in the CLC defined as including 'the registered owner, bareboat charterer, manager and operator of the ship'. Compensation for impairment of the environment other than loss of profits, as in the CLC, is limited to the costs reasonable measures to be, or actually undertaken.[451]

231. The shipowner is liable, apart from pollution, for preventative measures and further loss or damage these cause.

232. Claims under the Bunker Oil Convention are limited by either the 1957 or 1976 Limitation Conventions. For vessels over 1,000 gross tons only the registered owner must maintain insurance equal to the amounts applicable under the *Limitation of Liability for Maritime Claims Act* (Cth) 1989 (*see* paragraph 212) but not exceeding the 1976 Limitation Convention limits.

233. Article 7 gives direct rights of action against the insurer which maintains a right, as in the CLC, to limit even if this has been lost by the registered owner. The insurer may rely on any defences available to the shipowner and may avoid liability on proof that the damage arose from the wilful misconduct of the shipowner. Ships are required to carry insurance certificates when entering or leaving ports in

450. Bunker oil is defined as 'hydrocarbon mineral oil, including lubricating oil used for operation or propulsion of the ship, and any residues of such oil'. The *Protection of the Sea (Civil Liability for Bunker Oil Pollution Damage Act* 2008 (Cth) extends to external territories and has extraterritorial application; ss 5 and 6 and is concurrent with State and Territory laws s. 10. The liability under the Convention overlaps with the CLC; s. 9.

451. *See Protection of the Sea (Civil Liability for Bunker Oil Pollution Damage) Act* 2008 (Cth) s. 11.

Australia as are Australian operational registered ships.[452] The Bunker Oil Convention adopts the CLC time limits for claims.[453]

§5. COLLISION

234. Collisions involving vessels usually arise from such an incident or incidents with another vessel or vessels, jetties and wharves, bridges, underwater objects or pipes such as oil gas or other types of construction.[454] This is distinct from grounding which is where the vessel makes contact with the seabed or shore. Only collisions as apart from groundings or stranding are considered here. Collisions may give rise to civil liability for personal and property injury or damage which may include pollution, criminal sanctions, and marine insurance issues.

Where the common law establishes both proximity and reasonable foreseeability of risk between persons then a general duty of care is proved and breach of that duty sets up a right to an action in negligence. In the context of a collision, persons such as master and crew, shipowner, charterer, pilot, or tug owner must prove liability for negligence, breach of the duty of care and resultant loss, damage or injury flowing from that breach.[455]

452. *See* Division 2 ss 16 and 17.
453. Claims may be taken before the courts of the state (country) where the pollution has occurred, or in the state where security has been posted.
In the alternative, claims may be taken before courts of the state here the preventative or minimizing measures have taken place. For general comment Bunker Oil Pollution Convention *see* S. Baughen, *Shipping Law* (4th ed., Cavendish 2009). *See also* N. Gaskell & C. Forrest, *Marine Pollution Damage in Australia: Implementing the Bunker Oil Convention 2001 and the Supplementary Fund Protocol 2003*, UQLJ 27, 2 (2008): 103. Under the Hazardous and Noxious Substances by Sea Convention (HNS) a shipowner must take out insurance to cover its liability for any damage caused by hazardous or noxious substances in connection with carriage by sea on board the ship; *see* Shipping: Laws of Australia, 173–174. For a list of noxious and harmful substances *see* Art. 1(5)(a) of the HNS Convention. *See also Protection of the Sea (Harmful Anti fouling Systems Act* 2006(Cth) which gives effect to the International Convention on the Control of Harmful Anti-fouling Systems on Ships.
454. *See* generally *Australian Maritime Law* (M. White ed., 2d ed. Federation Press 2000); M. Davies & A. Dickey, *Shipping Law* (3d ed., Thomson Reuter 2004); A.W. Street, *Collisions and Groundings*, in *Australian Maritime Law* (M. White Sydney ed., Federation Press 1991). D.A. Butler & W.D. Duncan, *Maritime Law in Australia* [6.1]–[6.7.3] (Legal Books 1992). *See also* H.M. Holdert & F.J. Buzek, *Collision Cases-Judgements and Diagrams* (Lloyd's of London Press 1984).
455. *See Caltex Oil (Aust) Pty Ltd v. The Dredge 'Willemstad'* (1976) 136 CLR 529, dredge damaging underwater oil pipeline in Botany Bay, Sydney. *See also Baggermaatschappij Boz & Kalis BV (t/a Westham Dredging Co) v. Australian Shipping Commission* (1980) 30 ALR 387 for analysis by the HC of the 'reasonable man' common law concept contrasted with the requirements under the *International Regulations for Prevention Collisions at Sea 1972* (*see* below). *see* Dredge, *WH Goomai' v. Australian Oil Refining Pty Ltd*, 94 FLR 298 (NSWCA) (1989). *Shipping: Laws of Australia* [34.3.123] where the defence to a claim for breach of duty giving rise to contributory negligence may be based on the doctrine of the 'agony of the moment' or 'alternative danger' (p. 124). For recent case where collision and limitation of liability were the subject of arrest proceedings in Admiralty in both Chinese and Australian jurisdictions *see Atlasnavious Navegacao v. The Ship; Xin Tai Hai (No2)* [2012] FCA 1497 and *CMA CGM v. Ship Chou Shan* [2014] FCA 74 (*see* ADMIRALTY).

235. The *International Regulations for Preventing Collisions at Sea 1972*, commonly known as the Collision Rules, are set out in the Navigation Act 1912 (Cth).[456] The Collision Regulations cover thirty-eight rules and four annexes. The latter deal with matters such as the positioning and technical details of lights and shapes to be displayed, additional signals for fishing vessels in close proximity, technical details of sound appliances and distress signals. Only a brief outline of the Collision Regulations is given here.

Under the *Navigation Act* 2012 (Cth), the Regulations apply to all ships, wherever they are located, which are not specified in the *Navigation Act* 1912 (Cth) section 2(1).[457] Part A, Rule 1–3, is of general application. The Regulations apply to all vessels on the high sea and in all waters connected to them that are navigable by sea-going vessels.[458] The definition of a vessel includes non-displacement craft, such as hovercraft and seaplanes.[459] The term a 'vessel restricted in her ability to manoevre' means a vessel so restricted under the Rules and includes a survey vessel, one engaged in cable or pipeline laying, dredging, aircraft recovery, mine sweeping, and towing of a restrictive nature.[460] Exceptions may be made in respect of special or purpose built vessels where compliance with the Regulations is determined by the Federal Government to be impracticable.[461] Nothing in the Regulations exonerates any vessel, owner, master, or crew from the consequences of failing to comply with them or neglecting any precaution required by the ordinary practice of seamen or by the circumstances of the case.[462]

236. Any action to avoid collision must, if the circumstances allow, be positive, made in ample time and with regard to good seamanship.[463] A vessel hearing a fog signal of another vessel forward of her beam or unable to avoid a close-quarters situation with such a vessel is required to reduce her speed to the minimum for keeping on course. If necessary all way should be taken off and in any event the vessel is required to navigate with extreme caution until the danger of collision is over.[464]

237. Breach of the Collision Regulations constitutes a criminal offence. Under the *Navigation Act* 2012 (Cth) where loss of life or personal injuries are suffered by

456. *See Navigation Act* 2012 s. 14(1), giving effect to the Convention on the International Regulations for preventing Collisions at Sea 1972 ATS 5. *See* corresponding State legislation; Navigation (Collision) Regulations 1983 (NSW); Marine (Collision) Regulations 1982 (NT); Queensland Marine (Prevention of Collisions) Regulation 1992; Prevention of Collisions at Sea Regulations 1977 (SA); Marine (Collision) Regulations 1983 (Tas); Marine (Navigation and Operation of Vessels) Regulations 1988 (Vic); Prevention of Collisions at Sea Regulations 1983 (WA).
457. *See Navigation Act* 2012 (Cth) s. 14(1) definition of vessel and applying the Collision Regulations. *See also Navigation Act* 2012 *(Cth)* Ch. 6 Pt3 s. 175(2).
458. Part A, r. 1.
459. Rule 3.
460. Rule 3(g).
461. Rule 1(c).
462. Rule 2(a).
463. Rule 8. *See* H.M.C. Holdert & F.J. Buzek, *Collision Cases – Judgements and Diagrams* (Lloyds of London Press 1984) for a useful illustrated compendium of collision cases.
464. Rules 20–31; *see also* Annexes I and II.

any person on board a ship due to the fault of that ship or any other ship or ships, the liability of the ships' owners is joint and several (i.e., individual). The *Navigation Act* 2012 (Cth) provides that in the case of collision a ship shall not be deemed to be in fault solely by reason of the fact that the ship has breached the Collision Regulations. The Act also imposes a general duty on masters and persons in charge of vessels to give assistance to any person in danger at sea. Failure to comply with this provision without reasonable cause constitutes an indictable offence on the part of the person in charge of the ship. In the case of a collision between two ships the collision shall not be deemed to have been caused by the wrongful act, neglect, or default of the master or person in charge of the ship who fails to stand by and render assistance to the other ship. The Collision Regulations do not apply to a ship in the territorial sea of Australia, sea on its landward side or inland waters to the extent that a law of a State or Territory makes provision for giving effect to the Prevention of Collisions Convention.[465]

238. Conviction of a person for an offence under the Collision Regulations does not relieve that person from civil liability resulting from their negligence.[466] Proof of a breach of the Collision Regulations may, therefore, be useful evidence of negligent navigation in a case for civil damages.[467] Where the Collision Regulations have been broken, or a master is alleged not to have navigated in accordance with the *Navigation Act* the fact of such occurrence does not automatically give rise to liability for collision damage. Now that the statutory presumption of fault has been abolished the court has to examine what took place before the collision and from this extract what is termed the last or operating cause of the event. There may be considerable overlap of faults leading to the collision at issue and it may be difficult for a court to decide when one stage came to an end and the other began.[468]

239. The division of loss in all modern cases involving collision is the result of the Collision Convention of 1910[469] which introduced a rule based on proportionate

465. *Navigation Act* 2012(Cth) assigning liability for loss of life (s. 176(3)(a)), not at fault due to breach of Regs.(s. 179), requirement to assist at sea (s. 181), indictable offences (s. 177–s. 178), render assistance at sea (s. 184), a master of a vessel to report any serious danger to navigation on or near his course (s. 187(1). *See* Navigation Regulation reg. 15.
466. *See Navigation Act* 2012 (Cth) s. 14(1) 'civil penalty provision'.
467. *See* below. *See* on recovery for economic loss resulting from a collision the HC decision in *Caltex Oil (Australia) Pty Ltd v. The Dredge Willemstad* (1976) 136 CLR 529 and the difficulty of reconciling the Privy Council decision in *Candlewood Navigation Corporation Limited v. Mitsui Osk Lines Limited (The Mineral Tramsporter)* [1986] C 1. Notwithstanding the decision in *The Mineral Transporter*, purely economic loss is still recoverable in Australia courts; *see* Ch. 4.
468. *See The Hagen* [1973] 1 Lloyd's Rep 257; *see* H.M.C. Holdert & F.J. Buzek, *Collisions Cases-Judgements and Diagrams* 172 (Lloyds of London Press 1984). On inquiries into collisions *see* the foundering of the 'Lake Illawarra', Report No. 157 conducted by a Court of Marine Inquiry under the now repealed Pt IX of the *Navigation Act* 1912 (Cth); *see* A.S. Ogilvie, *Courts of Marine Inquiry in Australia*, ALJ 53, 129 (1979) 129 for commentary on the 'Illawarra' disaster which involved a zinc carrier vessel striking and causing the part collapse of the Tasman Bridge in Hobart Tasmania in 1975. The Australian Transport Safety Bureau, set up by the *Australian Safety Investigation Act* 2003 (Cth), is responsible for independent investigation of all transport accidents, including collisions and groundings; *see* website at www.atsb.gov.au.
469. *See Maritime Conventions Act* 1911 (UK) s. 1 enunciating Art. 4 of the Collision Convention 1910.

fault. The *Navigation Act* 1912 (Cth) applies this rule for Australian purposes and provides that where, by fault, two or more ships cause damage or loss to one or more of the ships, their cargoes or freight, or any property on board, the liability makes good for the damage or loss that shall be in proportion to the degree each ship was in fault. If, in all the circumstances of the case, it is not possible to establish degrees of fault, the liability shall be apportioned equally.[470]

240. In a collision situation, a master of a vessel may do or omit to do something which may contribute to the collision without being regarded as being deficient in ordinary skill and care. This concept, termed the 'doctrine of alternative danger' is based on the rationale that the creator of the danger is not permitted to be overly critical of a master of another vessel responding to that danger.[471] To illustrate: Ship A manoeuvres negligently and suddenly puts ship B in serious danger. The master of B, acting in the agony of the moment without time for further thought, gives an order which he believes will avoid the impending collision. If the order turns out to be the proximate cause of the collision it has been held that B's negligence will not be taken into account and ship A has to bear the whole loss. The 'doctrine of alternative danger' can only be relied on if the action of the master was taken in the 'agony of the moment', with the danger imminent with no time for the master to grasp the situation or to have acted freely. Where the danger was not imminent or there was sufficient time to decide action, any miscalculation on the master's part will be regarded as negligence and the usual division of loss will apply.

241. In practice, the courts require very strong evidence to show that the plaintiff's negligence came last. In most cases, the negligence of both parties will be regarded as having happened at the same time so that the loss will be divided. What is known as the 'clear line' rule was put forward by Lord Birken head as follows:

> while no doubt where a clear line can be drawn, the subsequent negligence is the only one to look to, there are cases in which the two acts came so closely together and the second act of negligence is so mixed up with the state of things brought about by the first act that the party secondly negligent, while not held free of blame under the rule, might, on the other hand, invoke the prior negligence as being part of the cause of the collision so as to make it a case of contribution.[472]

---

470. *See Navigation Regulations* reg. 15 which replaces s. 259 of the *Navigation Act* 1912 *(Cth)* and provides for two or more vessels being liable in proportion to their degree of fault, where damage or loss is caused to one or more such *other* vessels, their freight nor the property on board such *other* vessels. Under the old s. 259 of the 1912 Act, the equivalent provision was not limited to *other* vessels but also applied to the vessel at fault as well. Read literally, reg. 15 would appear not to be available to determine the proportionate liability between two vessels for damage or loss suffered by those two vessels.

471. *See The Bywell Castle* (1879) 4 P.DF. 219.

472. *Admiralty Commissioners v. SS Volute* [1922] 1 AC 129 at 144. For illustration of an 'agony of the moment' *see Webster & Co v. Australasian United Steam Navigation Co Limited* [1901] St R Qd 207.

The *Navigation Regulations* provides that division of loss as a result of a collision will be apportioned in the following ways. Where two or more ships cause loss or damage to one or more ships or to any property on board the liability to make good the loss or damage is in proportion to the degree of fault of each ship. Where it is not possible to establish different degrees of fault, the liability is to be apportioned equally. Nothing under this provision renders any ship liable for loss or damage to which it has not contributed. This section has no effect on any contractual arrangement or statutory provision which enables the right of any person to limit their liability.[473]

§6. SALVAGE

242. Salvage[474] is a service that saves or contributes to the ultimate safety of the vessel, cargo, or wreck, or the lives of persons on the vessel, when it is in danger at sea or in tidal waters, or its shores. It must be a voluntary service and not one performed under a legal duty or for self-preservation. The person providing the service, known as the salvor, is entitled at a payment known as the salvage reward. Before any entitlement to a reward arises there must be a danger to the vessel, life, or object salved, the property or life salved must be of a type capable of being subject to salvage, the service must be voluntary and successful or have contributed to a successful salvage.[475]

243. The *Navigation Act* 2012 (Cth) provides that where services are rendered within Australian waters in saving life from any ship, or elsewhere in saving life from any ship registered in Australia, the owner of the ship, cargo, or equipment saved, is required to pay a reasonable amount of salvage (i.e., the reward). The Act also provides that where any vessel is wrecked or stranded or in distress at any place on or near the coasts of Australia, and services are rendered in assisting that ship or saving any wreck, the owner of the ship or wreck is similarly obliged to make payment.[476] 'Salvage' includes all expenses properly incurred by the salvor in carrying

---

473. *See Navigation Regulations* reg. 15.
474. *See* generally M. White, *Shipping: Laws of Australia* Ch. 12. *See* M. White, *Salvage, Towage and Wreck*, in *Australian Maritime Law* 247 (M. White ed., 2d ed., Federation Press 2000); *Shipping: Laws of Australia* Ch. 12. The *international Convention on Salvage* has force of law in Australia by the *Navigation Act* 2010 (Cth) s. 226(3)(a).*See* A Sullivan note on *Svitzer Salvage v. Z Energy Limited and Another*[2013] NZHC 17; ' *The Interaction Between the Law of Salvage, the Law of Contract and the Salvage Convention*', 30(1) ANZMarLJ 70–74 (2016).
475. *See Fisher v. The 'Oceanic Grandeur'* (1972) 127 CLR 312.
476. Wreck (which is not dealt with here) is defined by the Navigation Act 1912 (Cth) s. 294 as including 'jetsam, flotsam, lagan and derelict found in or on the shores of the sea or any tidal water, and any articles or goods of whatever kind which belonged to or came from any ship wrecked, stranded, or in distress, or any portion of the hull machinery or equipment of any such ship' *see* M.W.D. White, *Shipping Law: Laws of Australia,* Ch. 13 for a detailed account of the law relating wreck and prize (neither of which are dealt with here).

out salvage services. 'Tidal waters' means a part of the sea, or part of a river within the ebb and flow of ordinary spring tides, but does not include a harbour.[477]

Regulation 17 of the *Navigation Regulation* 2013 provides that Articles 8, 12–19, 21–23, and 30 of the *International Convention on Salvage (Salvage Convention)* (1989) *1953 UNTS 193; [1998] ATS 2,* and the common understanding concerning Articles 13 and 14 of the Salvage Convention have force of law in Australia. These Articles cover conditions for a salvage reward, life salvage, apportionment between salvors, contracts, respective duties, payments, and misconduct. In addition, compliance by a shipmaster to render assistance to any person found at sea in danger of being lost does not affect their right to make a claim in respect of a savage operation.[478]

244. To qualify as a salvor a person must be, at the relevant time either personally engaged in salvage service, entitled to possession of a vessel used to provide salvage service, or the owner or person entitled to possession of other property which was used to provide a salvage service.

What is paid as a salvage reward (or award) depends on the circumstances. These include the value of the salved property, the degree of danger to life and property and the value of property saved. Also of relevance will be the degree of danger and risk to the salvors and the skill and time involved, the costs and inconvenience to them.[479] Salvors are entitled to limit their liability for injury, loss, or damage arising from a salvage operation.[480]

245. Salvage agreements are commonly used to determine the rights (including reward) and liabilities under acts of salvage. The most widely used of these is Lloyd's Open Form (LOF). Under LOF 2011, the salvor is bound to use their best endeavours to save the vessel, life, and property 'while performing the salvage services to prevent or minimize damage to the environment'. LOF 2011 like its predecessor LOF 80 follows the principle of 'no cure, no pay'. LOF 2011 gives effect to the *International Convention on Salvage 1989* so that the requirement under the

477. *The Navigation Act* 2012 (Cth) Ch.7 Pt 3 does not apply to any salvage operation: (1) taking place in inland waters and involving vessels of an inland nature; (2) taking place in such waters not involving a vessel; (3) to the extent salvage involves cultural property and is situated on the seabed.; *see also* ss 229, 238, 239. Jurisdiction over salvage claims is determined under the *Admiralty Act* 1988 (Cth); *see* below.

478. For the general obligation to render assistance to persons in distress at sea *see Navigation Act 2012* s. 181(1).Ch 7; Pt 3 Div. 2 of the *Navigation Act* 2012 addresses salvage claims made against the Crown.

479. *See Fisher v. The Ship 'Oceanic Grandeur'* (1972) 127 CLR 312; *see also Brown v. The Ship 'Honolulu Maru'* (1924) 24 SR (NSW) 309; *Putwain v. English, Scottish & Australian Bank (The Gothenburg)* (1877) 4 QSCR 133 (PC); *Bingle v. The Ship 'The Queen of England'* (1862) 1 SCR (NSW) Eq 47; *Brown v. The Ship 'Darnholme'* (1922) 23 SR (NSW) 195; *Stuart v. The Ship 'Columbia River'* (1921) 21 SR (NSW) 674; *Hodson v. Owners of 'Super Sport'* (1990) 26 FCR 157.

480. Under the *Limitation of Liability for Maritime Claims Act* 1989 (Cth), Sch. 1, Art. 1(1).

Salvage Convention to provide for payment to protect the marine environment from pollution is incorporated in the salvage contract.[481]

246. An exception to the principle of 'no cure, no pay' developed after 1980 regarding the efforts of salvors to prevent oil pollution from vessels they attempted to salve, particularly problems with oil tankers. Oil escapes during salving may result in the salvor becoming liable or destruction of a vessel by government order thwarting the operation and so negating the salvor's entitlement to salvage. As a result LOF 1980 introduced the twin concepts of the 'enhanced award' and the 'safety net'. These both apply to the salvage or attempted salvage of wholly or partly loaded oil tankers loaded. Clause 1(a) imposed a duty on the salvor while salving to use its best endeavours to prevent oil escaping from the vessel. The prevention of oil pollution during salvage was isolated as a factor that would 'enhance' any eventual award. If a salvor lost an entitlement due to unsuccessful operations LOF 1980 provided a 'safety net' whereby the salvor should be awarded expenses reasonably incurred with a profit element of 15% payable by the shipowner not the cargo interests. This would not apply if the negligence of the salvor caused the failure of the salvage enterprise.[482]

247. Articles 13 and 14 of the 1989 Salvage Convention contain modified versions of the 'enhanced award' and the 'safety net' which are incorporated into LOF 1990. Unlike LOF 1980 these provisions are not limited to loaded tankers. Article 13(1)(b) lists 'the skill and efforts of the salvors in preventing or minimizing damage to the environment, as one of the factors to be considered in assessing any salvage award but does not specifically give this factor priority over others listed. As the provision is worded to reward success it does not cover the skill and efforts of salvors that fail in attempting to minimize damage to the environment.[483]

248. In *United Salvage Pty Ltd and Others v. Louis Dreyfus Armateurs SNC and Others* [2007] 240 ALR 630, United Salvage, an international salvage operator, with a tug owner provided salvage services to a grounded vessel ' *La Pampa*' in Gladstone Harbour, Queensland. The vessel was a capsize bulk carrier with an agreed salved value of AUD 37,914,691.94. The three tugs commenced a coordinated salvage operation which resulted in the vessel being refloated. Article 13 of the International Salvage Convention on Salvage 1989 provided the criteria for fixing the salvage reward. United Salvage claimed that the third respondent was the 'beneficial owner' of the vessel. The primary judge fixed the award for salvage in favour

481. For a commentary on LOF *see* D.A. Butler & W.D. Duncan, *Maritime Law in Australia* para. 7.9 (Legal Books 1992); G. Darling & C. Smith, *LOF 90 and the New Salvage Convention* (Lloyd's of London Press 1991).
482. *See* S. Baughen, *Shipping Law* 304 (4th ed., Cavendish 2009). But *see* LOF 2011.
483. *See* S. Baughen, *Shipping Law* (4th ed., Cavendish 2009) 305 and for details of the Salvage Convention's provisions for 'safety net' and 'special compensation' in respect of salvors and assessment of compensation to them under Arts 13, 14, 14(2), and 14(3) *see* 305–307. For consideration of these provisions by the House of Lords *see The Nagasaki* Spirit [1997] 1 Lloyd's Rep 323 and *see* note (1997) LMLQ 321.

of United Salvage and the tug owner at AUD 850,000 but gave no judgment against the third respondent.

249. In dismissing the appeal the Federal Court held that the court could not interfere with the assessment of the award by the primary judge unless it could be shown he had acted on some wrong principle or misunderstood the facts of the case. The primary judge was correct in finding that he was not satisfied that there was any real probability or danger of global failure. The primary judge accounted for the possibility of global failure, as he did for the release of oil, blockage of the channel, damage to adjoining structures, and the consequences if there had been a global failure. The risk of damage to the environment was premised on the salvor's success on the issue of global failure. The primary judge reasons indicted that he accepted there was a remote but not a real risk of the vessel breaking up. He expressly acknowledged the potential risk of liability to third parties arising from the potential of the vessel blocking the port and polluting the environment but following from his findings of fact that risk was remote. The Federal Court found the primary judge to be correct to reject the submission that the salved value of AUD 38 should have been used as a benchmark and the award fixed at a percentage of at least 10% of that value.

§7. TOWAGE

250. Towage involves the use of one vessel to expedite the voyage of another when nothing more is required than the acceleration of her progress.[484] A contract of towage, usually in a standard form such as the United Kingdom Towing Provisions,[485] requires the exercise if diligence, care, and reasonable skill in carrying out the obligations by both parties to the agreement. Salvage and towage services are distinct; the first being voluntary and no guaranteed payment, the second on the basis of contractual payment. If a tow becomes a danger to the towing vessel without the tug's fault and the additional risk is undertaken by the tug beyond agreement's provisions as a result, then the tug is entitled to a salvage reward.[486]

251. In *PNSL Behad v. Dalrymple Marine Services* (2007) 210 FLR 243, the Federal Court held that there is no relevant relationship between a contract to provide a towing service and the transportation of goods. As such, there is no reason to

---

484. *See The 'Princess Alice'* [1875–1876] 1 All Cas 58, 63. *Salvage, Towage and Wreck*, in *Australian Maritime Law* (M. White ed., 2d ed., Federation Press 2000). N.Gaskell, *The Law of Tug and Tow and Offshore Contracts* (3rd ed.) S. Raney, in D.R. Thomas (ed.) 18 J Intl Mar L 322 Law Text (2012).

485. For application of these provisions *see The Australian Coastal Shipping Commission v. The Owners, Master and Crew of the PV 'Wyuna'* (1964) 111 CLR 303. For Australian towage cases *see The Ship Texaco Southampton v. Burley* [1982] 2 NSWLR 336 (CA); *Australian Steamships Pty Ltd v. Koninklijke Java-China Pakevaart Lynen NV Amsterdam* [1955] VLR 108; *Howard Smith Industries Ltd v. Melbourne Harbour Trust Commissioners* [1970] VR 406; *Taylor v. Geelong Harbour Trust Commissioners* [1962] VR 190; *The Tudor* [1968] 1 Lloyd's Rep 500 (HC).

486. *See The Emile Galline* [1903] 106.

conclude that the purpose of the *Trade Practices Act* 1974 (Cth) section 74(3) extends to removing towing contracts from the scope of section 74(1) and (2). A negligent defendant cannot rely on the UK Standard Conditions since section 68 of the *Trade Practices Act* 1974 (Cth) made the exemption clause in the Conditions void.[487]

§8. PILOTAGE

252. A pilot is described in the *Navigation Act* as 'a person who does not belong to, but has conduct of a ship'.[488] A marine pilot is an independent skilled professional and is, therefore, required under the contact to exhibit such skill in the discharge of such duties.[489] Under the *Navigation Act* 1912 (Cth), a pilot is under the authority of the master and the master is responsible for the conduct of the ship as still retains that responsibility while the ship is being piloted. Where pilotage is compulsory the owner or master is liable for any loss or damage caused by the ship, by its faulty navigation, as if the pilotage were not compulsory.[490] Pilotage and control of ships is governed by Commonwealth and State legislation.[491]

253. In *Amarantos Shipping Co v. State of South Australia and Others* [2004] SASC 276, Aramantos's bulk carrier collided with a jetty, causing damage to the ship and equipment on it, property owned by the South Australian Ports Corporation (SAPC). The ship at the time was under compulsory pilotage, the pilot being employed and supplied by the SAPC which also supplied tugs assisting the vessel. Amarantos (the shipowner) sued the State of SA for costs of repairing the ship, claiming that SAPC was negligent. The State of SA (standing in for the SAPC) denied liability relying on section 36 of the *Harbours and Navigation Act* 1993 (SA) and arguing that section 2 of the *Merchant Shipping (Liability of Shipowners and Others) Act* 1900 (Imp) (the 1900 Act) applied to limit any liability to the shipowner. The State counter claimed arguing that the plaintiff shipowner was strictly liable for the damage to the jetty, relying on section 21 of *Harbours and Navigation Act* and section 24 of the *South Australian Ports Corporation Act* 1994 (SA). The shipowner argued that the State Acts were ineffective and was entitled to limit its liability under the 1900 Act.

254. The Full Court of the Supreme Court of South Australia held that the *Navigation Amendment Act* 1979 (Cth) repealed section 1 (at least) of the 1900 Act. The

487. Section 74(3) provides that services must be provided with due care and skill. Section 68 includes provision that any clause exempting these terms is void but now *see Competition and Consumer Act* 2010 (Cth) ss 60, 63.

488. *Navigation Act 2010(Cth) s14(1).*

489. *See Fowles v. Eastern & Australia Steamship Co Ltd* [1916] 2 Ac 556, at 562–563; *Oceanic Crest Shipping Co v. Pilbara Harbour Services Pty Ltd* (1986) 160 CLR 626.

490. *Navigation Act 2010 (Cth) s326(4).*

491. *See Maritime Services Act* 1935 (NSW); *Pilotage Act* 1971 (NSW); *Darwin Port Authority Act* 1981 (NT); *Harbours Act* 1936 (SA); *Marine Act* 1958 (Tas); *Marine Act* 1988 (Vic); *Pilot's Limitation of Liability Act* 1962 (WA); *Shipping and Pilotage Act* 1967 (WA).

Limitation of Liability for Maritime Claims Act 1989 (Cth) set down a legislative scheme inconsistent with the survival 1900 Act.[492] The 1989 Act indicated an intention to cover the field as it created a single scheme for shipowners to limit liability, subject to the exceptions provided. The 1989 Act repealed or rendered inoperative the provisions of the 1900 Act and regulated the claim by the shipowners to limit liability.[493]

§9. ADMIRALTY

255. The *Admiralty Act* 1988 (Cth) reforms and clarifies a branch of maritime law which had the hallmark of an anachronistic and ill-defined jurisdiction in Australia.[494] Power to enact the *Admiralty Act* is based on section 76(iii) of the Constitution which allows the Federal Parliament to confer jurisdiction in all matters of Admiralty and maritime jurisdiction and section 51(xxxix) which empowers the Federal Parliament to regulate ancillary and incidental matters.[495] The *Admiralty Act* 1988 (Cth) retains the existing and generally accepted division of admiralty action against ships, that is, the distinction between actions in rem based on maritime liens and statutory rights of action in rem based on causes of action arising out of the general law and involving the ownership or operation of ships. The action in rem is directed against property, usually a ship. The Act confers jurisdiction over claims on maritime liens but does not codify or define the substantive law.[496] The *Admiralty Act* 1988 (Cth) does, however, provide in detail for statutory rights in rem

492. Applying *Kirmani v. Captain Cook Cruises Pty Ltd (No. 1)* (1985) 169 CLR 351.
493. The State laws dealing with liability for damage caused to property of the Crown or SAPC by a vessel were not inconsistent with s. 410B of the *Navigation Act* 1912 (Cth). Section 4 of the *Australia Act* 1986 (Cth) validly repealed ss 735 and 736 of the *Merchant Shipping Act* 1894 (Imp) in their application to the States, s. 4 of the *Australia Act* 1986 (UK) having the same effect; applying *Attorney-General (WA) v. Marquet* (2003) 78 ALJR 105.
494. The *Admiralty Act* 1988 (Cth) is based on a report and recommendations of the Australian Law Reform Commission (ALRC), *Civil Admiralty Jurisdiction Report*, ALRC 33 (Canberra: AGPS, 1986). This Report made a thorough study of the admiralty law in other common law countries. In general, the *Admiralty Act* 1988 (Cth) follows the *Supreme Court Act* 1981 (UK) and the *Arrest Convention* 1952. The *Admiralty Act* 1988 (Cth) repeals the *Colonial Courts of Admiralty Act* 1890 (Imp) and amends the *Merchant Shipping Act* 1894 (Imp); for details *see* J. Crawford, *Admiralty: Laws of Australia* 34.4, paras 4–10. For a review of the ALRC Report *see* B. Davenport, *Proposed Reforms of Admiralty Jurisdiction in Australia*, 3 LMCLQ 317 (1987). On Admiralty generally *see* J. Crawford, *Shipping: Laws of Australia* 34.4 and the *Admiralty Act* 1973 (NZ) which in turn are modelled on the *Arrest Convention* 1952. The *Admiralty Act* 1988 (Cth) repeals the *Colonial Courts of Admiralty Act* 1890 (Imp) and amends the *Merchant Shipping Act* 1894 (Imp); for details *see* J. Crawford, *Admiralty: Laws of Australia* 34.4, paras 4–10. For a review of the ALRC Report *see* B. Davenport, *Proposed Reforms of Admiralty Jurisdiction in Australia*, 3 LMCLQ 317 (1987). On Admiralty generally *see* J. Crawford, *Shipping: Laws of Australia* 34.4. *See* D J Creaman. *'The Early History of Admiralty Jurisdiction'*(2014) ANZMarLJ 28(1) 16–24.
495. Other provisions in the *Admiralty Act* 1988 (Cth) rely on s. 76(ii) which deals with jurisdiction arising under other laws made by the Federal Parliament. On the scope of the Admiralty jurisdiction and the relationship with the Federal Constitution *see Civil Admiralty Jurisdiction* (1986), 35–82.
496. *See* A. Phillipides, *Shipping: Laws of Australia* 34.3 Ch. 7.

and sets out the maritime claims under which actions in rem can be brought in Australian courts, defines the circumstances in which ships, including surrogate or 'sister' ships can be arrested on such claims.[497]

256. In *Safezone Pty Ltd v. Ship 'Island Sun'* (2004) 215 ALR 690, the plaintiff company applied for a warrant for the arrest of the ship 'Island Sun' as a surrogate ship of MV 'World Adventurer'. In order to obtain the warrant, the plaintiff was required under section 19(b) of the *Admiralty Act* 1988 (Cth) to establish that the owner of the 'World Adventurer' was also the beneficial owner of the 'Island Sun'. The plaintiff asserted that the owner of the 'Island Sun' was a wholly owned subsidiary.

257. The Federal Court held, in refusing the warrant to the plaintiff company, that the concept of beneficial owner of a surrogate ship, for the purposes of section 19(b) of the *Admiralty Act*, does not cover a company whose wholly owned subsidiary is the legal owner of the ship.[498]

258. The *Admiralty Act* 1988 (Cth) defines a ship[499] for the purposes of the legislation in broad terms and specifically includes hovercraft and moveable oil rigs, but specifically excludes seaplanes, inland waterway vessels (i.e., one used or intended to be used exclusively on Australian inland waterways) and vessels under construction. A foreign ship, defined as ship which cannot be registered under the *Shipping Registration Act* 1981 (Cth) is subject to admiralty jurisdiction even where the maritime claim arises in respect of the use or intended use of the ship on inland waters.[500] The Act extends to all ships and all claims wherever arising.[501]

259. A maritime claim is defined in reference to either a proprietary or general maritime claim.[502] A proprietary maritime claim is defined as claims involving disputes over title to or possession of a ship, mortgage claims, co-ownership disputes, claims to enforce statutory liens (i.e., the right against a vessel resulting from a judgment in rem) and associated claims to interest. In such cases, the right of action itself defines the ship concerned; so a link is required to a specified 'relevant person'.[503] Since proprietary maritime claims usually involve determining or enforcing claims or title or possession of the ship in question surrogate or 'sister' ship is

---

497. For the Admiralty Rules *see* SR 1988.
498. Applying *Malaysia Shipyard v. 'Iron Shortland' as a surrogate for the ship 'Newcastle Pride'* (1995) 131 ALR 738; *Kent v. The Vessel Maria Luisa as Surrogate for the Vessels 'Monika' and 'Boston Bay'* (2003) 130 FCR 12.
499. *Admiralty Act* 1988 (Cth) s. 3(1). *See The Gas Float Whitton* (No. 2) [1897] AC 337; *see also Navigation Act 2010 (Cth)* s. 14(1).
500. *Admiralty Act* 1988 (Cth) s. 5(4).
501. *Admiralty Act* 1988 (Cth) s. 5(1).
502. *Admiralty Act* 1988 (Cth) s. 4. By not including 'damage done to a ship' as a head of jurisdiction within the general maritime claims under s. 4(3) of the Act this gives effect to the House of Lords decision in *The Eschercheim* [1976] 1 WLR 430.
503. *Admiralty Act* 1988 (Cth) s. 19. On maritime liens *see* A. Phillipides, in *Shipping: Laws of Australia* 34.3 Ch. 7.

accordingly excluded.[504] General maritime claims substantially constitute the bulk of maritime claims within admiralty jurisdiction which covers salvage, including life salvage, cargo, or wreck found on land.[505]

260. In *CSL Australia Pty Ltd v. Formosa* (2009) 261 ALR 441, slippery slurry on the deck causing injury was claimed to be a defect in a ship. The Federal Court held that under section 4(3)(c) a defect in a ship is not limited to inherent defect in the design or structure of the ship. Where a ship was made temporarily defective for safe use by a layer of slippery slurry on the deck that was a defect within the meaning of section 4(3)(c) of the *Admiralty Act.*

261. In *Programmed Total Marine Services Pty Ltd v. The Ship Hako Fortress* [2012] FCA 805,(2012) ALR 139 Programmed Total Marine Services Pty Ltd (PMTS) arrested four vessels, including the 'Hako Fortress'. PTMS claimed that it had not been paid for manning services, including crew to the four vessels. The respondent claimed that PTMS had no claim under the Admiralty Act 1988 (Cth) section 4(3). PTMS by the respondent to be the employer of the crew.[506] McKerarher J in the Federal Court of Australia held that the fact that PTMS paid the wages of the crew for the vessels did not give PTMS any surrogated maritime lien against the vessels.[507]

In *CMA CGM SA v. Ship Chou Shan* [2014] FCA 74 the defendant ship collided with the *MV CMA CGM Florida* about 100 nautical miles from the Chinese coastline and inside the PRC's EEZ. Three weeks after the collision the owners of the *MV CMA* commenced proceedings in relation to the collision and applied to Ningo Bo Maritime Court. The Chou Shan was arrested in Port Hedland, WA. The Chou Shan applied to the Federal Court after the vessel was released on additional security by its owners. Chou Shan applied to the Federal Court for stay of proceedings on the basis that the Federal Court was an inappropriate forum and the proceeding was vexatious and oppressive as it concerned the same subject matter before the Ningbo Maritime Court in China.

The Federal Court considering the evidence and noting the operation of the laws covering collision, pollution, and limitation of liability applying in China granted Chou Shan a stay of application.[508]

---

504. *Admiralty Act* 1988 (Cth) s. 19.
505. *Admiralty Act* 1988 (Cth) s. 4(3) 9(g).
506. *See* J. Crawford, fn to para. 117 of the ALRC Report 338 and S. Hetherington, Annotated Admiralty Legislation (Law Book Co Ltd 1989) at 65 cited by J. McKerracher at [25].
507. J. McKerracher at [64] citing *The Petone* [1917] P198 per J. Hill at 208–209.
508. For the detailed outline of the relevant Chinese law provided by Mr X Cheng on behalf of the Chou Shan's owners *see CMA CGM SA v. Ship Chou Shan* [2014] FCA 74 at [39]–[61].*See also Altlas Navegacao LDA v. The Ship 'Xin Tai Hai' (No 2)* [2012] FCA 1497 involving Chinese and Australia jurisdictions over a collision and arrest. Ares J held that neither China nor Australia had any substantive connection to the parties. However, the jurisdiction was founded as of right by the Xin Tai Hai being in Australian waters. There was no basis for finding the plaintiff's purpose in bringing the Australian proceedings was improper. In dismissing stay of proceedings by the Xin Tai Hai's owners Rares J held that Australia was not a clearly inappropriate forum (at [127]–[128]). *See* M Davis *International and Commercial Maritime Law Yearbook* (2012) 1 comment on *Atlasnavious Navegacao Ldn v. Ship Xin Hai Tai (No 2)* [2012] FCA 1497.For presentations from the Federal

A question arises whether a vessel under arrest can still trade between Australian ports. In *Dem Norske Bank(Luxembourg) SA v. The Martha II* [2000] FCA 241 an application was made by the time charterer to permit the vessel to sail, while under arrest, from Port Jackson to Newcastle to unload cargo. Sheppard J refused to permit the vessel to make such a voyage on the basis the vessel could leave the jurisdiction if so permitted. In *Tai Shing Maritime Co SA v. The Samsun Veritas as surrogate for the Tai Hawk*[2008] FCA 1546, McKerracher J adopted a 'pragmatic approach' by permitting the *Samsun Veritas* under arrest in Port Hedland to proceed to Dampier, even if that permitted it to sail outside territorial waters, pointing to the very urgent and paramount public interest considerations in the case, the absence of any application to set aside the arrest and release the ship, and the presence of representatives from both the plaintiff and Marshall on board. In contrast, in *News Maritime v. Hyundai Cosmos*[202] FCA 1164 Tamberlin J rejected an application to move an arrested ship to enable unloading of coal cargo at Port Gladstone on the basis that to permit the vessel's movements could unnecessarily complicate the administration of the vessel's custody.[509]

In *Wilmington Trust* Company *(Trustee) v. The Ship'Houston'* [2016] FCA 1349 The Wilmington Trust Company began proceedings against the defendant. The plaintiff's claim, bought within sections 16 and 18 of the *Admiralty Act 1988* (Cth), sought relief in respect of a BARECOM 2001 bareboat charter citing hire owed to the plaintiffs and repossession of the *Houston.* The vessel was US flagged and registered in Wilmington Delaware. In granting the plaintiff's claim Siopis J. held that it fell within an action in rem and was a proprietary maritime claim within s(4))(a) of the *Admiralty Act 1988.* This section, the judge held, embraced a claim where a third party (as in this case) which did not assert its own right to ownership of a vessel but relied on that of a third party.[510]

262. The *Admiralty Act* 1988 (Cth) substantially extends the jurisdiction under the repealed *Colonial Courts of Admiralty Act* 1890 (Imp) to bring Australia into line with comparable overseas jurisdictions such as the United Kingdom and Singapore. Maritime claims under the *Admiralty Act* 1988 (Cth) now include the following:[511]

Court Sydney 25 Jul. 2017 on judicial powers sale of vessels *see* http://www.fedcourt.gov.au/law_and practice/national practice areas/admiralty.

509. *For decisions cited in the Den* Norske case by J. Sheppard *see The Bazias 3* [1993] QB 675; *The Myro* [1978] 1 Lloyd's Rep 11; *Malaysian Shipyard v. The Iron Shortland* [1995131 ALR 738. For discussion of these cases *see Transport: Laws of Australia,* Law Book Co (20016 revision) Dr S. Tutty; *see also* R.E. Cooper, *Crewing Vessels While under Arrest,* 4(1) MLAANZ Journal 25 (1999).

510. J. Siopsis at [34] citing Owners of the Ship *'Shin Kobe Maru' v. Empire Shipping Company Inc* (1994) 181 CLR 404 at *Wilmington Trust Company (Trustee) v. the Ship'Houston'* [2016] FCA 1349; *see also Elbe Shipping SA v. The Ship Global Peace* 920060 154 FCR 439. *See also* J. Allsop at [70] in reference to s. 4(2)(a) of the *Admiralty Act* 1988.

511. *Admiralty Act* 1988 (Cth) s. 4(2); s. 4(3)(f) includes 'claims arising out of agreement [relating] to the carriage of goods or persons by ship or for the use or hire of a ship, whether by charter party or otherwise'. *See also* D.C. Jackson, *Enforcement of Maritime Claims* (Lloyd's of London Press 1985).

(a) all claims for loss or damage attributable to shipowners or operators and arising from the operation of a ship;
(b) all claims for goods, materials, or services supplied or to be supplied to a ship;
(c) pollution damage claims;[512]
(d) claims for unpaid insurance premiums; and
(e) claims to enforce arbitral awards arising from maritime claims.

512. *See International Maritime Conventions Legislation Amendment Act* 2001 (Cth) Sch. IA amending *Admiralty Act* 1988 (Cth) s. 3(1) meaning of Limitation Convention by *Limitation of Liability for Maritime Claims Act* 1989 (Cth) s. 3(1).

Part III. Other Transport

Chapter 1. Carriage by Road

§1. General

263. The principles that govern the carriage of passengers and goods by land, like the rules applying to carriage generally, are formed by their historical origins. The duty of a common carrier to safely carry and deliver passengers and goods entrusted to it and to answer for any loss or damage to those goods or injury to those passengers, developed as part of the law of bailment, well before greater stress was laid upon the contractual element.[513] The duty of a carrier to safeguard the goods is considered at common law to exist apart from contract, and is imposed not as a consequence of the contract of carriage, but because the carrier has been put in possession of another's goods. One of the consequences of this is that the owner of goods may successfully sue a carrier for loss or damage to goods even though no contract of carriage can be proved.[514] Despite the virtual extinction of the common carrier for the purposes of Australian law, principally by the effect of disclaimers in standard form contracts of carriage, the distinction between common and private carriers is necessary to understand the evolution of the current law. The carriage of passengers is considered subsequently as a separate issue.

§2. Common and Private Carriers

I. Common Carriers

264. A common carrier is one who undertakes for reward to transport passengers and the goods of any who wish to employ the carrier's services. Even though a carrier limits the kind of goods it is prepared to carry and/or the rate at which they are carried, the carrier may still remain a common carrier. Similarly, the status is not lost if the carrier holds itself ready to carry goods between two fixed or variable termini.[515] In the carriage of passengers by land, common carriers are not insurers

513. *See* O.S. Kahn-Freund, *The Law of Carriage by Inland Transport* 194 (4th ed., Stevens 1965).
514. *See* N.E. Palmer, *Bailment* 19 (2d ed., LBC 1991).
515. *Johnson v. Midland Railway* (1849) 4 Ex 367 [154 ER 1254], B. Parke at 373.

in regard to persons and are only liable for injuries to goods.[516] However, the use of disclaimers in standard form contracts of carriage has effectively eliminated the common carrier for the purposes of Australian law. State legislation, based on the *Carrier's Act* 1830 (UK), regulates the position of the common carrier.[517]

II. Private Carriers

A. General

265. Carriers by road are, almost without exception, private carriers. Unlike a common carrier, a private carrier is under no obligation to carry goods offered for carriage.[518] However, the distinction between common and private carriers is no longer relevant because of the use of disclaimers in standard forms of contracts of carriage.[519] Ferry operators would appear to be ordinarily common carriers by water.[520]

B. Liability for Negligence

266. A private carrier may be liable for negligence.[521] The onus is on the carrier to show that its servants exercised reasonable care in relation to the consignor's property. If the goods are lost or damaged in transit it is for the carrier to show that either the carrier or its servants were not negligent, or that such negligence did not

516. Such liability may be excluded by the terms of the contract of carriage; *see Kelly v. Australasian Steam Navigation Co* (1885) 6 LR (NSW) 233 [2 WN 40] (FC). However, where the transport service is supplied by a corporation to a consumer under the terms of s. 74(1) of the *Trade Practices Act* 1974 (Cth) the duty to render such services with due care and skill cannot be excluded. Such terms that purport to do so are void under s. 68 of the *Trade Practices Act* 1974 (Cth).

517. *See Common Carrier's Act* 1902 (NSW); *Carriers Act* 1891 (SA); *Common Carriers Act* 1874 (Tas); *Carriers and Innkeepers Act* 1958 (Vic); *Carriers Act* 1920 (WA). For a general discussion of the definition and position of the common carrier by road *see* N.E. Palmer, *Bailment* 969–984 (2d ed., LBC 1991). The National Rail Corporation and the States' rail authorities are not common carriers.

518. *See* N.E. Palmer, *Bailment* (2d ed., LBC 1991); *Belfast Ropework Co v. Bushell* [1918] 1 KB 210; *Kilners Ltd v. John Dawson Investment Trust Ltd* (1935) 35 SR (NSW) 274 [52 WN 88] (FC), C.J. Jordan at 279; G.W. Paton, *Bailment in the Common Law* 230 (Stevens 1952); *Cowper v. JG Goldner Pty Ltd* (1986) 40 SASR 457; *Securitas (NZ) Ltd v. Cadbury Schweppes Hudson Ltd* [1988] 1 NZLR 340 (CA).

519. Note the judicial tendency in the United Kingdom courts not to attach the liability of common carriers to carriers by road. Palmer notes that 'the species is not wholly extinct': N.E. Palmer, *Bailment* 971 (2d ed., LBC 1991) citing *Hunt & Winterbotham (West of England) Ltd v. BRS (Parcels) Ltd* [1962] 1 QB 617 [[1962] 2 WLR 172; [1962] 1 All ER 111] (CA) and *Great Northern Railway v. LEP Transport & Depository Ltd* [1922] 2 KB 742 (CA).

520. *See Direct Transport Co Ltd v. Detroit & Windsor Ferry Co Ltd* [1936] 1 DLR 423 (HC Ont), affirmed in *Direct Transport Co Ltd v. Detroit & Windsor Ferry Co Ltd* [1936] 4 DLR 807 (CA Ont); *Robert v. Laurin* (1882) 2 LC Jur 378 (CA); *Culver v. Lester* (1901) 21 CLT 295 (CC Ont).

521. *John Carter (Fine Worsteds) Ltd v. Hanson Haulage (Leeds) Ltd* [1965] 2 QB 495 [[1965] 2 WLR 553; [1965] 1 All ER 113] (CA): or, of course, for breach of any express or implied contractual term.

contribute to the loss.[522] Whether the carrier's servants have been negligent is essentially a question of fact. However, the carrier's duty with regard to the fitness of its vehicle for carriage is a heavy one. Therefore, when the carrier breaches any statutory provisions relating to fitness of the vehicle for carriage, this raises a strong presumption of negligence.[523]

267. A private carrier will be liable if its servant, having been entrusted with the goods, steals or commits any intentional or negligent harm, whether the servant is acting for the carrier's benefit or not. Therefore, a carrier is liable not only where goods are stolen by its servant at the carrier's instigation,[524] but also where the servant steals them independently and for personal gain alone,[525] and where the servant, by its negligence, makes it possible for some third party to take the goods.[526]

268. A carrier and its servants are under a duty to ensure that goods entrusted to them for carriage are saved in the event of fire, breakage, or theft, whether or not caused by the negligence of either the carrier or its servants. A carrier will be liable to pay damages to the owner of the goods if it does not do all it can to mitigate damage to the goods.[527]

C. Contracting Out

269. A private carrier's obligations can be varied or modified by contractual agreement.[528] Commonly, standard form agreements of private carriers exclude their sole liability, that of negligence. However, an exemption clause will not be construed as relieving a private carrier from negligence unless it does so

522. *See Joseph Travers & Sons Ltd v. Cooper* [1915] 1 KB 73 (CA).
523. *EA Lee & Sons Pty Ltd v. Abood* (1968) 89 WN (NSW) (Pt 1) 430 (Dist Ct) (vehicle capsizing for unexplained reason); *AF Colverd & Co Ltd v. Anglo-Overseas Transport Co Ltd* [1961] 2 Lloyd's Rep 352 (QB) (driver leaving body of van unlocked, removing ignition key but leaving cab unlocked). But *see* cases in which a carrier was held not to have been negligent: *Hobbs v. Petersham Transport Co Pty Ltd* (1971) 124 CLR 220 [45 ALJR 356]; *Thomas National Transport (Melbourne) Pty Ltd v. May & Baker (Australia) Pty Ltd* (1966) 115 CLR 353 [40 ALJR 189; [1966] 2 Lloyd's Rep 347]; *Gallagher Ltd v. British Road Services Ltd* [1974] 2 Lloyd's Rep 440 (QB). There is no absolute warranty of roadworthiness akin to the common law warranty of seaworthiness imposed on a shipowner. *See also* the refusal of the Privy Council to assimilate the position of a ship at sea to that of a motor car on land in *Trickett v. Queensland Insurance Co Ltd* [1936] AC 159 [[1935] All ER 729] (PC), the Court 165–166.
524. *Barwick v. English Joint Stock Bank* (1867) LR 2 Ex 259.
525. *Morris v. CW Martin & Sons Ltd* [1966] 1 QB 716 [[1965] 3 WLR 276; [1965] 2 All ER 725]; *Moukataff v. British Overseas Airways Corporation* [1967] 1 Lloyd's Rep 396.
526. *Abraham v. Bullock* (1902) 86 LT 796 (CA).
527. *White v. John Warrwick & Co Ltd* [1953] 1 WLR 1285 [[1953] 2 All ER 1021] (CA); *Canada Steamship Lines Ltd v. The King* [1952] AC 192 [[1952] 1 All ER 305]; *Smith v. South Wales Switchgear Ltd* [1978] 1 WLR 165 [[1978] 1 All ER 18] (HL). On the construction of exemption clauses.
528. *See* J. Livermore, *Exemption Clauses and Implied Obligations in Contracts* (LBC 1986).

expressly.[529] Such an exemption will not exclude liability as a consequence of wilful negligence or misconduct on the part of servants or agents, unless that is also expressly excluded.[530] Total loss of goods carried has been held to be covered by an exemption clause in a contract of carriage.[531] The exemption clause would apply even if the loss had been due to theft by the carrier's servants, unless such action could be treated as that of the carrier itself.[532]

270. Where there is a breach of an implied term in a contract of carriage by the carrier, the contract will be construed to ascertain if this breach prevents reliance by the carrier on the exempting terms. In *Thomas National Transport (Melbourne) Pty Ltd v. May & Baker (Australia) Pty Ltd* (1966) 115 CLR 353 [40 ALJR 189; [1966] 2 Lloyd's Rep 347], the High Court held that the carriers were in breach of an implied term of the contract that the respondent's goods would be taken to the depot by the driver and that the contract, on its construction, did not permit the storage of goods in the driver's garage where they were damaged.[533]

271. What amounts to notice of terms and conditions of carriage is a question of fact. In *DJ Hill & Co Pty Ltd v. Walter H Wright Pty Ltd* [1971] VR 749, the Court found that there was insufficient notice of an exemption clause purporting to exempt the carrier from liability for negligence. In that case, the Court found no evidence of any course of prior dealings where the parties mutually regarded the terms and conditions on the back of the receipt form as part of the contract between them.[534]

272. A carrier, whose servant or agent converts the goods entrusted to the carrier, is liable to the owner of the goods, unless an exemption clause in the contract of carriage precludes liability. In *Rick Cobby Haulage Pty Ltd v. Simsmetal Pty Ltd* (1986) 43 SASR 533, the carrier attempted to rely on an exemption clause for loss or damage to goods while in transit or storage when the goods were misappropriated by a subcontractor. The Supreme Court of SA held that the exemption clauses did not apply because the carrier had not proved that the goods were in transit or in storage when the loss occurred as required by the exemption clauses.[535] In that case, even if the goods were in transit or storage, loss by misappropriation did not take

529. For such conduct to be wilful, a conscious choice must be proved to have been made; *see Transport Commissioner v. Neale Edwards Pty Ltd* (1954) 92 CLR 214 [28 ALJ 106].
530. *Metrotex Pty Ltd v. Freight Investments Pty Ltd* [1969] VR 9 (FC).
531. *Metrotex Pty Ltd v. Freight Investments Pty Ltd* [1969] VR 9 (FC).
532. *Thomas National Transport (Melbourne) Pty Ltd v. May & Baker (Australia) Pty Ltd* (1966) 115 CLR 353 [40 ALJR 189; [1966] 2 Lloyd's Rep 347], McTiernan, Owen & J.J. Taylor at 365–366.
533. *Thomas National Transport (Melbourne) Pty Ltd v. May & Baker (Australia) Pty Ltd* (1966) 115 CLR 353 [40 ALJR 189; [1966] 2 Lloyd's Rep 347], C.J. Barwick at 360, McTiernan, Taylor & J.J. Owen at 365, J. Windeyer dissenting.
534. Distinguishing *Hardwick Game Farm v. Suffolk Agriculture & Poultry Production Association Ltd* [1966] 1 WLR 287 [[1966] 1 All ER 309] (CA).
535. *Rick Cobby Haulage Pty Ltd v. Simsmetal Pty Ltd* (1986) 43 SASR 533, J. Bollen at 540 (J. Jacobs agreeing), J. Mohr dissenting.

place during or in connection with the work under the contract, and so was not covered by the exemption clause.[536]

D. *Subcontractors*

273. The right to subcontract is invariably an express term in a contract of carriage. In the absence of such a term, the contract might be performed by the employment of a subcontractor unless the carrier has undertaken expressly or impliedly to perform the contract itself.[537] Where the nature of the goods to be carried requires particular skill and handling,[538] or where the goods are valuable and attractive to thieves, the implication is that the carrier shall not subcontract without express authority.[539]

274. Standard form contracts of carriage usually expressly authorize a carrier to employ another carrier to perform the contract and give such other carrier similar powers to subcontract. These conditions also require the subcontractor to indemnify the carrier against liability arising where the goods are in transit and that of any failure by the subcontractor to collect the goods within a reasonable time. The subcontractor is also required to take out insurance policies which are acceptable to the carrier against liabilities arising under the conditions of contract. It is also common to include in the subcontract a term indemnifying the subcontractor against claims by any person in excess of the subcontractor's liability under the subcontract. A carrier may subcontract its duties expressly and by so doing transfer indemnity to a third party.[540] The issue of third-party liability under a 'Himalaya' clause is considered in the context of carriage of goods by sea.[541]

E. *Liability of the Carrier as a Warehouseperson*

275. A carrier's liability lasts only for the period of carriage. Where a carrier holds goods before or after their carriage, these are held as a warehouseperson and not as a carrier.[542] The liability of a warehouseperson is that of a bailee and, as such,

536. Following *Delco Australia Pty Ltd v. Darlington Futures Ltd* (1986) 43 SASR 519 (FC), distinguishing *Life Savers (Australasia) Ltd v. Frigmobile Pty Ltd* [1983] 1 NSWLR 431 (CA).
537. *John Carter (Fine Worsteds) Ltd v. Hanson Haulage (Leeds) Ltd* [1965] 2 QB 495 [[1965] 2 WLR 553; [1965] 1 All ER 113] (CA), L.J. Davies at 523; *Garnham Harris & Elton Ltd v. Alfred W Ellis (Transport) Ltd* [1967] 1 WLR 940 [[1967] 2 All ER 940] (QB), J. Paull at 942.
538. *Edwards v. Newland & Co* [1950] 2 KB 534 [[1950] 1 All ER 1072] (CA).
539. *Garnham Harris & Elton Ltd v. Alfred W Ellis (Transport) Ltd* [1967] 1 WLR 940 [[1967] 2 All ER 940] (QB).
540. *See Broken Hill Pty Co Ltd v. Hapag-Lloyd A/G* [1980] 2 NSWLR 572 (a sea carrier entitled to subcontract its duties and transfer an indemnity to a land carrier; land carrier entitled to recover from the sea carrier on claim against the land carrier by the cargo owners, the sea carrier being entitled to be indemnified by the cargo owners under the terms of the bills of lading).
541. *See The Himalaya* (1859) 1 LT 307.
542. *Chapman v. Great Western Railway Co* (1880) 5 QBD 278, the Court at 281. 'Bailment'; N.E. Palmer, *Bailment* 983–984 (2d ed., LBC 1991).

a carrier is only liable for its own negligence. A carrier becomes an involuntary bailee where it remains in possession of the goods at the end of the carriage due to failure of the consignee to take delivery of the goods within a reasonable time. Where goods are stolen from a carrier's warehouse when the transit is at an end, or are destroyed by fire without negligence on the part of its servants, the carrier is not liable.[543] If a road carrier, who had no proper storage, informed the consignee of the fact and disclaimed responsibility for damage arising from this deficiency, the court would probably hold that the carrier was not a warehouseperson (provided no rent was charged) but was an involuntary bailee.[544] Unless the carrier holds the goods expressly and impliedly as a warehouseperson before carriage commences, transit begins, and the goods are possessed as a carrier, when they are delivered to the carrier or to actual or ostensibly authorized agents or employees.[545] Where there is acceptance by a third party or employee without the express or implied authority of the carrier, the goods are not regarded as having been delivered to the carrier.[546]

F. Delay

276. Unless protected by an express term in the contract, a carrier is under a duty to use all reasonable care to deliver goods within a reasonable time.[547] For a carrier to be liable in damages for delay a plaintiff must show failure to deliver within a reasonable time and negligence on the part of the carrier or its employees.[548] A carrier will not be liable for delay beyond its reasonable foreseeability and control.[549] But liability will follow where the carrier negligently either fails to send goods on or holds them beyond a reasonable time at their destination.[550]

G. Deviation

277. At common law no carrier is permitted to deviate from its usual or agreed route.[551] A private road carrier will be liable in such circumstances where no special contract exists. This situation will be exceptional since a private road carrier is normally protected in a contract of carriage by an exemption clause which is subject to the canons of construction laid down by the courts.[552]

---

543. *Brooks Wharf & Bull Wharf Ltd v. Goodman Bros* [1937] 1 KB 534 [[1936] 3 All ER 696] (CA).
544. *See* N.E. Palmer, *Bailment* 984, Ch. 13 (2d ed., LBC 1991).
545. *Soanes Bros v. Meredith* [1963] 2 Lloyd's Rep 293, J. Roskill at 307.
546. *Crows Transport Ltd v. Phoenix Assurance Co Ltd* [1965] 1 WLR 383 [[1965] 1 All ER 596] (CA).
547. *Raphael v. Pickford* (1843) 5 Man & G 551 [134 ER 680].
548. *Taylor v. Great Northern Railway Co* (1866) LR 1 CP 385.
549. Such as the act of a third party: *Taylor v. Great Northern Railway Co* (1866) LR 1 CP 385; imperfect addressing of goods by consignor: *Briddon v. Great Northern Railway Co* (1853) 28 LJ Ex 51; a strike by the carrier's employees: *Sims & Co v. Midland Railway Co* [1913] 1 KB 103; an act of God: *Briddon v. Great Northern Railway Co* (1853) 28 LJ Ex 51.
550. *Gordon v. Great Western Railway Co* (1881) 8 QBD 44.
551. *Taylor v. Great Northern Railway Co* (1866) LR 1 CP 385.
552. *See* J. Livermore, *Exemption Clauses and Implied Obligations in Contracts* (Law Book Co 1986).

H. Misdelivery

278. Where a carrier delivers the goods to any other person than the consignee it is liable for breach of contract and conversion on the basis of misdelivery.[553] If a carrier obeys the consignor's instructions and the goods are delivered to a person who commits a fraud on a consignor, the carrier will not be liable for misdelivery.[554] Delivery to the consignee's address is due performance by the carrier even if the person who takes delivery is not so authorized by the consignee,[555] unless the circumstances should have made the carrier suspicious.[556] A carrier becomes an involuntary bailee where it has unsuccessfully tried to deliver goods to the address indicated and is then only liable for negligence.[557]

I. Transit and Stoppage in Transit

279. Standard contracts of carriage by road specifying where transit begins and ends may be altered by notice from the owner of the goods. Standard contracts usually provide that transit begins when the consignment is handed in at the carrier's place of business or point of collection and ends when the consignment is tendered at the usual place of delivery at the consignee's address within the usual delivery hours of the area. Transit will end where the consignment cannot be delivered or is held by the carrier 'to await order' or 'to be kept until called for' and such instructions are not given or the consignment is not called for and removed within a reasonable time.

280. If the owner of the goods alters the carrier's instructions then the carrier must follow these new directions if it is satisfied that the person giving them is the owner when the orders are given.[558] Delivery to the carrier is deemed to be delivery to the buyer, subject to any contrary agreement made by the parties to the contract of sale.[559] Where the owner becomes insolvent the owner can exercise its right of stopping the goods in transit and requesting the carrier to redeliver them to the owner.[560] When notice of stoppage in transit[561] is given by the owner, the carrier is

---

553. *Stephenson v. Hart* (1828) 4 Bing 476 [130 ER 851].
554. *British Traders & Shippers Ltd v. Ubique Transport Ltd* [1952] 2 Lloyd's Rep 236 (KB).
555. *Heugh v. London & North Western Railway Co* (1870) LR 5 Ex 51.
556. *Stephenson v. Hart* (1828) 4 Bing 476 [130 ER 851].
557. *Heugh v. London & North Western Railway Co* (1870) LR 5 Ex 51.
558. *Scothorn v. South Staffordshire Railway* (1853) 8 Ex 341 [155 ER 1378].
559. *Sale of Goods Act* 1954 (ACT), s. 36; *Sale of Goods Act* 1923 (NSW), s. 35; *Sale of Goods Act* 1972 (NT), s. 35; *Sale of Goods Act* 1896 (Qld), s. 34; *Sale Goods Act* 1895 (SA), s. 32; *Sale of Goods Act* 1896 (Tas), s. 37; *Goods Act* 1958 (Vic), s. 39; *Sale of Goods Act* 1895 (WA), s. 32.
560. *See* Sale of Goods Act (NSW) s. 42; (Vic) s. 46; (Qld) s. 41; (WA) (SA) s. 39; (Tas) s. 44; (ACT) s. 43 (NT) s. 41.
561. To be effective, such notice must be given under such circumstances as to allow the possessor of the goods (or their principal) to advise their servant or agent accordingly. *See Sale of Goods Act* 1923 (NSW); K.C.T. Sutton, *Sales and Consumer Law* 617–618 (4th ed., LBC 1995).

under a duty to redeliver the goods to the owner at the latter's expense. Failure or refusal to do so by the carrier makes it liable to an action for conversion.[562]

281. A private carrier has a specific lien on the goods it carries only if there is a particular agreement to that effect.[563] A carrier (both common and private) by common law may acquire the right to sell the goods after a reasonable time (an 'active lien') and additionally a right to hold goods against freight due for other goods (a 'general lien'). Under standard form contracts of carriage it is usual for the common law lien to be extended to make it active and general, so that a general lien is available against the owner of the goods and enforceable by sale of such goods if charges are not met within a reasonable time after the carrier gives notice to the owner of the goods of the exercise of the lien.[564] A general lien cannot be exercised until the goods reach their destination or the unpaid seller stops them in transit. This right of the unpaid seller has priority over the carrier's general lien.[565] If the carrier remains in possession of the goods at the end of the transit as a warehouseperson, its lien continues. The carrier must take reasonable care of goods held under the exercise of its lien and keep them where they can be conveniently repossessed by the consignor or consignee on payment of the debt due under the lien.[566] The carrier's right to exercise liens under its function as warehouseperson is regulated by statute.[567]

J. Measure of Damages

282. Where no agreement to the contrary exists, a carrier who is responsible for loss or injury to goods arising naturally from its default is liable to compensate the owner.[568] The measure of damages as a general rule is the difference in the market value of the goods at the time and place at which they were due to be delivered and when they were delivered.[569] A carrier is not liable for indirect or consequential

562. *Litt v. Cowley* (1816) 7 Taunt 169 [129 ER 68].
563. *Electric Supply Stores v. Gaywood* (1909) 100 LT 855. This contrasts with the common carrier, which has a right at common law to hold goods against payment of freight: *Skinner v. Upshaw* (1702) 2 Ld Ray 752 [92 ER 3]; *Goldsbrough v. McCulloch* (1868) 5 WW & A'B(L) 154 (SC Vic); *Kilners Ltd v. John Dawson Investment Trust Ltd* (1935) 35 SR (NSW) 274 [52 WN 88] (FC); *Brilawsky v. Robertson & Cannell* (1916) 10 QJPR 113 (SC).
564. *George Barker (Transport) Ltd v. Eynon* [1974] 1 WLR 462 [[1974] 1 All ER 900] (CA).
565. *US Steel Products Co v. GW Railway* [1916] 1 AC 189; *see* N.E. Palmer, *Bailment* 1014 (2d ed., LBC 1991). For a discussion of particular liens *see* N.E Palmer, *Bailment* 943–955 (2d ed., LBC 1991), for example, a workman has a particular lien (a right to retain an item repaired or worked on) against the fee or charge owed by the customer.
566. *See Great Western Railway Co v. Crouch* (1858)3 H & N 183 [157 ER 437], J. Willes at 201–202.
567. For liens exercisable by the carrier *see Mercantile Law Act* 1962 (ACT), ss 17–32; *Warehousemen's Liens Act* 1935 (NSW); *Warehousemen's Liens Act* 1959 (NT); *Warehousemen's Liens Act* 1973 (Qld); *Warehouse Liens Act* 1990 (SA); *Warehousemen's Liens Act* 1959 (Vic); *Warehousemen's Liens Act* 1952 (WA). No corresponding legislation exists in Tasmania: *see* N.E. Palmer, *Bailment* 877 (2d ed., LBC 1991).
568. *Hadley v. Baxendale* (1854) 9 Ex 341 [156 ER 145], B. Alderson at 354–355; *Victoria Laundry (Windsor) Ltd v. Newman Industries Ltd* [1949] 2 KB 528 [[1949] 1 All ER 997] (CA).
569. *C Koufos v. Czarnikow Ltd* [1969] 1 AC 351 [[1967] 3 WLR 1491; [1967] 3 All ER 687].

damages or loss of a particular market unless there is a special contract to this effect. Similarly, a carrier cannot be made liable for any loss of profits or damages incurred by the owner due to the latter's inability to carry out a contract of sale.[570] A carrier will only be liable for loss of exceptional profits if it can be proved that it was aware of the facts which would result in such a loss if it were guilty of delay.[571]

§3. Carriage of Passengers

283. A private carrier for reward is under a duty to exercise reasonable care in the carriage of its passengers, independent of any contract.[572] As a carrier of passengers is not a bailee it does not guarantee the safety of its passengers. However, a private carrier must exercise reasonable care to carry them safely, including any person lawfully on the carrier's vehicle.[573] Such a duty may be excluded or modified by the terms of any contract.[574]

284. A carrier of passengers does not warrant that its vehicles are sound or that they will be fit for the purpose of carriage.[575] However, commercial vehicles are required by statute to adhere to required safety standards: (*see* paragraphs 264–308). A carrier will be liable for harm caused by any defect that a reasonable and careful examination would reveal.[576] The breakdown of a vehicle is prima facie evidence of negligence on the part of the carrier.[577] A passenger would not appear to acquire a right of action for damages for breach of statutory duty only because the carrier fails to comply with regulations as to the construction and use of motor vehicles.[578]

285. A carrier is under a duty to take reasonable care in relation to procedures for passengers entering or alighting from a carrying vehicle. The carrier's obligations are based on principles equally applicable to the carriage of passengers by road and rail. In the case of a passenger entering or alighting from a carrying vehicle, whether or not a carrier is negligent is a question of fact.[579] If passengers are invited

---

570. *See Heskell v. Continental Express Ltd* [1950] 1 All ER 1033 (KB), J. Delvin at 1048.
571. *Horne v. Midland Railway Co* (1873) LR 8 CP 131 (FC).
572. *Maloney v. Commissioner for Railways (NSW)* (1978) 52 ALJR 292 [18 ALR 147] (HC); *Hayes v. Brisbane City Council* (1979) 5 QL 269 (Dist Ct); *Price v. Ramsay* (1882) 16 SALR 95 (FC).
573. *Gregory v. Railways Commissioner (Cth)* (1941) 66 CLR 50 [15 ALJ 283]; *Kelly v. Australasian Steam Navigation Co* (1885) 6 LR (NSW) 233 [2 WN 40] (FC); *King v. Victorian Railways Commissioners* (1892) 18 VLR 250 [13 ALT 293] (FC); *Whitchurch v. Commissioner of Railways* (1901) 4 WALR 53; *Daly v. Commissioner of Railways* (1906) 8 WALR 125 (FC).
574. *Gregory v. Railways Commissioner (Cth)* (1941) 66 CLR 50 [15 ALJ 283]; *Kelly v. Australasian Steam Navigation Co* (1885) 6 LR (NSW) 233 [2 WN 40] (FC).
575. *John Carter (Fine Worsteds) Ltd v. Hanson Haulage (Leeds) Ltd* [1965] 2 QB 495 [[1965] WLR 553; [1965] 1 All ER 113] (CA).
576. *King v. Victorian Railways Commissioners* (1892) 18 VLR 250 [13 ALT 293] (FC); *O'Connor v. British Transport Commission* [1958] 1 WLR 346 [[1958] 1 All ER 558] (CA).
577. *Barkway v. South Wales Transport Co Ltd* [1950] AC 185 [[1950] 1 All ER 392]; *Christie v. Griggs* (1809) 2 Camp 79 [170 All ER 1088].
578. *Barkway v. South Wales Transport Co Ltd* [1950] AC 185 [[1950] 1 All ER 392].
579. *Shirt v. Wyong Shire Council* [1978] 1 NSWLR 631 (CA), J.A. Samuels at 648, affirmed in *Wyong Shire Council v. Shirt* (1980) 146 CLR 40 [54 ALJR 283; 60 LGRA 106; 29 ALR 217].

to alight without the vehicle being stopped then the carrier will be negligent.[580] Negligence will be evidenced if the vehicle moves or jerks during the entrance or alighting of a passenger.[581] A carrier of passengers must take reasonable care that the carrying vehicle does not start while passengers are in the process of entering or alighting.[582] A passenger standing on the step or platform of a carrying vehicle, or a passenger who attempts to alight while it is moving, may be guilty of contributory negligence.[583] The stopping of a carrying vehicle may constitute an invitation to passengers on it to alight.[584]

286. A carrier does not relinquish its obligation to take reasonable care to carry passengers safely if the passenger, in alighting, is put in a position of clear danger, without that passenger being warned or without the carrier providing him or her with an opportunity to avoid the risk.[585] A carrier may incur liability to passengers on a bus who are injured as a result of a start button being rung on board the vehicle by another passenger in the absence of the bus conductor or driver.[586] A carrier has special obligations in relation to securing doors and windows for the safety of passengers. Failure by an employee of a carrier to secure a carrying vehicle's doors before it moves off may be evidence of negligence,[587] as may the striking of a passenger on a platform by the open door of a train.[588] The opening of a door by a passenger while the vehicle is travelling between stations or stops may constitute an act which would not have occurred if ordinary care was used.[589] Where there is a failure by a carrier's employee to secure a door to a passenger vehicle before the commencement of a journey and another employee slams it shut so causing a passenger injury, negligence may be inferred.[590] Showing that a door came open after a passenger leant on it does not prove contributory negligence on the part of the passenger.[591] A notice posted in a carrying vehicle requesting passengers not to put their heads or arms out of windows does not become a condition of the contract of carriage, even where it can be proved to have been drawn to the actual notice of the passengers.[592]

580. *Thomson v. Commissioner for Railways* (1863) 2 SCR (NSW) 292 (FC).
581. *London & North Western Railway Co v. Hellawell* (1872) 26 LT 557 (Ex); *Stockdale v. Lancashire & Yorkshire Railway Co* (1863) 8 LT 289; *Angus v. London Railway Co* (1906) 22 TLR 222 (CA).
582. *Geirk v. Connolly* (1887) 13 VLR 446 [9 ALT 23] (FC); *Davies v. Liverpool Corporation* [1949] 2 All ER 175 (CA).
583. *Hall v. London Tramways Co Ltd* (1896) 12 TLR 611 (CA).
584. *Vautier v. Melbourne Tramway & Omnibus Co Ltd* (1896) 18 ALT 143 (FC Vic).
585. *Thomson v. Commissioner for Railways* (1863) 2 SCR (NSW) 292 (FC).
586. *Hall v. London Tramways Co Ltd* (1896) 12 TLR 611 (CA); *Vardasz v. Melbourne & Metropolitan Tramways Board* (1971) 1 CCR (Vic) 186.
587. *Gee v. Metropolitan Railway Co* (1873) LR 8 QB 161; *Brookes v. London Passenger Transport Board* [1947] 1 All ER 506 (KB).
588. *Hare v. British Transport Commission* [1956] 1 WLR 250 [[1956] 1 All ER 578] (QB).
589. *Potter v. Victorian Railway Commissioners* (1882) 14 ALT 87 (SC Vic).
590. *Dickson v. Commissioner for Railways* (1922) 30 CLR 579 [16 QJPR 130].
591. *Gee v. Metropolitan Railway Co* (1873) LR 8 QB 161.
592. *Cashmore v. Chief Commissioner for Railways & Tramways (NSW)* (1915) 20 CLR 1 [15 SR (NSW) 396; 32 WN 43]; *King v. Victorian Railways Commissioners* (1892) 18 VLR 250 [13 ALT 293] (FC).

287. A carrier of passengers is under a duty to provide them with reasonable accommodation.[593] Damages may be claimed for loss or injury directly caused by overcrowding.[594] Permitting a person who is clearly drunk to travel on the carrier's vehicle does not constitute negligence on the part of the carrier. However, in such circumstances, the carrier is obliged to protect other passengers from injury and annoyance by the drunken person.[595] In contrast, the carrier is not liable for the acts of persons over whom it has no control.[596]

288. A carrier is liable in negligence for damage and injury incidental to the carriage of passengers. A carrier is negligent if it permits a passenger to take with her or him onto the carrying vehicle any article or object likely to injure other passengers.[597] The degree of care to be exercised in an emergency by a carrier will depend on the circumstances of each case.[598] In addition to the duty owed to passengers, a carrier owes a duty of care to pedestrians and other traffic to drive with reasonable care. The standard of judging that reasonable care is that of an ordinarily, sensible, and prudent driver.[599]

289. In the absence of a contract, a private carrier is under no duty to accept passengers' luggage for carriage. Whether a carrier accepts passengers' luggage as a private or common carrier depends on the carrier's representation and its facilities for carrying such luggage.[600] A carrier must provide reasonable facilities for the carrying of passengers' luggage where the goods are safe from damage or theft.[601] Goods are not regarded as passengers' luggage for the purposes of carriage unless they are for the passengers' personal use and are of a kind usually taken by a passenger away from home.[602]

---

593. *Jones v. Great Northern Railway Co* (1918) 34 TLR 467 (Div Ct).
594. *Redpath v. Railway Commissioners* (1900) 21 LR (NSW) 234 [17 WN 47] (FC).
595. *Adderley v. Great Northern Railway Co* [1905] 2 IR 378.
596. *M'Cormick v. Caledonian Railway Co* (1904) 41 SC LR 282 (railway company held not bound to protect a drunken passenger who had alighted from a railway carriage and who had been fatally injured after falling onto the railway line and being run over by a passing train).
597. *East Indian Railway Co v. Kalidas Mukerjee* [1901] AC 396 (PC). *See also* TORTS 33.2 'Negligence.' For carriage of dangerous goods *see* para. 38.
598. *See London Railway Co v. Patterson* (1913) 29 TLR 413 (HL) (reasonable precautions to protect all passengers required by rail carrier in the case of fog).
599. *Vardasz v. Melbourne & Metropolitan Tramways Board* (1971) 1 CCR (Vic) 186.
600. A duty to accept such luggage will normally be the case, and an implication on the part of a carrier to carry luggage may be made: *Macrow v. Great Western Railway Co* (1871) LR 6 QB 612.
601. *Upperton v. Union-Castle Mail Steamship Co Ltd* (1902) 19 TLR 123, affirmed in *Upperton v. Union-Castle Mail Steamship Co Ltd* (1903) 89 LT 289 (CA) (lavatory on board ship held not to be a suitable location for passenger's luggage). 'Reasonable facilities' would appear to imply a location where the goods could not be damaged or stolen.
602. *Britten v. Great Northern Railway Co* [1899] 1 QB 243 (bicycle not regarded as ordinary luggage for carrying on a railway and so not personal luggage to be carried free under railway company's regulations). In most cases, the regulations and contractual provisions of the private carrier would govern what would be regarded as passenger luggage as distinct from goods.

§4. FEDERAL ROAD TRANSPORT LEGISLATION AND REGULATION

I. Freedom of Interstate Trade

290. The Commonwealth has power to legislate in relation to interstate road transport legislation pursuant to the trade and commerce power in section 51(i) of the Constitution, subject to the restriction of section 92. Section 92 provides that trade and commerce between the States shall be absolutely free.[603] The phrase 'trade and commerce including the business of carrying goods and passengers for reward' means that although the Commonwealth can regulate interstate transport it cannot restrict or prevent it. For example, in *Hughes & Vale Pty Ltd v. New South Wales [No. 2]* (1955) 93 CLR 127 [29 ALJ 157], the requirement of interstate road traffic to pay more than a reasonable sum for the use of roads was held to infringe section 92.[604] The balance between reasonable regulation and prohibition of interstate trade has been extensively explored by the courts, as has the issue of what constitutes part of interstate road transport.[605]

II. Competition Law

291. Where 'services' are supplied by a corporation to a consumer in the course of a business, section 60 of the *Australian Consumer Law* formerly section 74(1) of the *Trade Practices Act* 1974 implies a guarantee that the services will be rendered with due care and skill[606]. Section 63 of the *Australian Consumer Law* (formerly section 74(3) of the *Trade Practices Act* 1974) provides that 'services (in the context of section 60) does not include services provided under a contract for or in relation to the transportation or storage of goods for the purposes of a business, trade, profession, or occupation carried in or engaged in by the person for whom the goods are transported or stored.

Although the effect of section 63 is not to imply a warranty into a contract for the storage or transportation of goods for commercial purposes, the courts have taken a broader view of this limitation (particularly the words 'in or in relation to').For example in *PNSL Bhd v. Dalrymple Marine Services Pty Ltd* [2008] 1 Qld R 514;[2007] QCA 429, the Queensland Court of Appeal held that the exclusion

603. *James v. Commonwealth* [1936] AC 578; 55 CLR 1 [10 ALJ 162; [1936] 2 All ER 1449] (PC).

604. *Hughes & Vale Pty Ltd v. New South Wales [No. 2]* (1955) 93 CLR 127 [29 ALJ 157], J. Williams at 189–190.

605. *Russell v. Walters* (1957) 96 CLR 177 [31 ALJ 162]; *Simms v. West* (1961) 107 CLR 157 [35 ALJR 290; [1963] Qd R 156; 56 QJPR 29]; *IXL Timbers Pty Ltd v. A-G (Tas)* (1939) 109 CLR 574 [36 ALJR 328]; *Tamar Timber Trading Co Pty Ltd v. Pilkington* (1968) 117 CLR 353 [41 ALJR 365]; *Holloway v. Pilkington* (1972) 127 CLR 391 [46 ALJR 253]; *Pilkington v. Frank Hammond Pty Ltd* (1974) 131 CLR 124 [48 ALJR 61; 2 ALR 563]; *see Boyd v. Carah Coaches Pty Ltd* (1979) 145 CLR 78 [54 ALJR 33; 27 ALR 161]; *Stoneham v. Simkin* [1977] VR 357 [14 ALR 85]; *Stoneham v. Ryan's Removals Pty Ltd* (1978) 143 CLR 79 [53 ALJR 212; 23 ALR 1]. On the issue of 'border hopping' *see* P. Brazil, *Border Hopping and Section 92 of the Constitution*, 34 ALJ 77 (1960).

606. *See* R. Miller, *Miller's Annotated Trade Practices Act-Australian Competition and Consumer Law* [1.74.5]–[1.74.15] (Thomson Reuters) (subscription service).

clause in the *Trade Practices Act* 1974 did not apply to the towage of a vessel laden with coal[607]. Additionally, where the proper law of the contract is that of an Australian State or Territory that restricts or limits liability for breach of warranty implied by section 63, that State or Territory law will govern the consequences of any breach.[608]

III. Uniform Road Transport Law

292. The *National Transport Commission Act* 2003 (Cth)[609] established the NTC replacing its predecessor the National Road Transport Commission (NRTC). The NTC has the ongoing responsibility to develop, monitor, and maintain uniform or nationally consistent regulatory or operational reforms relating to road, rail, and intermodal transport. It also undertakes to provide the making of regulations in accordance with the Agreement.[610] This Agreement, which was entered into on 30 July 1993 between the Commonwealth, New Zealand, the States, and the ACT and NT, adopted and committed the respective governments to the objectives of improving both road safety and transport efficiency and reduction in the costs of administration of road transport, together with a scheme of development of uniform or consistent road transport law by the NRTC.[611]

293. The NTC regulations set out the model legislation developed by the NTC and agreed by the Australian Transport Council relating to road, rail, and intermodal transport.[612] Included are road transport regulations and other legislative instruments (whether in enacted or model form) developed by the NRTC and agreed by the Australia Transport Council.[613] The Australian Transport Council, established on 11 June 1993, has as its membership the Commonwealth, NZ, the States and the ACT and NT represented by the Prime Minister, Premiers, and Chief Ministers.[614]

294. The Australian Transport Council must prepare a strategic draft plan at least once a financial year for the NTC.[615] The Australian Transport Council is to provide to the members every six-year period following the enactment of the *National*

607. *PNSL Bhd v. Dalrymple Marine Services Pty Ltd* [2008] 1 Qd 511; [2007] QCA 429. J.A. Williams at [31]–[36] noting that the application of the former *Trade Practices Act* 1974 (Cth) was not strictly necessary to consider as the appellants were liable in negligence.
608. *Australian Consumer Law* s. 67 (formerly *Trade Practices Act* 1974 (Cth) s. 74(2A). See *also Watts v. Downard-Pickford (North Queensland) Pty Ltd* (1994) 179 388; *Grace Bros Pty Ltd v Rice* (1981) 71 FLR 129. Both cases were decided before the enactment of s 74(2A).
609. Repealing the *National Road Transport Commission Act* 1991 (Cth); see *National Transport Commission (Consequential Amendments and Transitional Provisions) Act (Cth)* 2003 Sch. 1, s. 4.
610. *National Transport Commission Act* 2003 (Cth) s. 3(a), (b), s. 4.
611. Initially termed the 'Heavy Vehicle Agreement'; s. 3(b)(ii).
612. Section 3(b)(i), (ii).
613. Section 3(b)(ii).
614. Section 4.
615. Section 23.

Transport Commission Act 2003 (Cth) a written report which includes recommendations as to whether the NTC should continue and if the *National Transport Commission Act* 2003 (Cth) should be repealed or amended and reasons for the recommendations.[616]

§5. Operation of Model Legislation

295. Regulations made under the *National Transport Commission Act* 2003 (Cth) set out model legislation and road transport legislation[617] which accords with the Intergovernmental Agreement (the Agreement). The Agreement requires the Commonwealth to submit road transport legislation for inclusion in schedules to Regulations under the Act which implement this requirement.[618] The Regulations provide a single reference point for the road transport legislation. The States, Territories, and the Commonwealth where appropriate may either reference or enact the substance of the model legislation in their own law so establishing a nationally agreed regulatory framework.[619]

296. Each of the Regulations sets out in a schedule an item of road legislation previously developed by the former NRTC and which, in consultation with the jurisdictions, has been identified for this purpose and put in an appropriate form by the NTC.[620] Several Regulations set out road transport legislation (including amendments) which has been enacted into template law. These include Acts and Regulations made by the Commonwealth for ACT, in particular, covering the area of road transport charges, heavy vehicle registration, vehicle operations, and transport of dangerous goods by road and rail. The Regulations will eventually be the only reference point for implementation by all jurisdictions irrespective of the previous form of road transport legislation.[621]

297. The *National Transport Commission Act* 2003 (Cth) provides that the road transport legislation scheduled to the Regulations does not have the force of law.[622] The schedules only operate as a depository for nationally agreed reforms which are then implemented by the jurisdictions. However, the Regulations are legislative instruments for the purposes of the *Legislative Instruments Act* 2003 (Cth).[623]

---

616. Section 53.
617. Sections 52, 7(1).
618. IGA Cl. 13.
619. IGA Cl. 13. *See* Commonwealth Numbered Regulation-Explanatory Statement particularly Attachment B at austlii.edu.ay/cgi-bin/simodisp/au/legis/cth/num_reg_e.
620. As provided by IGA Cl. 14.
621. Section 7(2)(a).
622. The Regulations are not subject to challenge; *see Legislative Instruments Act* 2003 (Cth) s. 44(2) and Sch. 2 r. 7 nor sunsetting; s. 54(2) Legislative Instrument Regulations 1994 (Cth) Sch. 3 r. 4.
623. *See* the *Legislative Instruments Act* 2003 (Cth).

I. Heavy Vehicles

298. The Heavy Vehicle Agreement (originally the 1991 Agreement); *see* (paragraph 74) laid down principles in definitions to be followed by the parties, including 'Road Charge', 'Access Charge', 'Mass Distance Charge', and 'PAYGO'. The definition of a vehicle in the Heavy Vehicle Agreement was one having a Gross Vehicle Mass of more the 4.5 tonnes.[624]

299. The NTC as noted above issues Regulations which include coverage of heavy vehicle operation.[625] The Heavy Vehicle Regulations have as general objects the improvement of road transport safety, minimization of the adverse impacts of road transport on roads, bridges and road infrastructure, the environment and community, and the promotion of effective and efficient observance of road transport law. In particular, the Regulations provide for an effective and efficient compliance with the requirements of road transport law, a system promoting improved outcomes for road safety, the environment, road infrastructure and traffic management and reduction of unfair competitive advantage by improved compliance with and accountability for the requirements of road transport law.[626]

300. Access restrictions are provided for oversize and overmass vehicles such as B-doubles and road trains and network access for other restricted access vehicles.[627] Regulations also limit driving hours for drivers of heavy goods vehicles.[628]

The regulations provide a system recognizing a chain of responsibility of parties who have a role in the transport of goods or passengers by road and make parties accountable for their acts and omissions. These chains of responsibility oblige all parties to take positive steps to prevent breaches of mass, dimension, and loading laws, reducing pressures on road operators and leading to an improved compliance and safer roads. The chain of responsibility requires anyone in control of transport

624. National Road Transport Commission Act 1991 (Cth) Sch. 1, Pt 1 provisions now repealed but incorporated by the National Transport Commission Act (Cth) s. 3(b)(ii) and *see* National Transport Commission (Consequential Amendments and Transitional Provisions) Act (Cth) 2003 Sch. 1, s. 4.

625. *See* National Transport Commission (Road Transport Legislation-Heavy Vehicle Standards Regulations) Regulations 2006 (SLI 25 of 2006) Regulations National Transport Commission (Road Transport Legislation-Higher Mass Limits) Regulation 2006 (SLI of 2006), National Transport Commission (Road Transport Legislation-Restricted Access Vehicle*s Regulations 2006 (SLI 26 of 2006).*

626. *See Heavy Vehicle National Law Transport Act* 2013 (Tas); *Heavy Vehicle Accreditation Scheme Validation Act* 2013 (Tas).

627. *See* National Transport Commission (Road Transport Legislation-Mass and Loading) Regulations 2006 (SLI 25 of 2006); National Transport Commission (Road Transport Legislation-Restricted Access Vehicles Regulations) Regulations 2006 (SLI 26 of 2006).

628. National Transport Commission (Road Transport Legislation-Driving Hours Regulations) Regulations 2006 (SLI 20 of 2006).

operations (not just the driver) to be held responsible for breaches of road laws and may be legally liable.[629]

In February 2014 the Heavy Vehicle National Law, covering all vehicles over 4.5 tonnes, commenced in the ACT. NSW, Queensland and SA, Tas, and Vic, without the participation of WA and the NT. The law covers matters relating to vehicle standards, mass dimensions and loadings, fatigue management, the Intelligent Access Program, heavy vehicle accreditation and on road enforcement. The Heavy Vehicle National Law is administered by the National Heavy Vehicle Regulator based in Brisbane.[630]

II. Vehicle Charges

301. National charges for heavy vehicles based on defined charging principles were originally enshrined in the *Road Transport Charges Act (ACT) Act* 1993 (Cth) and have been incorporated in the Regulations.[631] The jurisdictions are obliged to determine annual registration charges for vehicles of 4.5 tonnes or over and the charges for the grant of a permit to operate a vehicle, or a combination of a vehicle. The Regulations contain key definitions for the purposes of the charging regime.[632]

III. Vehicle Operations

302. The aim of the Regulations for vehicle operation is the same as those under the *Transport Reform (Vehicles and Traffic) Act* 1993 (Cth) that is, they are designed to improve the safety and efficiency of transport on roads and other areas that are open to and used by the public, and to reduce the costs of administration of that transport. Light vehicle standards and roadworthiness are governed by the Road Transport Reform (Vehicles and Traffic) Regulations. The *Motor Vehicles Standards Act* 1979 (Cth) is the source of standards for the design and construction of motor vehicles.

629. *See Heavy Vehicle Transport Act 2009* (Tas) s. 3. *See* http://www.ntc.gov.au for projected developments in the National Heavy Vehicles Compliance Review and the role of the National Heavy Vehicle Regulator.

630. National Heavy Vehicle Regulator 'Heavy Vehicle National Law and Regulations' available at https//www.nhvr.gov.au/law-policies/heavy-vehicle-national-law-and-regulations, (viewed 1 Apr. 2016).

631. *See National Transport Commission Act 2003* (Cth) s. 3(b)(ii).

632. Definitions include MRC (mass rating for charging), operating mass, truck, prime mover, long combination prime mover, medium combination truck, semi trailer, bus, special purpose vehicle, compliance plate, indivisible load, load carrying vehicle, and loaded mass. *See* National Transport Commission (Road Transport Legislation – Road Transport Charges Act) Regulations 2006 (SLI 32, 34) and National Commission (Road Transport legislation-Road Transport Charges Act) Amendment Regulations 2006 (No. 1) (SLI 31, 33).

IV. Australian Road Rules

303. The Australian Road Rules regulations[633] apply to vehicles and road related areas and occupy much of the areas previously covered by State and Territory legislation. The regulations include coverage of speed limits, turns, direction signals, give way procedures, traffic signs and road markings, lights on vehicles, public buses, and tow trucks. The regulations define a road as an area open to or to be used by the public and is developed for the main use of driving or riding motor vehicles. Separate regulations deal with driver licensing again providing uniform provision where disparate State and Territory legislation previously applied.[634]

The Australian Government Department of Infrastructure and Regional Development states:

> Vehicle registration and driver licensing are the responsibility of State and Territory governments. Each State and Territory vehicle registration and driver licensing authority participates in the Ausroads Registration and Licensing Task Force, as does Commonwealth Department of Infrastructure and Regional Development. The Task Force promotes harmonization and consistency for vehicle registration across Australia and facilitates collaboration between jurisdictions. It also develops and promotes national policies and procedures to harmonise driver licensing schemes and ensure the seamless transfer of driver licences across jurisdictional borders.[635]

The NTC describes the *Australian Road Rules* as:

> [the Australian Road Rules] form the basis of the Road Rules of each Australian state and territory. For the most part, each state and territory has copied the Rules into their own laws, however not every provision of the Rules has been copied exactly in each state and territory, Also there are a number of provisions in the Rules that specifically leave certain matters for determination to state and territory governments.

V. Dangerous Goods

304. The Uniform Code for the Carriage of Dangerous Goods had been taken up by existing State and Territory laws[636] before the regulations to cover this area

633. *See* National Transport Commission (Road Transport Legislation-Australian Road Rules) Regulations 2006 Sch. 1; National Transport Commission (Road Transport Legislation-Australian Road Rules) Regulations 2006 (SLI 13 of 2006) and (SLI 12 of 2006).
634. *See* National Transport Commission (Road Transport Legislation-Driver Licensing) Regulations 2006 (SLI 19 of 2006).
635. *See* Australian Government Department of Infrastructure and Regional Transport 'Austroads Registration and Licensing Task Force'; at https//ww.ntc.gov.au/roads/rules-compliance/the Australian-road-rules/ (viewed April 2016).
636. *See Dangerous Goods (Road Transport) Act* 2009 (ACT), *Dangerous Goods (Road and Rail Transport) Act* 2008 (NSW), *Dangerous Goods (Road and Rail Transport) Act* 2003 (NT), *Dangerous Goods Safety Management Act* 2009 (Qld), Dangerous Substances *(Dangerous Goods Transport)*

were set out by the NTC which in turn used the provisions *Road Transport Reform (Dangerous Goods) Act* 1995 (Cth) as a template.[637]

305. The regulations provides for safety in the transport of dangerous goods by road and rail. 'Dangerous goods' are defined as a substance or article prescribed as dangerous goods. 'Transport' in relation to dangerous goods include the loading or unloading of the goods for the purpose of transport by road or rail. The regulations do not apply to dangerous goods that are in a container designed to and which form part of the fuel or battery system of a vehicle's engine, fuel burning appliance or other part of a vehicle's propulsion equipment.

306. Exemption from the regulations may be granted when it is not reasonably practical for compliance with its provisions and granting the exemption would not be likely to create a risk of death or injury to a person or harm the environment greater than if there were compliance or where exemption would not cause unnecessary administrative or enforcement difficulties. A person assisting in a situation in which an emergency or accident involves dangerous goods is exempted from civil liability.

307. A person is required to be accredited under the regulations to hold a licence or use a licensed vehicle for the carriage of dangerous goods. It is breach of the regulations if dangerous goods are not transported in a safe manner.

VI. Compliance and Enforcement

308. Compliance and enforcement provisions under the regulations[638] include enforcement and penalties, the appointment of officers and their powers, evidentiary provisions, procedural matters, and reviews and appeals. The regulations may provide for the granting of exemptions from provisions of the regulation and create offences for breach of the regulations.

VII. State and Territory Law

309. For State and Territory road law *see Laws of Australia: Transport* 34.1, [34.1.440]–[34.1.510]

Regulations 2008 (SA), *Dangerous Goods (Road and Rail Transport) Regulations* 1998 (Tas), *Dangerous Goods (Transport by Road and Rail) Regulations* 2008 (Vic), *Dangerous Goods Safety (Road and Rail Transport of Non-Explosives) Regulations* 2007 (WA).

637. *See National Transport Commission Act* 2003 (Cth) s. 3(b)(ii). *See National Transport Commission (Road Transport Legislation-Dangerous Goods Regulations) Regulations* 2006 (18 of 2006).

638. *See* National Transport Commission (Road Transport Legislation-Compliance and Enforcement Regulations) Regulations 2006 (SLI 25 of 2006).

Chapter 2. Carriage by Rail

§1. Federal Legislation

310. While the Commonwealth Government has no direct constitutional power over railways (except for military purposes), it does have power to acquire or construct railways in a State either by agreement or with the consent of that State.[639]

I. Commonwealth and Railway Management

311. In 1997/1998, the Commonwealth Government sold to three private operators interstate freight and passenger services that the National Rail Corporation in 1993 had taken over from the earlier Australian National Railways Commission.[640] In 1998, the ARTC was formed [*see* below] which took over the mainline interstate track which had been run by the National Rail Corporation. The Commonwealth has, therefore, retreated from direct involvement in rail management in Australia. The Commonwealth Government has no direct constitutional power over railways (except for military purposes) but it does have power to acquire or construct railways in a State by agreement or with the consent of that State.[641]

II. State Authorities: Rail Provision

A. New South Wales

312. Rail Corp has as its principal objectives under the *Transport Administration Act* 1988 (NSW) to deliver a safe and reliable railway passenger service in NSW in an efficient, effective, and financially responsible manner, and to ensure the part of the NSW rail network vested in or owned by Railcorp enables safe and reliable railway passenger and freight services to be provided in an efficient, effective, and responsible manner.[642] Railcorp is also to maintain reasonable priority and certainty of access for railway passenger services, to promote and facilitate access to the rail network it owns[643] and to be a successful business and so operate at least as

---

639. Constitution, s. 51(xxxiii), (xxxiv). The Commonwealth reserves the right under the *Australian National Railways Commission Sale Act* 1997 (Cth) Pt 2, to use the national rail system for defence purposes.
640. *The National Rail Corporation Agreement Act* 1992 (Cth) gave effect to an agreement made on 30 Jul. 1992 between the Commonwealth, NSW, Qld, Vic, and WA setting up the National Rail Corporation. The National Rail Corporation was jointly owned by the NSW and Victorian Governments. The National Rail Corporation and the NSW owned freight operator, Freightcorp was jointly sold in June 2002 operating privately as Pacific National.
641. Constitution, s. 51(xxxii), (xxxiv).
642. *Transport Administration Act* 1988 (NSW) s. 5 10(a), (b).
643. This provision (s. 2(b) under s. 5(5)) does not apply to any part of the NSW rail network that is subject to an ARTC lease or licence (*see* [82] above).

efficiently as any comparable business and maximizing the net worth of the States investment in Railcorp.[644]

313. Railcorp is required to have regard to the interests of community in which it operates and conduct its business operations to comply with ecologically sustainable development[645] and to show a sense of responsibility towards regional development and decentralization in Railcorp's operations.[646]

B. *Queensland*

314. Aurizon, formerly QR National, is a publicly listed freight rail company previously owned by the Queensland government. Its assets were transferred to QR National Ltd in July 2010. QR was rebranded as Aurizon in December 2012. QR was split in two in July 2010 with QR taking over the coal business and bulk mineral and grain haulage in Qld and WA and containerized freight between Cairns, Brisbane, Sydney, Melbourne, Adelaide, and Perth. The objectives for rail under the *Transport Infrastructure Act* 1994 (Qld) are to establish a regime that contributes to overall transport effectiveness and efficiency, provides for adequate levels of safety, contributes to lower transport costs by allowing the maximum flexibility in rail transport operations consistent with safety objectives.[647] The objectives also include allowing railway managers to make decisions on a commercial basis and provide a framework under which Qld Rail may operate under the *Government Owned Corporation Act* 1993 (Qld).[648] Qld Rail is not a common carrier.[649]

The transport of Dangerous goods in Qld is governed by the Uniform Code for the Carriage of Dangerous Goods and the *Dangerous Goods Safety Management Act* 2009 (Qld).[650]

C. *South Australia*

315. The *Railways (Operation and Access) Act* 1997 (SA) has as its objectives the operation of a rail system in South Australia that is efficient and responsive to the needs of industry and the public and to facilitate the efficient allocation of resources in the rail transport segment of the transport industry.[651] The objectives

644. *See Transport Administration Act* 1988 (NSW) s. 5(c).
645. *Transport Administration Act* 1988 (NSW) s. 2(e), *see Protection of the Environment Act* 1991 (NSW) s. 6(22).
646. *Transport Administration Act* 1988 (NSW) s. 5(2)(f).
647. *Transport Infrastructure Act* 1994 (Qld) s. 2(2) (d)(i)–(iii).
648. *Transport Infrastructure Act* 1994 (Qld) s. 2(2)(d)(v), (vi).
649. *Transport Infrastructure Act* 1994 (Qld) s. 248. Conditions of carriage of goods and access provisions are governed by standard conditions and Australian Rail Track Corporation requirements.
650. *See* now *National Transport Commission (Road Transport Legislation-Dangerous Goods Regulations) Regulations* 2006 (12 of 2006).
651. *Railways (Operation and Access) Act* 1997 (SA) s. 3(a), (d).

also include the facilitation of competitive markets in the provision of railway services and the promotion of access to railway services on fair commercial terms and on a non-discriminatory basis.[652] The regulator under the *Railways (Operation and Access) Act* 1997 (SA) is the Essential Services Commission.[653]

D. Tasmania

316. The Tasmania Government took over the rail network from the previous private operator (Pacific National) in 2009. The *Rail Company Act* 2009 (Tas) provides for the establishment and registration under the *Corporations Law* of a State-owned company to acquire, own, and operate a rail business in Tas.[654] The Act provides for the transfer between the company and Crown (or vice versa) of rail infrastructure and related assets, liabilities, and contracts.[655]

The *Emu Bay Railway (Operation and Acquisition) Act* 2009 (Tas) authorizes the purchase by the Tasmanian Government of the West Coast Railway, including the rail business and assets from the previous owner and operator (Pacific National).[656]

E. Victoria

317. The *Rail Management Act* 1996 (Vic) provides the regime for rail management in Victoria.[657] The Act abolished V/Line Freight and made as its successor the Public Transport Commission (PTC).[658] The urban rail system is operated by Metro under the PTC. Associated rail infrastructure may be declared under the Act to be rail infrastructure.[659] Access to the rail network is dealt with under the *Rail Management Act* 1996 (Vic) setting out the obligations of the access provider and the regime for access management dispute by which the Essential Services Commission determines such disputes.[660] Access providers are under pricing calculations for rail transport services.[661] Rail and tram operators using lease or licence in connection with a rail or tram passenger service are subject to terms and conditions.[662]

---

652. *Railways (Operation and Access) Act* 1997 (SA) s. 3(c), (e).
653. Railways (Operation and Access) Act 1997 (SA) s. 9; *see* Essential Services Act 2002 (SA).
654. *Railway Company Act* 2009 (Tas) s. 3., 3(a).
655. *Railway Company Act* 2009 (Tas) s. 3(c). Part 5 of the Act provides for regulations to be made by the Minister or the Secretary of the Department of Infrastructure, Energy, and Resources (DIER).
656. *Emu Bay Railway (Operations and Acquisition) Act* 2009 (Tas) by s. 12 amending the *Rail Infrastructure Act* 2007 (Tas) and the *Boundary Fences Act* 1908 (Tas) and by s. 13 repealing the *Emu Bay Railway Act* 1976 (Tas).
657. *Rail Management Act* 1996 (Vic) s. 1.
658. *Rail Management Act* 1996 (Vic) s. 106A.
659. *Rail Management Act* 1996 (Vic) s. 3.
660. *Rail Management Act* 1996 (Vic) s. 38ZZX. The Essential Service Commission was set up by the *Essential Services Commission Act* 2001 (Vic).
661. *Rail Management Act* 1996 (Vic) s. 38ZZY.
662. *Rail Management Act* 1996 (Vic) s. 65.

F. Western Australia

318. The *Railways (Access) Act* 1998 (WA) states as the main object as the establishment of a rail access regime that encourages the efficient use of, and investment in, rail facilities by facilitating a contestible market for rail operations.[663] The *Railway (Access) Act* provides for the conduct of rail operators; the industry participant is not a common carrier.[664] The *Railways (Access) Act* 1998 (WA) enables the Minister to establish a Code to give effect to the Competition Principles Agreement in respect of railway infrastructure to be available for use by persons other than the railway owner to carry on rail operations under agreements with the railway owner or determinations made by arbitration.[665]

The rail lines in the south-west of Western Australia are leased to a private operator WestNet Rail and mining companies manage rail lines in the Pilbara region.[666]

III. Standard Conditions of Rail Carriage

319. Pacific National in its Standard Conditions of Carriage used in NSW, Qld, and Vic clearly states it is not a common carrier[667] and is entitled to subcontract part or all of its obligations or terms.[668] Pacific National's employees, agents, and subcontractors and each rail access authority and their employees, agents, and subcontractors have the benefit of the contract as if they were parties as benefited persons.[669] Goods means any goods accepted on behalf of the customer, or picked up with those goods (including packaging, pallets, or containers) and any rolling stock accepted from or on behalf of the customer.[670] A consumer as defined by the *Trade Practices Act* 1974 (Cth) retains any rights under that Act.[671] Pacific National makes no express warranties under the contract and excludes all conditions and warranties and terms implied by law nor guarantees the time of departure or arrival of the goods and does not have to inform the customer of that arrival.[672]

320. Pacific National may charge for any additional expenses it incurs as a result of an incorrect declaration by the customer of the weight, volume, description, or packaging of the goods and the cost of repackaging or reloading of goods to comply with any laws. Also where there is cancellation by the customer of any services such charges will also apply demurrage or detention charges will apply as the result

663. *Railways (Access) Act* 1998 (WA) s. 2A. *See also Rail Freight System Act* 2000 (WA).
664. *Rail (Access) Act* 1998 (WA) ss 21–25; z7.
665. *Railways (Access) Act* 1998 (WA) s. 4. *See* Pt 3 for functions of Regulator.
666. *Rail Management Act* 1996 The Kalgoorlie-Adelaide rail section is owned by the Australian Rail Track Corporation.
667. These Standard Conditions were helpfully provided by Ms Maria Festa media officer on behalf of Asciano/Pacific National. Cl. 2.1. For State and Territory Law *see* Laws of Australia: Transport 34.1.
668. Cl. 1.3.
669. Cl. 1.4.
670. Cl. 1.5.
671. Cl.2.1.
672. Cl. 2.2.

of the customer's act or omission preventing Pacific National from using any rolling stock, vehicle, or other item of equipment. Customers will also be liable for storage or any other charge in relation to the goods, and a late payment fee and any expenses incurred in connection with overdue accounts.[673]

321. The customer promises Pacific National and other benefited persons that they have sole ownership of the goods or if there are other owners the customer acts as their agent and that they agree to the handling, transport, and storage of the goods and the supply of services on the terms of this contract.[674] The customer indemnifies Pacific National against any claim in connection with the contract, the supply of services or the handling, transport, or storage of the goods from any person other than the customer (including the sender where the customer is not also the sender).[675] The customer promises that the consignment note has been completed accurately and all the information provided is accurate[676] and that the goods are packaged to withstand handling, transport, and storage and that all the laws in connection with the goods have been complied with[677] and the packing, loading, and restraint of the goods ensure that the goods can be lawfully handled, transported, and stored.[678] The customer also promises that all laws have been complied with in connection with any rolling stock, vehicle, or equipment supplied by the customer, including holding the necessary accreditation as a railway operator in each jurisdiction through which the equipment is likely to travel.[679] The customer promises that he or she has not asked Pacific National to handle, transport, or store goods in any way that could be unlawful.[680] The customer undertakes to indemnify Pacific National for any loss or damage (including property) caused to any person as a result of the customer's breach of contract (including breach promises). These indemnities operate irrespective of whether any loss or damage arises from a wilful, deliberate, or unauthorized act or omission by Pacific National or by any benefited persons.[681]

322. The customer must obtain all necessary rights for Pacific National to supply the services, including access to any private sidings and roads[682] and take proper care of all rolling stock, vehicles, and other equipment belonging to Pacific National or any benefited person while in the control of the customer.[683] The customer must comply with all reasonable directions given by Pacific National or a benefited person and notify Pacific National in writing in advance of any special exemption, examination, authority, or permit required in relation to the goods and the way they

673. Cl. 4.4.
674. Cl. 5.2(a).
675. Cl. 5.2(b).
676. Cl. 5.2(c).
677. Cl. 5.2(e).
678. Cl. 5.2(d).
679. Cl. 5.2(f).
680. Cl. 5.2(h).
681. Cl. 5.2(j).
682. Cl. 6.1(a).
683. Cl. 6.1(b).

are packed and loaded.[684] Where the customer is responsible for packing and loading the goods the customer must ensure all goods and any rolling stock, vehicles, or other equipment and are restrained safely, securely and in accordance with all laws and any reasonable loading and restraint requirements (including any applicable rail corridor, station and siding loading gauges and dimensions).[685] The customer must also ensure that the mass of goods within the container, rolling stock or vehicle is within the carrying capacity and is evenly and safely distributed and restrained and in accordance with all laws and any requirements (including limitations) of the relevant rail access or road authority.[686] Where the customer is responsible for packing, loading, or unloading they must ensure the goods, containers, rolling stock, and vehicles are packed, loaded, and unloaded safely.[687] If the customer fails to comply with the above packing or unloading provisions Pacific National has the discretion at the customer's cost repack or reload the container, rolling stock or vehicle or require the customer to do so; refuse to carry the goods or delay its carriage; remove the goods from Pacific National's rolling stock or vehicle, or require the customer to remove the goods.[688]

323. Dangerous goods are those classified as such under the Australian Dangerous Goods Code, or if they might injure people or damage property or the environment. They include goods that are or may become poisonous, corrosive, volatile, explosive, flammable, or radioactive.[689] If Pacific National or any of the benefited persons reasonably consider that the dangerous goods may cause injury or damage, they may at the customer's cost destroy or dispose of the goods or take any other appropriate action in relation to the goods.[690] Neither Pacific National nor any of the benefited persons will be liable to the customer for the above actions.[691] The customer will always bear all risk of loss of or damage to, or arising in connection with, dangerous goods.[692] The customer must pre-book all dangerous goods; collect dangerous goods on the day of arrival at destination; comply with the Dangerous Goods Code (including making all declarations); and give Pacific National a full and accurate written inventory of dangerous goods, including if requested an emergency procedures guide.[693]

324. The customer authorizes Pacific National to use any method for handling, transporting, or storing the good; deviate from any usual route of transport or place of storage; weigh or measure the goods; open any container or inspect the goods to determine their nature, conditions, ownership, or destination; claim a general or particular lien over the goods and any related documents for outstanding payments for

684. Cl. 6.1(d).
685. Cl. 6.2(a).
686. Cl. 6.2(b).
687. Cl. 6.3(a).
688. Cl. 6.4(a).
689. Cl. 7.1.
690. Cl. 7.3.
691. Cl. 7.4.
692. Cl. 7.5.
693. Cl. 7.2.

the goods; sell any goods held by Pacific National for outstanding payments by public auction or private sale; in the case of perishables and dangerous goods immediately in other cases one month.[694] The customer is liable for any costs, liability, loss, or damage (including increased costs in maintenance) resulting from the customer's possession or use (including for the purpose of packing, loading or unloading) of Pacific National's rolling stock, vehicles, and equipment. Where these are supplied by the customer to Pacific National the customer is liable for all costs, liability, loss, or damage relating to their use by Pacific National.[695]

325. Pacific National will attempt to deliver to the address (including a private siding or private road) nominated by the customer. Delivery will be deemed to have been effected when Pacific National receives a signed receipt or delivery docket.[696] If that address is unattended delivery is deemed to have occurred and Pacific National may leave the goods. If that address is unattended or Pacific National cannot deliver the goods for any reason, Pacific National may at its discretion; dispose of dangerous goods immediately; store the goods, or redeliver the goods to the customer, and if it elects to do so charge the customer any costs Pacific National may incur.[697] If the customer does not accept delivery of the goods or Pacific National stores the goods for more than thirty days after giving the customer then Pacific National may dispose of or sell the goods on any terms after giving notice to the customer that this is to occur and apply any proceeds of sale against Pacific National's charges and costs of disposal or sale. Any remaining balance from the proceeds of sale must be paid to the customer on demand.[698]

326. If the customer believes Pacific National is liable it must notify Pacific National immediately and send written notice of claim within seven days. If Pacific National does not receive such notice within that time it will have no liability to the customer who will remain liable to pay Pacific National's charges.[699] Pacific National will have no liability to the customer even if the claim is given within seven days if the customer does not commence legal proceedings against Pacific National within twelve months after the date of ordering the services.[700] Services are supplied at customer's risk and it bears all risk of loss or damage to or arising in connection with the goods. The customer acknowledges its responsibilities under laws relating to the goods and the way they are loaded and packed and will at all times comply with all such laws. Pacific National and the benefited persons are not liable for any delay, loss, or damage arising from the supply or failure to supply services (including any loss of, deterioration in, misdelivery of, or failure to deliver goods) for any reason whatsoever, including breach of contract, negligence, breach of duty as bailee or Pacific National's wilful act or default.[701] Pacific National and

694. Cl. 8.1.
695. Cl. 9.1; 9.2.
696. Cl. 10.1.
697. Cl.; 10.3.
698. Cl. 10.4(b).
699. Cl. 11.1.
700. Cl. 11.2.
701. Cl. 12.2.

the benefited persons have the benefit of these exclusions and limitations of liability even if any loss or damage arises on the basis of the above exclusions and limitations. These exclusions and limitations also apply to any claims for consequential losses, including loss of profits.[702] Pacific National limits any liability to the customer from any cause whatsoever at its discretion to refunding the amount paid for the services; resupplying the services; or paying the cost of having the services resupplied.[703] Title and risk in the goods remains with the customer (as between the customer and Pacific National) even while the goods remain in Pacific National's possession.[704]

§2. Australian Rail Track Corporation Agreement

327. The ARTC Agreement sets out the terms and conditions under which an accredited operator may operate on the rail network (as defined).[705] Under the Agreement, the ARTC grants the operator the use and availability of the network it owns and train paths (track access rights).[706] An accredited operator is one that is accredited under the *Rail Safety Acts* in each State and Territory in which the operator runs its service on the network. An accredited owner is one, including the ARTC, similarly accredited.[707] The ARTC disclaims responsibility for any loss, additional cost, or other damage suffered by an operator in the event that a train path or an operator's train is not delivered on time to its ultimate destination.[708] The ARTC warrants an operator right of access to the network.[709] The operator in its turn warrants that the rolling stock it operates is in good and safe operational standard and condition and the other equipment it uses is of safe standard.[710] The operator agrees to comply with the Code of Practice Commonwealth Network Operations and the Dangerous Goods Code.[711]

328. The ARTC is not to discriminate, in complying with the Agreement, between government and non-government users of the network and between any two governments or two non-government users. The ARTC is also to treat all operators similarly in respect of similar services they purchase.[712] The operator is required to give an indemnity to the ARTC from all claims regarding:

(1) death or injury of any person;

702. Cl. 12.4.
703. Cl. 12.5.
704. Cl. 1.
705. *See* Sch. 1 to the Agreement.
706. Cl. 2.1.
707. Cl. 1.1.
708. Cl. 2.3.
709. Cl. 5.2.
710. Cl. 5.4.
711. Cl. 5.5.12.1.
712. Cl. 5.6.

(2) any loss of, or damage to, or destruction of, any property of the ARTC (including the network), the operator or any other person; arising out of; and
(3) the use by the operator of the network, the failure of any system or equipment owned or operated by the ARTC.[713]

I. Access Regime for Rail

329. The Australian Access regime is set out in Part III of *Competition and Consumer Act (Cth)* 2010. The process under Part III first determines whether or not a service is 'essential', and second, providing arbitration where the parties are unable to agree on access arrangements or pricing.[714] Essential is not defined in Part III which requires a person to seek a declaration of a particular service[715]. A service can only be declared if access to the service would promote a material increase in competition in another market; it would be uneconomical for anyone to develop another facility to provide the service; the facility to which access is required is of national significance; access to the facility can be provided without undue risk to human health or safety; there is not an existing effective access regime in relation to the service and access would not be contrary to the national interest. The 'service' is simply a right or benefit provided, granted, or conferred in relation to a facility which in Part III means a physical asset or a set of such assets essential for service provision which shows features of a natural monopoly.[716]

A service has been held to include services at a major airport and the use of a rail track network. In *BHP Billiton Iron Ore Pty Ltd v. National Competition Council* [2008] HCA 45 a dispute existed over access to BHP Billiton's iron ore extraction, processing, and shipping operations in WA. The High Court confirmed that while BHP Billiton may have used the line to which access was sought as an integrated part of its process for iron ore extraction, processing, and shipping, access to rail lines could not be denied on the basis that it involved the use of production process.[717]

713. Cl. 15.1.
714. *Competition and Consumer Act* 2010 s. 44F. For details of the access procedure and status of declarations under Part III *see Laws of Australia: Transport* Law Book Co [34.1.570].
715. *Competition and Consumer Act* 2010 s. 44G.
716. *Re Sydney Airports Corporation Ltd* (2000) 156 FLR 10.
717. *BHP Billiton Iron Ore Pty Ltd v. National Competition Council* [2008] HCA 45.

Chapter 3. Carriage by Air

§1. Introduction

330. The *Civil Aviation (Carriers' Liability) Act* 1959–1991 (Cth) gives force of law in Australia to three international agreements to which Australia is a party concerning international carriage by air of passengers and goods: the Warsaw Convention, the Hague Protocol, and the Guadalajara Convention. Intrastate carriage of passengers by air by holders of airline or charter licences in the course of commercial transport operations under a contract of carriage is controlled by State legislation. The State Acts that apply to such carriage adopt the Commonwealth provisions applying to interstate carriage of passengers, so that a uniform scheme applies to both types of carriage by air under Commonwealth and State legislation.[718]

331. The right of the Commonwealth to exercise general control over civil air carriage was firmly established in *Airlines of New South Wales Pty Ltd v. New South Wales* (1964) 113 CLR 1. In 1963, Airlines of NSW Pty Ltd (a subsidiary of Ansett Transport Industries Ltd) challenged the validity of the *State Transport (Co-ordination) Act* 1931 (NSW) in relation to the provisions governing State licensing of aircraft engaging in intrastate air flights. The NSW Commissioner for Transport had decided to cancel licences held by the plaintiff company for particular intrastate services and reallocate these to a rival company, East-West Airlines; in return the plaintiff company was granted some of the unprofitable routes operated by East-West Airlines. Airlines of NSW Pty Ltd claimed that the Commonwealth *Air Navigation Act* and *Regulations*, including the Federal licensing of air transport services, covered all air navigation within the Commonwealth and the additional licensing system set up by NSW was inconsistent with Commonwealth law and, thus, invalid under section 109 of the Constitution. The High Court held that the provisions of the State Act were not inconsistent with the Federal law and the Airlines of NSW Pty Ltd was not entitled to use aircraft within NSW without a licence under the State Act. The Commonwealth has the right to make navigational law applicable to all flying operations in Australia. The States, however, may still exercise licensing control for non-navigational reasons.[719]

---

718. *See Commonwealth Powers (Air Transport) Act* 1952 *(Tas); R v. Public Vehicle Licensing Appeal Tribunal* of *Tasmania: Ex parte ANA Pty Ltd. See also Commonwealth Powers (Air Transport) Act* 1952 (Qld); 1921 (SA).

719. *Airlines of New South Wales Pty Ltd v. New South Wales* (No. 2) (1964–1965) 113 CLR 54; *Rv. Burgess: Ex Parte Henry* (1936) 55 CLR 608. *See Transport: Laws* of *Australia* (LBC to date) paras 268–275. *See also* Industry Commission, *Intrastate Aviation Report* No. 25 (Canberra, 1992), 42–54. The 1991 Act never licensed air services. In New South Wales under the *Air Transport Act* 1964 (NSW) a licence is required by an operator for a regular public transport or charter service; in Qld commercial air transport operators require a licence under the *Transport Operations (Passenger Transport) Act* 1994 (Qld) but such services are open to competition; South Australia have never licensed intrastate air services and Vic has not done so since 1955; in the NT, all commuter air services were deregulated in 1992 by the *Aviation Repeal Act* 1992 (NT); in Tasmania the *Traffic Act* 1925 (Tas) provides for the licensing of regular air service and charter operators. However, intrastate air services in Tasmania have been de facto deregulated since 1997 with the demise of

§2. Warsaw Convention (Amended)

332. The Warsaw Convention 1929 on international carriage by air is given force of law in Australia by section 11(1) of the *Civil Aviation (Carriers' Liability) Act* 1959 (Cth).[720] Australia has ratified amendments made to the Convention by the Hague Protocol 1955, but not all countries that were parties to the Convention have done the same. Because these amendments apply only to carriage involving the territory of parties that have ratified the Protocol, the original Convention without the Protocol amendments continues to govern transport involving the territory of some States. The United States, for example, has not ratified the amendments made by the Hague Protocol. The Convention applies under the basic application provision, Article 1(1), to all 'international carriage', as defined, of persons, baggage or cargo by aircraft performed for reward, or performed gratuitously by an air transport undertaking (including carriage by a State) or by a legally constituted public body, but not including carriage under an international postal convention: Article 2. 'International carriage' is defined in Article 1(2) and (3) as carriage in which, according to the agreement between the parties, the place of departure and the place of destination are within the territory of two parties to the Convention, or within the territory of one such party, if there is an agreed stopping place in the territory of another country (whether that country is a party to the convention or not). The Convention, thus, applies only to transport involving States that are parties to the Convention.

§3. Successive Carriers

333. Where the first carrier and the passenger or consignor agree that carriage is to be performed by several successive air carriers, and regard the carriage as a single operation, the carriage is deemed to be one undivided carriage for the purposes of the Convention: Article 1(3). In such cases, each carrier who accepts baggage or cargo is subject to the rules of the Convention, and is deemed to be one of the parties to the contract of carriage in so far as the contract deals with the part of the carriage which is performed under its supervision: Article 30(1). The passenger or consignor has a right of action against the last carrier, and each may take action

---

what was then that State's sole operator Airlines of Tasmania. In Western Australia, the jet air network is open to competition, on other routes non-exclusive licences are issued to single operators, exclusive licences are issued to operators of remote subsidized services in the north of Western Australia; see *Transport Co-ordination Act* 1966 (WA).

720. The first Commonwealth aviation statute, the *Air Navigation Act* 1920 (Cth) empowered the Governor-General to make regulations to give effect to the Paris Convention of 1919 and, further, to make regulations providing for the control of air navigation throughout the Commonwealth and Territories. The Act was passed on the assumption that the Commonwealth Parliament possessed three main sources of primary power: (a) interstate and commerce power under s. 51(1) of the Constitution; (b) the external affairs power in s. 51(xxix); and (c) the power to make regulations for the Territories under s. 122. *See also R v. Burgess; Ex parte Henry* (1936) 55 CLR 605.

against the carrier that performed the carriage during which destruction, loss, damage, or delay took place (these carriers being jointly and severally liable to the passenger or the consignor and consignee): Article 30(3).

§4. Baggage Check

334. The carrier must deliver a baggage check for the carriage of baggage other than small personal items of which the passenger takes charge: Article 4(1). The baggage check must contain specified information about the baggage and the carriage, and a statement that the carriage is subject to the rules relating to liability established by the Convention: Article 4(3). Absence, irregularity, or loss of the baggage check does not affect the existence or validity of the contract of carriage, or the application to it of the Convention: Article 4(4). However, the carrier loses the benefit of exclusions and limitations of liability under the Convention if it accepts baggage without a baggage check having been issued, or if the baggage check does not contain the number of the passenger ticket, the number and weight of the packages, or the statement that the carriage is subject to the Convention's liability rules: Article 4(4).

§5. Air Waybill

335. A carrier of cargo has the right to require the consignor to make out and hand over an air waybill under Article 5 of the Convention, and a consignor has the right to require the carrier to accept the air waybill. Further requirements for the completion and signature of the air waybill are found in Articles 6 and 7. Article 8 sets out seventeen separate particulars which are to be included in the air waybill, concerning the carriage, the cargo, and the documentation itself. The air waybill is prima facie evidence of the conclusion of the contract, the receipt of the cargo, and the conditions of carriage: Article 11(1). As with the baggage check, absence, irregularity, or loss of the air waybill does not affect the existence or validity of the contract of carriage, or the application to it of the Convention: Article 5(2). The carrier loses the benefit of exclusions and limitations of liability under the Convention if they accept cargo without an air waybill having been made out, or if the air waybill omits certain of the particulars required by Articles 8 and 9.

336. Statements in the air waybill relating to the weight, dimensions, and packing of the cargo, and the number of packages, are evidence of the facts stated. Those relating to the quantity, volume, and condition of the cargo are not evidence against the carrier unless they relate to apparent condition of the cargo or have been, and are stated in the air waybill to have been, checked by the carrier in the presence of the consignor: Article 11(2). Information and documents necessary to meet formalities of customs and police must be provided by the consignor before the cargo can be delivered to the consignee, and the documents must be attached to the air waybill: Article 16(1). The consignor is liable to the consignee for damage occasioned by absence, insufficiency, or irregularity of such information or documents, unless the damage is due to the fault of the carrier or its servants or agents, and the carrier is under no obligation to inquire into their correctness or sufficiency: Article 16(1), (2).

337. The consignee is entitled, on arrival of the cargo at its destination, to require the carrier to hand over to them the air waybill and the cargo, on payment of charges due and compliance with the conditions of carriage set out in the air waybill (Article 13(1). The carrier must notify the consignee as soon as the cargo arrives at its destination: Article 13(2). The consignor has a right under Article 12 to dispose of the cargo by withdrawing it at departure or destination, stopping it on the journey, requiring it to be delivered at destination or on the journey to someone other than the consignee named in the air waybill, or requiring it to be returned to the place of departure. This right of the consignor ends when the right of the consignee to require delivery begins under Article 13, but revives if the consignee refuses delivery or cannot be communicated with: Article 12(4). The consignor's right is also subject to obligations not to prejudice the carrier or other consignors, and to pay expenses: *see* Article 12(1). The provisions of Articles 12, 13, and 14 can be varied by express provision in the air waybill, but only by such provision: Article 15(2).

338. Receipt by the person entitled to delivery of baggage or cargo without complaint is evidence that the baggage or cargo has been delivered in good condition and in accordance with the document of carriage: Article 26(1). If the carrier admits the loss of the cargo, or if the cargo has not arrived seven days after it ought to have arrived, the consignee is entitled to put into force against the carrier the rights which flow from the contract of carriage: Article 13(3). Provided they carry out their obligations under the contract of carriage, the consignor and the consignee can enforce their respective rights under Articles 12 and 13 in their own respective names, whether they are acting in their own interests or in the interests of others: Article 14. The relations of consignor and consignee with each other, or the relations of third parties claiming through them are not effected by Articles 12–14: Article 15.

§6. Liability for Destruction, Damage, or Loss

339. Liability is imposed on the carrier for damage sustained in the event of the destruction, or loss, or damage to, cargo and registered baggage, if the occurrence which caused the damage took place during the carriage by air: Article 18. For this purpose, the carriage comprises the period during which the baggage or cargo is in charge of the carrier: Article 18. The carrier is also liable for damage occasioned by delay in the carriage by air of baggage and cargo: Article 19. In cases covered by Articles 18 and 19, any action for damages, however founded, can only be brought subject to the conditions and limits in the Convention: Article 24(1). Article 18(2) and (3) define 'air transportation' as the period during which the baggage or goods are in the control of the carrier in an airport or on board an aircraft. In the case of landing outside an airport the carriers' liability for the goods is extended to 'any place whatsoever'.

340. Article 18 requires that the goods be shown to have been damaged while in the carrier's charge in an airport or on board. If there is a loss while the goods are not on board or were outside an airport, then Article 18(3) determines that the carrier is not responsible under the Convention for damage. Generally, when the carrier has physical possession of the goods in an airport or on board, it is 'in charge' of them. This may not be the case where cargo is placed at the disposition of the consignee while still on board the aircraft. Similarly, the carrier may be considered to be 'in charge' of the goods without having physical possession where these are with a handling agent. In *United International Stables Ltd v. Pacific Western Airlines* (1969) 5 DLR 367, a horse being carried with others broke loose from its stall aboard the aircraft. The captain had to kill the horse to avoid endangering the aircraft. In an action for the loss of the animal the carrier claimed that as the shipper had supplied handlers to accompany and look after the horses the carrier could not be held responsible for being 'in charge'. The Supreme Court of British Columbia, however, held that even where the cargo was being looked after by another, the carrier was still 'in charge' as Article 18 was intended to define when the carrier's liability began and ended.

341. The carrier is 'in charge' of the goods in an airport from the time the goods are delivered to it in the legal sense, until the carrier transfers the custody of the goods to the consignee. The carrier accepts the goods, in respect to cargo, when it issues an air waybill, this being evidence of receipt of the goods by the carrier under Article 11. Where goods are damaged while being stored on the carrier's premises the carrier is liable. The carrier will also be liable if goods are damaged when the cargo is being brought out to the aircraft by an airport truck or trailer.[721] The carrier does not stop being legally in charge of the goods simply because these leave the carrier's actual control. The common law cases do not give an indication of when a carrier ceases to be in charge of the goods. There are, however, general common law rules governing carriage that determine when transit ends. These rules are consistent with the existing cases dealing with 'carriage by air' and additionally may account for the absence of particular difficulties in cases of carriage by air dealt with by common law courts.[722]

342. In *Siemens v. Schenker International (Aust) Pty Ltd* (2004) ALR 322,[723] the High Court held by a majority that the limitation clause in the airway bill for goods carried by air which were subsequently damaged while being carried by road outside Tullamarine International Airport, Melbourne, applied not only to the air carriage but to the subsequent removal of the cargo by road to a bonded warehouse. In December 1996, Siemens Ltd purchased a large consignment of telecommunications equipment valued at over AUD 1.6 million from its parent company Siemens

721. *Young Jewellery Manufacturing Co v. Delta* 414 NYS 2d 528 (App Div 1979).
722. *Swiss Bank v. Brinks Mat* [1986] 2 Lloyd's Rep 79.
723. Kirby & J.J. McHugh's dissenting; on appeal from J. Barrett in the SC of NSW *Siemen v. Schenker International (Aust) Pty Ltd* (2001) 162 FLR 469. For a detailed commentary on the case in the HC *see* J. Livermore, *Siemens Ltd v. Schenker International (Aust) Pty Ltd: High Court of Australia Determines Air Waybill Limitation Clause Extends Beyond Destination Airport to Road Carriage*, J. Korean, Air & Space L. 19, 1 (2004): 213–233.

AG to supply and deliver a synchronous digital hierarchy transmission system required for a Telstra installation in WA. The equipment was purchased on an FCA (free to carrier) basis, so that, as between seller and purchaser, the property and risk passed at the 'FCA point' Tegel Airport, Berlin. Transport of the equipment was organized by Schenker International Deutschland GmbH. The consignment was consolidated on Singapore Airlines to Tullamarine Airport, Melbourne. After arriving at Tullamarine on 13 December 1996, the consignment was collected by an employee of Schenker Australia two days later and placed on a truck in readiness for its delivery to the Schenker Australia bonded warehouse about 4 km from Tullamarine's main gate. However, as a result of the negligence of the driver employed by Schenker Australia, part of the consignment fell off the truck before arrival at Schenker Australia's bonded warehouse and was damaged. In the action by Siemens Australia in the Supreme Court of NSW to recover damages, interests, and costs from Schenker Australia and Schenker Germany, the Supreme Court rejected the Schenker companies claim to limitation under the Warsaw Convention and alternatively under the house air waybill issued by Schenker Germany for the consignment, awarding Schenkers USD 1,688,059.50 damages. On appeal to the NSWCA that court set aside the orders of the lower court and found for Siemens for the limited amount of USD 74,680.[724] On appeal by Siemens to the High Court, it (by a majority) found for Schenkers. The High Court stated that the two primary issues from the appeal had to be considered. First, whether the Warsaw Convention, as incorporated into Australian law by the *Civil Aviation (Carriers' Liability) Act* 1959 (Cth), applied to limit the liability of the Schenker companies. Second, whether the limitation of liability in the air waybill issued by Schenker Germany for the consignment applied. In dismissing the appeal by Siemens with costs and upholding the judgment of the CA, the majority of the High Court ruled that the limitation in the Warsaw Convention did not apply but the limitation in the air waybill did apply.[725]

343. The general rule at common law is that the carrier's duties end when the goods are tendered to the consignee, whether accepted by them or not. Carriage will usually end by the handing over of the goods to the consignee. When the consignee refuses to accept the goods, the carriage may end without the handing over of the goods to the consignee. Where goods are not to be delivered at the consignee's premises, the common law principles are that transit ends when a reasonable time has passed after the arrival of the goods at the place of destination.

---

724. *Schenker International (Aust) Pty Ltd v. Siemens Ltd* [2002] NSWCA 172.

725. Two strong dissenting judgments were given by McHugh & J.J. Kirby. Both agreed that the limitation provision in Art. 18 of the Warsaw Convention did not apply. However, both held that the limitation provision in the air waybill did not apply either. A.C.J. McHugh, was of the opinion that the carriage of the consignment was not 'carriage to which the Warsaw Convention does not apply'. The fact that the Convention's liability provisions did not apply to the loss in question was beside the point. J. Kirby ruled that the relevant clause of the air waybill was concerned only with air carriage. The clause did not extend to impose a contractual limitation of liability on Schenker for loss caused by the negligence of Schenker International Australia's driver outside the airport. For a detailed analysis of the *Schenker* case *see* J. Livermore, *Schenker International (Aust) Pty Ltd v. Siemens Ltd: High Court of Australia Determines Air Waybill Limitation Clause Extends Beyond Destination Airport to Road Carriage*, 19(1) Korean J. Air & Space L. 215 (2004).

§7. WILFUL MISCONDUCT AND THE CARGO CARRIER

344. Article 25 of the Convention, in its original form, prohibited the carrier from relying on any clauses limiting or excluding liability for damage to goods or baggage if either it or its agents were guilty of wilful misconduct. The term 'wilful misconduct' gave rise to a number of problems of interpretation and resultant criticism. The Hague Protocol of 1955 amended Article 25 so that it must now be shown that the act or omission causing damage was done 'with intent to cause damage or recklessly and with knowledge that damage would result'. It defined 'wilful misconduct' in terms of a person's actions and not in terms of a legal concept. Although Article 25 penalized the carrier by prohibiting it from using limitations under Article 22 of the Convention other defences were still open to the carrier, such as Article 20 (all necessary measures) or Article 21 (contributory negligence). The amended Article 25 has produced as many problems of interpretation as its predecessor.

Article 25 gives the court to which the case is submitted the right to apply its own law. The court has to determine first, if the act complained of is considered 'wilful misconduct'; second, whether there is a causal connection between the act and the damage; third, the amount of proof required to establish knowledge on the part of the alleged wrongdoer; and, fourth, damages.

345. In *Goldman v. Thai Airways International Ltd* [1983] 1 WLR 1186, the English CA held in the context of a passenger injury claim that the word 'recklessly' could not be separated from 'and with knowledge that damage would probably result'. Therefore, the test under Article 25 must be regarded as subjected. In *Qantas Airways Ltd v.* SS *Pharmaceutical Co Ltd* [1989] 1 Lloyd's Rep 319, the defendant airline left a consignment of pharmaceutical products in the open during transshipment even though there has been a thunderstorm forecast and there were indications on the goods themselves that these were likely to be damaged if exposed to water. Qantas admitted liability and even wrote a letter to the plaintiffs apologizing for what they described as 'deplorably bad handling'. However, this did not prevent Qantas from seeking limitation of liability under Article 22. In the lower court, the judge found against Qantas and awarded full compensation to the plaintiffs. In the NSWCA, *Goldman* was cited with approval. It was not disputed that the test for the existence of knowledge for the purposes of Article 25 was subjective rather than objective. Qantas, while conceding that the damage resulted from acts or omissions of its servants or agents, called no evidence to explain what happened to the cargo or to account for the way in which it was handled. It, therefore, had to be established whether or not this failure to give evidence, together with the admission of fault and the proved facts, were enough to bring the case within Article 25. By a majority, the CA held that Article 25 was applicable and the plaintiffs were entitled to compensation for their entire loss.

346. The carrier can avoid liability by Article 20 as follows:

(1) If they prove that they and their agents have taken all necessary measures to avoid the damage, or that it was impossible for him or them to take such measures.

(2) If, in the case of the carriage of goods or luggage, they prove that the damage was caused by negligent pilotage or negligence in the handling of the aircraft or in navigation, and that, in all other respects, they and their agents have taken all necessary measures to avoid the damage.

§8. Liability for Cargo Loss and Damage Due to Delay

347. The air carrier is liable for damage caused by delay to passengers, baggage, and goods under Article 19 of the Convention. The carrier is presumed to be liable once the plaintiff shows that damage arose due to delay. The plaintiff must prove delay and damage and show delay as the proximate cause of the damage. Claims have to be made against the carrier in writing within fourteen days under the Convention and twenty-one days under the Hague Protocol. The majority of air carriers, that is, those using IATA General Conditions of Carriage, provide in their waybills that they are not bound by any indication of time that they have given for the completion of the carriage. The object of such clauses is to deny to the shipper of the goods the right to expect the performance of the carriage at a particular time.

348. In *Bart v. West Indian Airways Ltd* [1967] 1 Lloyd's Rep 239, the plaintiff sent a winning combination entry worth over 20,000 to Sherman's pools in England through a Guyana-based agent. Due to series of delays, the package missed its scheduled flight from Guyana and arrived in London too late to be included in the pool prize allocation. The carrier's argument, among others, that it was under no legally binding duty to deliver the package on a particular date, was rejected by the Guyana CA on the basis that the carrier was under a duty to perform the carriage within a reasonable time having regard to all the circumstances of the particular case. Bollers CJ argued that in the absence of a fixed time there would be an implied agreement between the shipper and the carrier that the goods would be conveyed by air within a reasonable time. However, under the air consignment note issued by the defendant airline, it was agreed that no time was fixed for completion of the carriage and no obligation was assumed by the carrier to carry the goods by any specific route or over any particular route or to make any connection at any point according to any particular schedule.[726] In *Barts'* case, Article 18 was applied to the issue of delay; carriage by air was held not to commence as soon as the cargo is received at the airline's terminal office. It would seem then if delay occurs because the carrier is late in transporting the goods from the terminal office to the airport, this is not delay within the meaning of the Convention. Article 14, in relation to who can sue the carrier, provides that the consignor and consignee can each enforce all the rights they have under Articles 12 and 13. In *Barts'* case the court ruled, applying Article 14, that only the consignor or consignee could sue the carrier, thus, ruling out the plaintiff whose winning coupon had missed the draw.[727]

726. [1967] 1 Lloyd's Rep 239, 275.
727. *See also Tasman Pulp and Paper Co v. Brambles JB O'Loghlen* [1981] 2 NZLR 225.

349. In most cases, the consignee will usually be the forwarding agent or freight forwarder or the buyer's bank, and it would appear undesirable that the buyer's remedy should have to rely on the ability and preparedness of the actual consignee to bring an action against the carrier. Under the Convention, the position of persons other than the consignor, consignee, or owner suffering damage as a result of delay or loss or damage to the goods is not clear. On a common law basis, an action for delay alone bought against the carrier as bailee of goods is likely to depend on the terms of the contract between the carrier and the consignor, that is, those contained in the consignment note and air waybill.

§9. Limitations of Liability and Special Declarations

350. Article 25 of the Convention gives carriers, shippers, and passengers the right to enter into a special agreement to increase the carrier's liability limits. In the case of cargo, the shipper can make a special declaration of the higher value of the goods before carriage. This gives the carrier notice that the shipment contains items of higher value. But the mere knowledge by the carrier of the higher value of a shipment may not give effect to a higher limitation liability for the shipper. It is necessary to declare the higher value of the cargo on the air waybill. A claim after the flight stating an approximate value is not the 'special declaration' under Article 25. The shipper must pay, if required, a supplementary sum if required by the carrier; if this is not done the higher declaration is ineffective. If a carrier admits that a higher declaration was made but no note of this is made on the air waybill, a carrier may still be held liable. It needs to be noted that problems may arise where the consignee is required to pay shipping charges at the destination. In this situation, the consignor cannot pay the supplementary charges in advance, as Article 22 requires. Those requirements may be satisfied by an offer to pay the supplementary sum.

§10. Recourse Between Successive Carriers

351. Where more than one carrier is involved, the situation is governed by Article 30 (successive carriers) and Article 31 (combined carriage), in determining which carriers are liable. Successive carriage has been defined as a factual, chronological partition of a single service as contemplated by the contracting parties. Successive carriage is expressly excluded from the scope of the Guadalajara Convention (Article 1(c)). Therefore, it is vital to distinguish between a successive carrier and an actual carrier. A successive carrier may be held fully liable for damage occurring during the carriage performed by another successive carrier. However, an actual carrier cannot be liable in excess of the limits laid down by Article 22 of the Warsaw Convention for the acts and omissions of the contracting carrier. Although Article 30 designates the carrier who is answerable to the passenger, consignor, or consignee, it does not determine which carrier will ultimately be liable for financial damages. Article 30A, however (inserted in the Convention by Montreal Protocol No. 4 of 1975), provides that nothing in the Convention shall prejudice the right of recourse against another person. Article 30(3) gives a right of action against the first carrier to the passenger or consignor and against the last carrier to the passenger or consignee entitled to delivery. Article 31 deals with combined carriage. Article 31(2) permits the parties to put in the air waybill conditions regulating transport modes other than air carriage, as long as the provisions of the Convention are followed in respect of the carriage by air. So the parties can apply the conditions similar to the Convention, but do so through conditions in the air waybill.[728]

§11. Limitation of Carrier's Liability

352. The carrier's liability is limited in the carriage of cargo and registered baggage to 17 SDR per kilogram of the weight of the lost or damaged package.[729] This is so unless the consignor has made, at the time when the package was handed to the carrier, a special declaration of the value at delivery, and has paid a supplementary sum if the case so required: Article 22(2). The carrier's liability is then limited to the declared amount, unless the carrier proves that the declared amount is greater than the actual value to the consignor at delivery: Article 22(2)(b). As regards objects of which the passenger takes charge, the carrier's liability is limited to 300 SDR: Article 22(3). When the Warsaw Convention was being drafted the delegates to the 1925 Paris Conference avoided using local currency for compensation to measure the carrier's liability. Instead, a gold standard was used in order to avoid the effects of devaluation, which might result if the limits of liability were expressed in local currencies. The limitation provided in Article 22 was originally expressed as the French Gold franc, the 'Poincare' franc. In 1972 and 1973, the US dollar was devalued against gold, giving a higher liability limit of USD 10,000 for passengers and a USD 9.07 per lb limitation for checked baggage and cargo and USD 400 per passenger for carry on baggage. As the value of gold increased, more units of local currency were required to purchase each ounce of gold. As a result of the erosion of currency, value limits under the Convention increased as more units of local currency were required to purchase gold units defined in the Convention.

353. Passenger levels of compensation for some time had been regarded as too low and in 1955 the Hague Protocol by Article 1.1 doubled the passenger limits and reference to the passenger limit and reference to the French gold franc was removed, reference being made simply to a 'currency unit'. However, the United State's Government regarded the Hague limits as too low and never ratified the Protocol. In 1965, the United States threatened to denounce the Warsaw Convention unless airlines agreed to raise their passenger limits to USD 75,000. As a result the Montreal Agreement 1965 came into being, which governs flights to and from the USA. In 1975, the High Contracting parties agreed to adopt the four Montreal Protocols, so abandoning the conversion based on a gold standard, replacing this with the SDR.

A major problem is the inconsistency in the methods of conversion adopted by different countries. A local (i.e., national court) can use either:

728. *Pick v. Lufthansa* 9 Avi 18 077 (NY City Ct 1965).
729. *Civil Aviation (Carrier's Liability) Amendment Act* 1991 (Cth) Sch. 2 (Art. 22(2)(b)).

(a) the official price of gold, or where there is none the latest 'official' price;
(b) the free market price of gold;[730]
(c) SDR's as under the Montreal Protocols. The Montreal Protocol was enacted in Australia by the *Civil Aviation Legislation Amendment (1999 Montreal Convention and other Measures) Act* 2008 (Cth);
(d) the current value of the French gold franc; and
(e) some other countries' currency.

354. The *Civil Aviation (Carriers Liability) Amendment Act* 1991 (Cth) which came into effect on 27 November 1991 enables the ratification of Montreal Protocols Nos 3 and 4. The Montreal Protocol No. 3 applies a 100,000 SDR limit to the carrier's liability limit applying to the international carriage of passengers by air. The Montreal Protocol No. 4 covers all international carriage of persons baggage or cargo by air for reward and specifically limits the carrier's liability for the carriage of cargo to 17 SDR's per kilogram (Article 22(2)(b). However, in November 1992, all Japanese airlines removed all liability limits on passenger compensation. These changes have been put into effect by the IATA Intercarrier Agreement of Passenger Liability (*see* below).

355. If an action is brought against a servant or agent of the carrier arising out of damage to which the Convention relates, the servant or agent is entitled to the benefit of the liability limits stated in Article 22, if they prove that they acted within the scope of their employment; Article 25A(a). The aggregate of the amounts recoverable from the carrier and their servants and agents in such a case is not to exceed the limits in Article 22; Article 25A(2). The extended benefit of the liability limits is not available if it is proved that the damage resulted from an act or omission of the servant or agent done with intent to cause damage or recklessly and with knowledge that damage would probably result: Article 25A(3).

§12. Passenger Ticket

356. The passenger ticket constitutes evidence of the conclusion and the conditions of the contract of carriage, Article 3(2). The ticket must be delivered before the passenger embarks for the relevant flight.[731] The absence, irregularity, or loss of the passenger ticket does not affect the validity of the contract of carriage which will be subject to the rules of the Convention. However, if the carrier accepts a passenger without a passenger ticket having been delivered they will not be entitled to protection of the Convention provisions excluding or limiting the carrier's liability: Article 3(2).

357. The purpose of the provision in Article 3(1) that the passenger ticket must contain the prescribed notice of the possible application of the Warsaw Convention

730. This was applied by the SC of NSW in SS *Pharmaceutical v. Qantas Airlines* [1989] NSWLR 319.
731. *Mannion v. Pan Am World Airways Inc.* Misc 2d 927 (NY Sup Ct 1980).

has been cited as giving the passenger fair warning of the carrier's limited liability,[732] in order to take measures such as buying insurance to obtain protection against the limitation of liability.[733] On such an assumption, the following propositions have been advanced by courts in the United States:

(1) the ticket must be delivered to the passenger or a close associate (spouse of parent);
(2) the ticket must be delivered in time for the passenger to take out insurance;
(3) a ticket not designed to bring the necessary information clearly to the passengers' attention may be regarded as so defective that it does not meet the requirements of the Convention.

358. In addition to the notice required by Article 3, most passenger tickets now contain a further notice headed: 'Advice to International Passengers on limitation of liability'. This is required by the Montreal Agreement 1966[734] in relation to carriage falling within the terms of the agreement; international carriage within either the amended or unamended Warsaw Convention where a point in the United States is a point of origin, point of destination, or agreed stopping place. The Agreement requires the printing of the advice to conform to prescribed specifications as to size of type, colour, and location.[735] A failure to print the advice or to comply with the format specifications can have no effect on the passengers' rights: the Agreement is essentially a contract between the air carriers which have become a party to it. Although the Agreement prescribes the terms of conditions of carriage to be adopted by signatory carriers, these do not include a reference to the advice.

359. In *Fattouch v. Gulf Air Co GSC* (2007)5 *DCL(NSW)* 234 the DC of NSW held that an agreement for international carriage was not created by the issue of a ticket to the plaintiff but only once he presented the ticket to the airline and embarked after seat allocation on the aircraft. In the case of a return air ticket, with multitude coupons, there is a series of contracts of international carriage made as the ticket is presented on each occasion. The place of destination is, therefore, determined according to the flight coupon for which the boarding pass is issued.

§13. Liability for Passenger Injury and Death

360. Article 17 of the Warsaw Convention has been given interpretation by various jurisdictions where damage or wounding or other bodily injury occurs after embarkation aboard an air carrier. Applying Article 17 to psychological as distinct from physical injury is exceptional and there is no clear support for its application

732. *Seth v. BOAC* 329 F2d 303 (1st Circ 1964).
733. *Mertens v. Flying Tiger Line Inc.* 341 F2d 851 (2nd Circ 1965).
734. CAB 18900.
735. *See Montreal Trust Co v. Canadian Pacific Airlines Ltd* (1976) 72 DLR (3d) 257. On the status of an airline ticket in contract law *see MacRobertson Miller Airlines Services v. Commissioner of State Taxation of State of Western Australia* (1975) 133 CLR 125.

in order to make an air carrier liable to the passenger or passengers involved. Carriers are liable to passengers and their personal representatives for damage sustained in the event of passenger injury and death. Article 17 of the Warsaw Convention provides:

> The Carrier is liable for damage sustained in the event of death or wounding of a passenger or other bodily injury suffered by the passenger if the accident which caused the damage so sustained took place on board the aircraft or in the course of any of the operations of embarking or disembarking.[736]

This provision is adopted into Australian law by the *Civil Aviation (Carriers' Liability) Act* 1959 (Cth).[737]

Legal liability of an airline for passenger injury or death raises issues of the type of injury involved, the entitlement to sue, and what jurisdiction determines the applicable law.

361. IIA and MIA: In October 1995. The IATA annual general meeting unanimously adopted the IATA Intercarrier Agreement of Passenger Liability (IIA) initially signed by seven airlines, including Qantas. Airlines participating in this Agreement agreed to take measures for it to waive the limits in international agreements for damages in the case of personal injury and death in 1996. IATA adopted a supplemental agreement, the Agreement on Measures to Implement the IATA Intercarrier Agreement (MIA). The MIA provides that participating carriers shall impose the following provisions in their conditions of carriage and tariffs where necessary:[738]

---

736. No change is made to the Warsaw Convention by Montreal Protocol No. 4. *See* Civil Aviation (Carriers' Liability) Act 1959 (Cth) Sch. 4. *See* G. Heilbronn, *Transport: Aviation, Laws of Australia.* Thomson Reuters (Sydney) [34.2.4380]–[34.2.4840]; P. Martin (ed) *Shawcross and Beaumont: Air Law* (4th ed., Butterworths subscription service) vol. 1, Div. VII at [522] *See* the IATA Intercarrier Agreement (IIA) and the Agreement to Implement the Intercarrier Agreement (MIA). *See also* Hannappel PCC, *The Right to Sue in Death Cases under the Warsaw Convention*, 6(2) Air Law 66 (1981). *See* T. Sakamoto, *The Fate of Passenger Liability Under the Warsaw Convention* and S. Okake, *Aviation Personal Injury Claim Settlement in Japan* both given at the International Conference on Air Transport and Space Application in a New World' June 1993, Tokyo. *See* B. Cheng, *Air Carrier Liability for Passenger Injury and Death and the Japanese Initiative and Response to the Current EC Consultation Paper*, 18 Air & Space L. 109 (1993); L.R. Edwards '*Liability of Air Carriers for Death and Personal Injury to Passengers*', 56 Air & Space L. 108 (1982); S.J. Levy, *The Rights of International Airline Passengers*, 1 Air & Space L. 275 (1976).
737. *Civil Aviation (Carriers' Liability) Act* 1959 (Cth) Sch. 5 records that the text in the Schedule contains the operative provisions of the Warsaw Convention as modified by Ch. 1 of the Hague Protocol and Ch. 1 of the Montreal Protocol No. 4 together with the remaining provisions of the Hague and Montreal Protocols. Pt IIIC of the Act (ss 25J–25N) deal with carriage to which Montreal No. 4 applies. Parts II, III, and IIIA deal respectively with carriage to which the Warsaw Convention applies, carriage to which the Warsaw Convention alone applies, and carriage to which the Guadalajara Convention applies. Pt VI of the Act (ss 26–41) deals with other carriage to which the Act applies, including carriage by Australian domestic carriers interstate or between a place in a Territory and another place in a Territory, and another place in Australia. *See also Povey v. Qantas Airways Ltd and Another* [2005] ALR 427 at 431–438.
738. *Civil Aviation (Carriers' Liability) Act* 1959(Cth) ss 12(3), (5)–(6), 24.

(1) (the carrier) shall not invoke any limitation of liability in Article 22(1) of the(Warsaw) Convention as to any claim for recoverable compensatory damage arising under Article 17 of the Convention;
(2) (the carrier) shall not avail itself of any defence under Article 22(1) of the Convention with respect to that portion of such claim which does not exceed 100,000 SDR; and
(3) except as otherwise provided in paragraphs 1 and 2 (the Carrier) reserves all defences under the Convention to any such claim. With respect to third parties, the carrier also reserves all rights of recourse against any other persons, including without limitation, rights of contribution and indemnity.

THE MIA also provided that at the option of the carrier the following provisions may be included in the conditions of carriage:

(1) (the carrier) agrees that subject to applicable law, recoverable compensatory damages for such claims may be determined by reference to the law of the domicile or permanent residence of the passenger;
(2) (the carrier) shall not avail itself of any defence under Article 20(1) of the Convention with respect to that portion of such claims which do not exceed 100,000 SDR, except that such waiver is limited to the amounts shown below for the routes indicated, as may be authorized by governments concerned with the transportation involved; and
(3) neither the waiver of limits nor the waiver of defences shall be applicable in respect of such claims made by public social insurance or similar bodies, however asserted. Such claims shall be subject to the limit in Article 22(1) of the Convention.

The Carrier will compensate the passenger or his dependents for recoverable compensatory damages received from any public social insurance or similar body.

The scope of Article 17 is subject to ambiguities as to the meaning which applies to the kinds of injuries and the circumstances in which they occur. Passengers, their personal representatives, and others, may sue under Article 173. Although the Warsaw Convention does not define 'passenger' it applies to all passengers whether holding tickets or not, as well as stowaways.[739] Article 17 applies to gratuitous as well as carriage for reward by an air transport operator.

362. Entitlement to sue: Who may sue on behalf of a deceased passenger and/or relative is outside the Warsaw Convention and left to the law of the country exercising jurisdiction in the matter. In Australia the right to sue is given to a wide range of relatives, even illegitimate children, or an adoptive or reputed father, as well as the deceased's personal representatives.[740]

363. In *McKenna v. Avoir Pty Ltd* [1981] WAR 255 the plaintiff claimed damages for the death of her son in an aircraft crash. The operator of the aircraft

---

739. *Civil Aviation (Carriers' Liability Act* 1959(Cth) s. 42 applying Pts II, III, and IV of the Act.
740. *See* n. 4.

admitted liability under the *Civil Aviation (Carriers' Liability) Act* 1961–1976 (WA). The Federal Act provided by section 35(8) that in awarding damages the court or jury were not limited to financial loss resulting from the death of the passenger. The plaintiff experienced grief and mental anguish as a consequence of her son's death and lost the benefit of certain household services performed by him. The West Australian Supreme Court held that damages were to be assessed on the basis on the same principles as claims under the Fatal Accidents Act. The plaintiff was entitled to damages for the lost benefit of household services performed by and financial benefits received from the deceased but was not entitled to damages for the grief and mental anguish she experienced as a result of his death.

364. Physical v. Psychological Injury:

In *South Pacific Air Motive Pty Ltd v. Magnus* (1998) 157 ALR 443 the case arose from an aircraft ditching in Botany Bay, New South Wales in 1994 carrying a group of students from Sydney to Norfolk Island. The operators of the aircraft were sued by a representative of a group of passengers and their parents who were variously alleged to have suffered physical and/or psychological harm as a result of the accident.

365. The majority of the Federal Court held that Part IV of the *Civil Aviation (Carriers' Liability) Act* 1959 (Cth) did exclude a cause of action in respect of claims by passengers independent of any physical injury. It was also held that the reference to 'personal injury' in section 28 of the Act rather than 'bodily injury' indicated that it was parliament's intention that the application of section 28 was not confined to physical injuries but also included psychological injuries.

366. The Federal Court held that the claims of the passengers for psychological damage independent of any physical injury were extinguished by section 34 of the Act. Part IV of the Act was not intended to be a complete code in respect of non-passengers who suffer loss or damage as a result of an air accident. Section 36 was not intended to preclude claims by non-passengers seeking damages for nervous shock under general law (e.g., tort). Therefore, these claims were not barred by the *Civil Aviation (Carriers' Liability) Act* 1959.[741]

367. In *Kotsambasis v. Singapore Airlines Ltd* (1997) 42 NSWLR 110 the appellant boarded a Singapore Airlines flight in Athens scheduled to fly to Sydney via

741. In *South Pacific Air Motive Pty Ltd v. Magnus* (1998) 157 ALR 443 J. Beaumont in a dissenting judgment suggested that the provisions of Part IV (governing non Warsaw Convention air carriage in Australia), especially s. 28 could entitle persons other than the passenger to sue for nervous shock resulting from the death or personal injury of a passenger. *See Cousins v Nimvale Pty Ltd* [2013] WADC 175. But *see* the decision in *Povey Qantas Airways Ltd and Another* [2005] ALR 427 holding that the liability of the carrier subject to Montreal Protocol No. 4 is in substitution for any civil liability under any other law in respect of the injury. Liability for death, wounding, and other bodily injury for liability under Art. 17 to apply to passenger death, wounding, or other bodily injury this must be caused by an accident which takes place on board the aircraft or while boarding or disembarking.

Singapore. She was seated on the port side wing near the window. Shortly after takeoff, she was leaning forward in her seat when a sudden jolt threw her back in her seat. The pain she felt in her back was subsequently held at first instance not to be accepted as an injury. Other passengers were screaming and she saw smoke coming from a starboard engine which had caught alight. There was an inboard announcement that there was an engine problem and that the aircraft would be returning to Athens once fuel had been jettisoned. The judge at first instance accepted the appellant's evidence that she was anxious and distressed and that she regarded the smoke from the engine as life-threatening and that she sustained a severe fright and believed that she might die. The NSW Court of Appeal held that the claim would not succeed as the term 'bodily injury' in Article 17 did not include purely psychological injury.

In *Pel-Air Aviation Pty Ltd v. Casey* [2017] NSWCA 32 the background to the claim against Pel Air arose in November 2009. Ms Karen Casey was a nurse who travelled on a small aircraft operated by Pel Air. She was accompanied by a doctor to Samnoa to evacuate a patient and her husband, and return to Melbourne. The aircraft was scheduled to refuel at Norfolk Island on the return journey. However, bad weather prevented the pilot from landing, as a result of which he ditched the aircraft in the sea. All six of the persons on board survived the ditching and were rescued after ninety minutes in the water off Norfolk Island. Ms Casey suffered significant physical injuries, including damage to her spine and her right knee. Additionally, she came to suffer from post traumatic stress disorder (PTSD), major depression, and anxiety.

The first issue in Pel Air's appeal to the NSW Court Appeal from the primary judge was whether they erred in concluding Ms Casey's PTSD constituted a 'bodily injury'. The second issue was whether that judge also erred in awarding damages to Ms Casey for non-economic loss, past and present care and treatment expenses. The central issue turned on the effect of excluding the consequences of her PTSD from the assessment of damages if that condition was not held to constitute a 'bodily injury'.[742]

At first instance Pel-Air accepted that Ms Casey's physical injuries constituted 'bodily injury' for the purposes of Article 17. The mental harm she suffered other than her PTSD was properly characterized because the evidence indicated under the Warsaw Convention that her physical injuries were at least in part a cause of her major depressive and anxiety disorders, and pain disorders. On review of Australian, English, and United States case authorities the primary judge concluded that a diagnosis of PTSD did not exclude the possibility that evidence in a particular case may establish that a person had suffered a bodily injury compensable under the Montreal Convention. The primary judge held that the PTSD from which Ms Casey suffered and had been unsuccessfully treated was a result of damage to her brain and other parts of her bodily processes.

The Court, on appeal by Pel-Air noted the ruling in the *Kotsombosis* case (above) that draftsmen in the Montreal Convention did not intend to impose absolute liability for all forms of injury[743]. In *Kotsombosis* Stein J added that where mental

742. *Pel-Air Aviation Pty v. Casey* [2017] NSWCA 32 at [5], [6].
743. At [25].

anguish followed and is caused by physical injury, recovery for both injuries is covered by the Convention. The Court in Pel-Air noted in *Weaver v. Delta Airlines Inc.* 56F Supp 2d 1190 the US DC of Montana found that PTSD suffered by an airline passenger as a result of an emergency landing constituted 'bodily injury' under Article 17[744]. However, the HL in *Morris v. KLM Royal Dutch Airlines; King v. Bristow Helicopters Ltd* [2002] 2 AC 628 claims relating to PTSD and clinical depression developed by a passenger after a forced helicopter landing did not succeed. It was held that a psychiatric condition did not of itself constitute a 'bodily injury' within Article 17 although their Lordships differed as to what is covered by that term.[745]

In allowing the cross appeal by Pel-Air the NSW Court of Appeal rejected Ms Casey's submission that her physical injuries caused her PTSD as there was, in its view, no evidence to support such an inference. As a result the award of damages to Ms Casey in respect of non-economic loss, past and present care and treatment expenses was denied.

Restricting the meaning of 'bodily injury' to the exclusion of PTSD and mental distress or depression in the *Pel-Air Aviation Pty Ltd* and *Morris* cases does not appear entirely logical. In *Pel-Air Aviation Pty Ltd* the NSW Court of Appeal chose to discount the expert medical submission that made a clear casual link between the claimant's physical injuries and subsequent PTSD and clinical depression. In the *Morris* case their Lordships, although prepared to limit the ambit of 'bodily injury' in Article 17 to physical injury, nevertheless, were unable to have an agreed interpretation of that term. If Article 17 was amended to include PTSD and mental distress this would result in uniformity and equitable application.

368. In *Paterson v. Airlink Pty Ltd* (2008) 7 DCLR (NSW) 373, the NSW DC ruled that death or personal injury of a passenger must be an accident within section 28 of the *Civil Aviation (Carriers' Liability) Act* 1959 (Cth) section 28 and be an unexpected or unusual event or happening external to the plaintiff. Plaintiff's reaction to the normal and expected operation of an aircraft cannot constitute an 'accident' under section 28. In this case, a portable step was moved while the plaintiff

744. At [31] The Montana District Court referred to 'recent scientific research explains that post traumatic stress disorder evidences actual trauma to brain cells structures'. *Weaver* was followed in In Re aircrash at *Little Rock, Arkansas on 1 June* 1999 118 F Supp 2d 916 (2000). However, in *Rosman v. Transworld Airlines* Inc 34 NY 2d 385[1974] the New York Court of Appeals held that passengers in a hijack were entitled to damages for physical injury but not for mental injury (at 397). In *Eastern Airlines Inc v. Floyd* 499 US 530 (1991) where passengers claimed damages for mental distress the US SC held (at [30]) that an air carrier was not liable under Art. 17 where an accident has not caused damage to a passenger not suffering death, physical injury, or physical manifestation of injury. The US SC refrained from expressing a view as to whether a passenger could recover for mental injuries as passengers in the case before it did not allege physical injury.

745. In *Morris v. KLM Royal Dutch Airlines; King v. Bristow Helicopters* [2002] 2 AC 628 a claimant alleged he suffered from PTSD after a forced helicopter landing and a subsequent peptic ulcer, another passenger claiming clinical depression after an indecent assault by another passenger. The HL allowed the claim for the peptic ulcer to succeed as 'bodily injury' but not the claims for PTSD and clinical depression as not constituting a 'bodily injury. As the NSW Court of Appeal their Lordships in Morris although agreeing on the outcome of the appeal differed in their views as what was covered by the term,' bodily in injury'; Mcfarlan, Ward & J.A. Gleeson at [32].

was disembarking from a small aircraft causing them to fall and sustain injuries was held to be an accident within the meaning of section 28.

In *Yeomans v. Carbridge Pty Ltd* [2011] SWDC 221 the plaintiff flew from Orange to Sydney on a Regional Express Airlines (Rex) flight which landed at Sydney Airport. On coming to a halt at the Sydney domestic terminal Rex did not give the benefit of an airbridge to take passengers from the aircraft directly into the terminal. It was necessary for the passengers to travel on a bus owned and operated by Carbridge. Having left the aircraft the plaintiff, in the course of entering the bus, was allegedly injured as a result of a defect in the bus's steps or perhaps its door. The plaintiff claimed damages for her injuries. Carbridge accepted the facts of plaintiff's claim but requested a summary judgment. Carbridge also submitted that it should be regarded as an agent of the carrier because it was taking the carrier's passengers from the aircraft to the terminal. The judge found that there was merit in the argument that an airline can be seen to have the duty to provide safe transfer of passengers from the aircraft to the terminal. He, therefore, held that the plaintiff was injured in the course of disembarkation.[746]

369. In *Hanna v. Singapore Airlines* (2007) 6 DCLR (NSW) 288, the plaintiff had a pre-existing medical condition, and so requested a seat in the emergency aisle of the aircraft so she could raise her feet. Her seat allocation was changed due to a computer malfunction, so she was given a cramped seat in the rear of the plane. During the flight she claimed she suffered injuries, including pedal oedema due to not being able to raise her feet. She sued Singapore Airlines under Article 17. The plaintiff claimed the accident that occurred to her when embarking was the computer malfunction causing the loss of her earlier seat allocation. The New South Wales DC, in striking out her claim, held that checking in was not embarking. Article 17 only applied when a passenger queued up to go through the boarding gate. A natural human reaction to flying does not constitute an accident under Article 17. The Court held that computer malfunction did not cause the plaintiff's medical condition, this was caused while she was on the aircraft in flight.

In *Gibson v. Malaysian Airline System Berhad* [2016] FCA 1476 a procedural application was made of the Federal Court in a class action proceeding arising out of the MH17 disaster in the Ukraine. On 17 July 2014, all 283 passengers and the crew on board a Boeing 777-200 aircraft en route to Kuala Lumpur operated by Malaysian Airlines were killed when it was shot down by a missile deployed by persons unknown. The daughter of one of the Australian passengers in the statement of claim did so as personal representative of the deceased. The proceedings by the applicant were made on her own behalf, but her originating application stated the claim was also a class action and she was suing in a representative capacity and on behalf of the representatives of the deceased passengers.

In noting that the claim was one for compensation under the *Civil Aviation (Carriers' Liability)* Act 1959 Perram J stated that the respondent airline's liability was governed by the provisions of the Montreal Convention to which Australia is party. The applicant's pleading of the class action gave rise, it was held, to matters which were not recognized in the scheme of compensation. Article 17 created a cause of

746. J. Elkiam at [15],[18].

action rather than recognizing a cause of action which exists independently[747]. Perram J held that in respect of Australian law there is no other cause of action available beyond that conferred by Article 17(1)[748] and Article 33(1), (2) of the Montreal Convention. Article 33 requires action for damage resulting from the death or injury of a passenger may be brought, at the option of the plaintiff, in the court of the domicile of the carrier or principal place of business, or where it has a place of business through which the contract was made, or before the court at the place of destination.[749]

Perram J found that Article 33 was not a procedural provision which could be waived. Article 33 was concerned with the topic of jurisdiction, and even if the respondent airline waived Article 33 this would not have the effect of clothing the Court with jurisdiction it did not have[750]. The statement of claim defined the class in a way that did not engage the ambit of Article 33 Therefore, the class was defined in a way which means the group members have no rights the Court has jurisdiction to enforce. What the applicant had pleaded revealed a lack of jurisdiction to hear the claims of the class as defined.[751]

I. Deep Vein Thrombosis

370. The liability of an airline for Deep Vein Thrombosis (DVT) of a passenger was given detailed examination by the High Court of Australia in *Povey v. Qantas Airways Ltd and Another* (2005) ALR 427. The appellant was a passenger on a Qantas flight from Sydney to London via Bangkok and return by British Airways Plc from London to Sydney via Kuala Lumpur. He alleged that during the course of the outward and return flights he suffered from DVT caused by the conditions and procedures relating to passengers on flights. These included what were said to be cramped seating from which it was not easy to move, the discouragement of movement about the cabin, and the offering of alcohol, tea, and coffee during the flights. The appellant argued that the 'accident' in Article 17 should not be given a narrow meaning and that it extended beyond operations of embarking and disembarking and covered some kinds of omissions in particular. It was contended 'accident' extends to omissions of warning (or the failure to warn) of the known dangers of, and precautions to be taken against the occurrence of DVT. 'Accident' also extends to the flight conditions encountered or to the combination of the failure to warn and the flight conditions.

371. The High Court noted that the *Carriage (Carriers' Liability) Act* 1959 (Cth) gives effect to the Warsaw Convention, the Hague Protocol 1955, the Guadalajara

747. J. Perram at [13] citing *United Airlines Inc v. Sercel Australia Pty Ltd* (2012) 266 FLR 37.
748. J. Perram at [14].
749. J. Perram at [15].
750. J. Perram at [24] citing *Rothmans of Pall Mall (Overseas) Ltd and Others v. Saudi Arabian Airlines Corporation* [1985] QB 368 at 376.
751. J. Perram [29].

Convention, and the Montreal Protocol No. 4. The liability of a carrier when the carriage is subject to the Montreal Protocol No. 4 is in substitution for any civil liability of the carrier under any other law (emphasis added) in respect of the injury.

372. The High Court also noted that the parties had accepted certain propositions which they took to be established by other courts, notably the *Supreme Court of the United States in Air France v. Saks* 470 US 392 (1985), *El Al Israel Airlines Ltd v. Tsui Yuan Tseng* 525 US 155 (1999), *Olympic Airways v. Hussain* 540 US 64(2004), and the *House of Lords in Sidhu v. British Airways Plc* [1997] AC 430. The argument was confined to what 'accident' means in Article 17.

373. The appellant firstly argued that no distinction should be drawn between 'events' or 'beginnings' on the one hand and 'non-events' or 'inaction' on the other. Second, that what was 'unexpected or unusual' was to be judged from the perspective of a reasonable airline passenger, not according to what may be the particular airline's policies and procedures, or what may be general industry practice. Third, it was argued that an 'accident' might occur during the whole flight where the reasonable passenger would expect an airline, knowing of a life-threatening risk, to warn passengers of that risk or the measure to avoid it, this would be an 'accident' that took place on the aircraft.

374. The respondent carriers argued that although it was neither necessary nor relevant to ask whether the cause of the accident was an act or omission or a combination of both, there must have been some unintended and unexpected occurrence which produced the hurt of loss by which damage was sustained. The carriers contended that a 'failure to warn' was not an occurrence, it was something which did not happen. What were alleged to be the relevant 'flight conditions' were not unintended or unexpected-they were the conditions which the appellant alleged to be 'the standard conditions and procedures relating to passenger travel' on the relevant flights.

375. The High Court noted that Article 17 relates to three different concepts. Article 17 refers to 'damage', to 'death or wounding of a passenger or any other bodily injury suffered by a passenger', and to 'the accident which caused the damage so sustained'. The damage sustained is treated as being distinct from the accident which caused the damage, and both the accident and the damage are treated as distinct from the death, wounding, or other personal injury. 'Accident' in the view of the High Court in the sense of 'an unfortunate event, a disaster, a mishap' is not to be read as sufficiently described as an adverse physiological consequence which the passenger has suffered. It might be asserted that its happening was not intended. DVT is and was not an accident. As both parties to the appeal accepted 'accident is a reference to something external to the passenger'.

376. The High Court agreed, as *Saks* indicated, the concept of 'accident' should not be over-refined. It is a concept which invited two questions: first, what happened on board (or during embarking or disembarking) that caused the injury of which complaint is made, and second was what happened unusual or unexpected. The course of events surrounding death or injury to an airline passenger may present difficulties in determining whether there has been an accident. In *Hussain* a passenger died on board an aircraft as a result of exposure to cigarette smoke. A flight attendant had refused requests to move the passenger to a seat further away from those who were smoking on board.

377. The United States Supreme Court acting as amicus curiae in supporting the respondents (the relatives and legal representatives of the deceased passenger) had put forward the question in proceedings as being whether the repeated insistence by an airline flight attendant that an asthmatic passenger remain in an assigned seat amidst life-threatening smoke in direct violation of standard industry practice and the policy of her airline is an unusual occurrence constituting an 'accident' under Article 17. The carrier, Olympic Airlines, on its part, described the question as being whether the court below improperly held that 'accident' under Article 17 can be satisfied when a passenger's pre-existing medical condition is aggravated by exposure to a normal condition in the aircraft cabin, even if the air carrier's negligent omission may have been in the chain of causation.

378. The High Court in *Povey* recognized *Hussain* as showing first, that each party sought to emphasize particular circumstances surrounding the passenger's death. Second, each sought to identify if something unusual or unexpected had happened on board the aircraft. The airline' in effect' sought to say that nothing had happened on board that was unusual or unexpected; even if the flight attendant did not react as she should, there was no accident.

379. The High Court noted that questions of the kind considered in *Hussain* did not arise in the case before it as central to the appellant's claim is that nothing happened on board the aircraft that was out of the ordinary or unusual. References to 'failure' to warn the High Court held were both irrelevant and unhelpful. These were irrelevant as they had to proceed from unstated premises about the origin of some duty to warn. There is no basis for introducing concepts of the common law of negligence to the construction or application of an international treaty like Montreal 47. The references to failure to warn are unhelpful as they suggest that the only point at which some relevant warning should have been given was on board the aircraft. It is not apparent that it should have been given at an earlier point in making travel arrangements, than on board the aircraft. The allegations made by the appellant, even if proved, would not establish a cause of action against the carriers.[752]

380. This conclusion, the High Court held, was consistent with the decisions reached in intermediate courts in the United States and in England about the application of the Warsaw Convention and subsequent treaties to cases of DVT.

752. At, 431. This would overrule the decision in *the South Pacific* case that the claims of non-passengers were not barred by the *Civil Aviation (Carriers' Liability) Act* 1959 (Cth) s. 28.

381. The decision by the Court of Appeal of England and Wales, *In Re Deep Vein Thrombosis* [2004] QB 234, held that the word 'accident' in the Warsaw Convention as modified by the Hague Protocol was to be given a natural and sensible, but flexible and positive meaning in its context for there to be an accident within the meaning of Article 17. The Court of Appeal held that inaction was a non-event which could not properly be described as an accident. Not warning of DVT and not giving advice on the precautions that would minimize that risk were not events. The conditions in which the passenger travelled on flights (with cramped seating and the like) were not capable of amounting to an event that satisfied the first part of the accident definition which 'took place on board the aircraft or in the course of embarking or disembarking'.

382. The High Court noted that the United States Courts of Appeal for the 5th and 9th Circuits had held that development of DVT was not in the circumstances of those cases an accident within Article 17. The High Court dismissed the appellant's claim against those airlines with costs.

II. Further Case Guidance in Applying Article 17

383. A number of cases have established further guidance for the establishment of principles in applying Article 17 to air carrier liability. According to *Evangalinos v. Trans World Airlines Inc* 550 F 2d 152 (1976) in borderline cases the basic factors are:[753]

(1) the extent of the carrier's control over the passenger;
(2) the activity being performed by the passenger; and
(3) the location of the passenger when the injury is sustained.

It has been argued that it is more in accord with the official French text to consider that 'lesion corporelle' (literally) bodily lesion damage includes mental injury.[754]

In *Dias v. Transbrassil Airlines Inc* 8 Avi 16,048 (1998) (SD NY) where a passenger contracted pneumonia from the poor quality of air in the cabin this was found to be an unexpected and unusual event external to the passenger. Depressurization

753. *See Blansett v. Continental Airlines Inc* 379 F 3d 177 (2004); *Rodriguez v. Ansett Australia Ltd* 383 F 3d 914 (2004).

754. *See* D. Stanculescu, *Recovery for Mental Harm under Article 17 of the Warsaw Convention: An Interpretation of Leison Corporelle*, 8 Hastings Int & Comparative L. Rev. 399 (1985) and J.N. Grippando, *Warsaw Convention-Federal Jurisdiction and Air Carrier Liability for Mental Injury: A Matter of Limits*, Geo Washington J. Int L. & Econ. 59 (1985). *See also Kalish v. Transworld Airlines* 14 Avi 17,936 (1997) (Civil Ct NY); *Husserl v. Swiss Transport Co* 13 Avi 17,936 (1975) (Dist Ct NY); *Seguritan v. North West Airlines Inc* 446 NYS 2d 397 (1962) (SC App Div); *Fischer v. North west Airline Inc 623 F Supp 1064 (1985) (Dist Ct III).*

of an airline cabin[755] and turbulent weather conditions causing passenger injury[756] have been ruled as accidents under Article 17 as has a bomb scare and search.[757]

384. In conclusion, Article 17 needs to be interpreted consistently, as should all international treaties incorporated into national domestic law. The cases dealt with in this examination provide strong indication that Article 17 will be given a flexible and balanced interpretation.

385. The cases noted, particularly *Evangalinos*, set down the key elements determining airline liability such as the extent of the carrier's control over the passenger, the activity performed by the passenger and their location in the aircraft.

386. The UK case *In Re Deep Vein Thrombosis* and the Australian High Court decision in *Povey* have ruled that DVT is not an accident and that inaction by an airline in giving advice on precautions to minimize DVT are not accidents within the meaning of Article 17. Nevertheless, prudent airlines have taken steps to warn long distance passengers of the need to undertake seated exercise and move about the cabin when safe to do so.

A. *Passenger and Baggage Screening*

387. The *Transport Legislation Amendment Act* (No. 2) 1995 (Cth) amends the *Air Navigation Act* 1920 (Cth), the *Civil Aviation (Carrier's Liability) Act* 1959 (Cth), and the *Crimes (Aviation) Act* 1991 (Cth) concerning air passenger and baggage screening and security measures at airports and on aircraft.[758] The security measures at airports and aircraft have been further extended by the *Aviation Transport Security Amendment Act* 2008(Cth).[759]

755. *See De Marines v. KLM-Royal Dutch Airlines 433 F Supp 656 (1985) (Dist Ct NY), affirmed De Marines v. KLM –Royal Dutch Airlines 580 F 2d 1193 (1978) (USCA).*
756. *Fleming v. Delta Airlines Inc* 359 F Supp 339 (1973) (Dist Ct NY).
757. *Salerno v. Pan American World Airlines Inc 606 F Supp 656 (1985) (Dist Ct NY). In Metz v. KLM-Royal Dutch Airlines* 15 Avi 17,843 (1979) failure by carrier to take adequate steps to protect a passenger's health after the onset of an attack was held to be negligence.
758. The *Transport Legislation Amendment Act (No. 2)* 1995 (Cth) came into force on 20 Jul. 1995: *see* Sch. Pts 1, 2, and 3. Part 2 requires carriers to produce evidence of current insurance against liability to passengers for death or personal injury (s. 41C). The amount so insured must not be less than AUD $ 500,000 in respect of domestic carriage to which Pt IV of the *Civil Aviation (Carrier's Liability) Act* 1959 (Cth) applies and 260,000 SDRs for any other carriage (i.e., International) (s. 41C(3); Pt 2 inserting Pt IV A after Pt IV of the 1959 Act the *Passenger Movement Charge Amendment Act* 1978 (Cth) and the *Passenger Movement Charge Collection Act* 1978 (Cth) are amended respectively by the *Passenger Movement Charge Amendment Act* 1995 (Cth) and the *Passenger Movement Charge Collection Amendment Act* 1995 (Cth).
759. *See Aviation Transport Security Act* (Cth) 2004.

§14. Bilateral Airline Agreements

388. The international framework for the operation of international commercial services is administered by multilaterally agreed rules established by the Convention on International Civil Aviation, termed the Chicago Convention, by the IATA and by principles governing bilateral air service agreements. Australia's approval of the Chicago Convention is made under the *Air Navigation Act* 1920 (Cth) as amended. The International Air Services Commission (IASC) set up by the *International Air Services Commission Act* 1992 (Cth) is an independent body with the duty of allocating international capacity and route entitlements among international carriers. Changes made under new regulations in 2003 to emphasize competition and speed up decision-making under the *International Air services Commission Act* 1992 (Cth) have already been noted.[760]

§15. Domestic Airline Deregulation

389. The deregulation of domestic airlines commenced on 31 October 1990 with the ending of the 'Two Airline Agreement'.[761] After that date, the operation of domestic airlines has been subject to the *Trade Practices Act* 1974 (Cth),now the *Competition and Consumer Act* 2010 (Cth). It should be noted that the States are still entitled to exercise the right to require an air transport operator wishing to engage in intrastate carriage to hold both State and Federal licences. The *Airlines Agreement Act* 1981 (Cth) was repealed by the *Airlines Agreement (Termination) Act* 1990 (Cth) section 3, and the 1981 Airlines Agreement between the Commonwealth and the two major domestic airlines was terminated. The Commonwealth in 1991 withdrew from the application of passenger capacity provisions in the *Airline Equipment Acts* 1958–1981 (Cth). Also in 1990 the Commonwealth announced the privatization of Australian Airlines[762] and control of domestic airfares through the Independent Air Fares Committee was abandoned with the abolition of the Commission. Qantas and Australian Airlines were merged on 14 September 1992 with the provisions of sale of part of Qantas being provided by the *Qantas Sale Act* 1992 (Cth) that repealed the *Australian National Airlines Act* 1945 (Cth) and the *Qantas Empire Airways Act* 1948 (Cth).[763]

---

760. *See* Ch. 1 the IASC.

761. The deregulation of the industry followed the recommendations of the May Report, *The Independent Review* of *Economic Regulation* of *Domestic Aviation* (Canberra 1986). For a comment on the Two Airline Agreement *see* J. Livermore, *The Legal Status of the Two Airline Agreement*, Air L. 90, 221 (1983). *See* P. Harbison, *Legal and Administrative Problems of Airline Deregulation: Australia, Australian Law and Legal Thinking in the 1990s* 299–324 (Faculty of Law, University of Sydney 1994).

762. *Australian Airlines (Conversion to* a *Public Company) Act* 1988 (Cth) ss 15, 16, Sch. 1.

763. Qantas was fully privatized in 1996. For foreign investment controls in Australian corporations, including airlines *see Foreign Acquisitions and Takeovers Act* 1975 (Cth) and *see* G. Heilbronn, *Aviation Regulation and Licensing* 272–273 (Law Book Co 2008).

[illegible]

[illegible]

[illegible]

[illegible]

Selected Bibliography

Allen, J. 'To Limit or Not to Limit: Limitation in West Australian Waters-A Call for Reform'. *24 A & NZ Mar. J* 93 (2010), 208.

Australian Government Publishing Service. *Final Report of the Constitutional Commission.* Canberra, 1988, 4.

Australian Law Reform Commission (ALRC). *Civil Admiralty Jurisdiction* Report 33 ALRC. Canberra: AGPS, 1986, 255.

Baker, C. & P. David. 'The Politically Unsafe Port'. *LMCLQR* 112, 1 (1986), 62.

Barnes, R. 'Barecom 2001: Bareboat Charter Revisited'. *LMCLQR* 528 (2002), 50.

Baughen, S. & N. Campbell. 'Hull Fouling-Charterparty Issues'. *LMCLQR* 129 (2006), 87.

Baughen, S. & S.J. Campbell. 'Apportionment of Risk and the Carriage of Dangerous Cargo'. *International Maritime Law* 8, 1 (2001).

Baughen, S. '"Shipowner" Implied Indemnity for Cargo Claims'. *LMCLQR* 15 (1996), 94.

Baughen, S. 'Bailments Continuing Role in Cargo Claims'. *LMCLQ* (1999) 393–405.

Baughen, S. 'Charterers' Bills and Shipowners' Liabilities: A Black Hole for Cargo Claimants?'. *Journal of International Maritime Law* (2004), 248.

Baughen, S. 'Dangerous Cargo and the Claimant's Dilemma'. *Shipping and Transport International* 5(1) (2005), 7–9.

Baughen, S. 'Does Deviation Still Matter?'. *LMCLQR* 70 (1991), 169.

Baughen, S. 'Laytime Definitions for Charterparties'. *Journal of International Maritime Law* 19, 5 (2014), 363.

Baughen, S. 'Off-Hire Claim and Arrest of Ship'. *Journal of International Maritime Law* 20, 5 (2015), 319.

Baughen, S. 'The "Clause Paramount" and the One Year Time Bar (the "Mariner")'. *LMCLQ* (1996), 173–175.

Baughen, S. 'Withdrawal with Cargo Still on Board: The Kos'. LMCLQ (2012), 343.

Baughen, S. *Shipping Law.* 4th edn. London: Cavendish, 2009, 233.

Baughen, S. *Summerskill on Laytime.* 5th edn. Sweet & Maxwell, 2013.

Baughen. S. 'Charterparty Bills of Lading-Cargo Interests' Liabilities to the Shipowner'. In *The Evolving Law and Practice of Voyage Charterparties*, edited by D. Rhidian Thomas. Informa, 2009, 217–250.

Bell, A.P. 'Sub-Bailment on Terms: A New Landmark'. *LMCLQR* 177 (1995), 189.

Bell, A.P. 'The Bills of Lading Act 1855 Today'. *JBL* 124 (1985), 132, 138.

Blay, S. & E. Clark. *Australian Law of Financial Institutions.* Sydney: Harcourt Brace, 1993, 145.

Selected Bibliography

Bonwick, G.J. & E.C. Steer. *Ship's Business.* 4th edn. London: Maritime Press, 1961, 123.

Boyd, S., A. Berry, B. Eder, D. Foxton & C. Smith. *Scrutton on Charterparties and Bills of Lading.* 21st edn. Sweet & Maxwell, 2008, 43, 50, 51, 55, 64, 68, 85, 87, 91, 94, 98, 103, 117, 121, 127, 132, 170.

Brazil, P. 'Border Hopping and Section 92 of the Constitution'. *ALJ* 34, 77 (1960), 290.

Brazil, P. *Liner Shipping Cargoes and Conferences.* Canberra: AGPS, 1993, 208.

Butler, D.A. & W.D. Duncan. *Maritime Law in Australia.* Sydney: Legal Books, 1992, 150, 207, 234, 245.

Carver, T. *Carriage of Goods by Sea.* 13th edn. London: Stevens, 1982, 64, 84, 169.

Cavanagh, S.W. 'The Ultimate Exclusion Clause'. *ALJ* 59, 67 (1985), 192.

Chandler III, G. 'The Electronic Transmission of Bills of Lading'. *J Mar L & Com* 571 (1989), 200.

Cheka, C.N. 'Conduct Barring Limitation'. *J Mar L & Com* 18, 487 (1987), 211.

Chorley, R.S.T. & O.C. Giles. *Shipping Law*, edited by N.J. Gaskell & Debattista. 9th edn. Clondon: Pearson Higher Education, 2013, 205.

Clarke, M. 'Transport Documents: Their Transferability as Documents of Title: Electronic Documents'. *LMCLQR* 359 (2002), 200.

Clarke, P. 'The Reception of the Eurymedon Decision in Australia, Canada and New Zealand'. *ICLQ* 29, 132 (1980), 190.

Cooke, J., T. Young, J. Kimball, D. Martowski & L. Lambert. *Voyage Charterparties.* 3rd edn. Informa 2007, 51.

Cooper, R.E. 'Crewing Vessels While under Arrest'. *MLAANZ Journal* 14, 1 (1999), 25.

Crawford, J. *Admiralty: Laws of Australia* 34.4, 205, 255.

Creaman, D.J. 'The Early History of Admiralty Jurisdiction'. *ANZMarLJ* 28, 1 (2014), 16–24.

Creamean, D. 'Marine Insurance'. In *Australian Maritime Law*, edited by M. White. 2nd edn. Sydney: Federation Press, 2000, 53.

Darling, G. & C. Smith. *LOF 90 and the New Salvage Convention.* Lloyd's of London Press, 1991, 245.

Davenbport, B.J. 'Misdelivery: A Fundamental Breach'. *LMCLQ* (2000), 386.

Davenport, B. 'Proposed Reforms of Admiralty Jurisdiction in Australia'. *LMCLQR* 3, 317 (1987), 255.

Davies, M. & A. Dickey. *Shipping Law.* 3rd edn. Lawbook Co, 2004, 46, 47, 50, 51, 55, 64, 66, 68, 70, 87, 91, 94, 104, 132, 211, 216, 217.

Davies, M. & G. Lawson. 'Limiting Shipowner's Liability for Economic Loss'. *ABLR* 16, 271 (1988), 202.

Davies, M. & P. Anderson. *Bareboat Charters.* 2nd edn. London: Lloyd's of London Press, 2005, 50.

Davies, M. 'A Chink (or Two) in the Bill of Lading Plaintiff's Jurisdictional Armour? Good News for Australian Maritime Arbitration'. *ABLR* 26 (1998), 152.

Davies, M. 'Australian Maritime Law Decisions'. *LIMCLQ* 394 (1998), 189, 199.

Davies, M. 'Fruits of the Blooming Orchard'. *ABLR* 19 (1991), 152.

Davies, M. 'The Elusive Carrier: Whom Do I Sue and How?'.*ABLR* 19, 230 (1991), 202.

Davies, M. 'Two Views on Free In and Out Stowed Clauses in Bills of Lading'. *ABLR* 22, 198 (1994), 163.
Davies, P.J. & N.E. Palmer. 'The Eurymedon Five Years On'. *JBL* 337 (1979), 190.
Davis, M. *International and Commercial Maritime Law Yearbook* (2012).
Debattista, C. 'Fundamental Breach and Deviation in the Carriage of Goods by Sea'. *JBL* 22 (1989), 169.
Debattista, C. *Sale of Goods Carried by Sea.* 2nd edn. London: M&! Books, 1998, 140.
Debattista, C. *UK Carriage of Goods by Sea Act 1992: Goodbye to Title to Sue Problems – Or Is It?.* Hong Kong: Maritime Law Association of Australia and New Zealand Conference, 1992, 133.
Department of Trade and Communications. *Status of Conventions – Australian Position.* Canberra, 1989, 226.
Department of Transport and Communications. *Draft Discussion Paper: Proposals for Reform of Australian Bills of Lading Legislation.* Canberra: A-G's Department, 1993, 104.
Derrington, S. 'Charterparties'. In *Australian Maritime Law*, edited by M. White. Sydney: Federation Press, 2000, 47, 50, 66, 68, 70, 87, 91.
Diamond, A. 'The Hague-Visby Rules'. *LMCLQR* 2, 225 (1978), 193.
Duggan, A.J. 'Offloading the Eurymedon'. *MULR* 9, 753 (1974), 189.
Edwards, L.R. 'Liability of Air Carriers for Death and Personal Injury to Passengers'. *ALJ* 56, 108 (1982), 359.
Ellinger, E.P. *Documentary Letters of Credit.* Sydney: Butterworths, 1973, 145.
Faber, D. 'Electronic Bills of Lading'. *LMCLQR* 2, 232 (1996), 200.
Faculty of Law. *Australian Law and Legal Thinking in the 1990s 1994 Sydney*, 392 University of Sydney, 242.
Garvin, S. 'Exempting Clauses and the Obligation to Provide a Seaworthy Vessel at Common Law'. *LMCLQR* 29 (2004)44.
Gaskell, N. & C. Forrest. 'Marine Pollution Damage in Australia: Implementing the Bunker Oil Convention 2001 and the Supplementary Fund Protocol 2003'. *UQLJ* 27, 2 (2008), 233.
Gaskell, N. 'Bills of Lading in an Electronic Age'. *LMCLQ* (2010), 233.
Gaskell, N. 'Limitation of Liability and Division of Loss in Operation'. In *Marsden & Gault on Collisions at Sea*, edited by S. Gault, S. Hazelwood, A. Tettenborn, E. Cole & T. Macey. 14th edn. Sweet & Maxwell, 2016.
Gaskell, N. 'The Law of Tug and Tow and Offshore Contracts'. *Journal of International Maritime Law* 18 (2012), 322, by S. Raney, in *Law Text*, edited by D.R. Thomas.
Gaskell, N., R. Asariotis & Y. Baatz. *Bills of Lading: Law and Contracts.* LLP, 2000.
Gilman, J. & R. Merkin. *Arnold's Law of Maritime Insurance and Average.* 17th edn. London: Sweet & Maxwell, 2008, 51.
Gorton, L. & R. Ihre R. *A Practical Guide to Contracts of Affreightment and Hybrid Contracts.* New York: Lloyd's of London Press, 1986, 48.
Gram, P. *Chartering Documents.* London: Lloyd's of London Press, 1981, 48.
Griggs, P., R. Williams & J. Farr. *Limitation of Liability for Maritime Claims.* 4th edn. Informa. 2004.

Selected Bibliography

Grippando, J.N. 'Warsaw Convention-Federal Jurisdiction and Air Carrier Liability for Mental Injury: A Matter of Limits'. *Geo.Washington J. IntL. & Econ.* 59 (1985), 382.

Hannah, F. & A. Phillipides. 'Carriage of Goods by Sea'. In *Australian Maritime Law*, edited by M. White. 2nd edn. Sydney: Federation Press, 2000, 46, 150.

Hannappel, P.C.C. 'The Right to Sue in Death Cases under the Warsaw Convention'. *Air Law* 6, 2 (1981), 66.

Harbison, P. 'Legal and Administrative Problems of Airline Deregulation'. In *Australian Law and Thinking in the 1990's.* Sydney: University of Sydney Law School, 1994, 392.

Heilbronn, G. *Aviation Regulation and Licensing.* Sydney: Thomson Law Book Co, 2008, 16, 24, 32, 33, 359, 392.

Heilbronn, G. *Transport: Aviation, Laws of Australia.* Sydney: Thomson Reuters [34.2.4380]–[34.2.4840].

Hetherington, S. *Annotated Admiralty Legislation.* Law Book Co Ltd, 1989.

Hetherington, S.W. 'Liability and Entitlement to Indemnity. The Antwerpen'. *LMCLQR* 1, 16 (1994), 192.

Hibbits, B. 'The Impact of the Iran-Iraq Cases on the Law of Frustration of Charter Parties'. *JIMLC* 16, 441 (1985), 100.

Holdert, H.M.C. & F.J. Buzek. *Collision Cases – Judgements and Diagrams.* London: Lloyds of London Press, 1984, 234, 236, 238.

Industry Commission. *Intrastate Aviation Report No. 25.* Canberra, 1992, 330.

Institute of Maritime Law. *Problems of the Shatt-al-Arab.* Southampton: Institute of Maritime Law, 1983, 100.

Jackson, D.C. *Enforcement of Maritime Claims.* London: Lloyd's of London Press, 1985, 262.

Kahn-Freund, O.S. *The Law of Carriage by Inland Transport.* 4th edn. London: Stevens, 1965, 263.

Kindred, K.M. 'Trading Internationally by Electronic Bills of Lading'. *Banking & Finance L. Rev.* 7, 265 (1992), 200.

King, P.E. 'The Carriage of Dangerous and Nuclear Cargoes'. *ABLR* 14, 86 (1986), 54.

Latimer, P. *Australian Business Law.* 19th edn. Sydney: CCH, 2000, 12.

Latimer, P. *Australian Business Law.* 20th edn. 2001, 14–15.

Levy, S.J. 'The Rights of International Airline Passengers'. *Air Law* 1, 275 (1976), 359.

Lewins, K. 'Australian Passengers Travel in Legal Equivalent of Steerage-Considering the Merits of a Passenger Liability Regime for Australia'. *ABLR* 38, 123 (2010), 217.

Lewins, K. 'Cruise Ship Operators, Australian Consumer Law and Civil Liability Acts'. *ANZMarLJ* 30, 1 (2016), Pt. 2, nn. 93–110.

Lewins, K. 'Sub-Bailment on Terms and the Australian Consumer'. *Murdoch Electronic Journal* 9 (2002) at http//www.murdoch.edu.au/law/93/lewins93.html., 189.

Lewins, K. *International Carriage of Passengers by Sea.* Sweet & Maxwell, 2016.

Livermore, J. & K. Eurjai. 'Electronic Bills of Lading and Functional Equivalence'. *Journal of Information Law and Technology* 2 (1998): 205 at http://elj.warwick.ac.uk/ jilt/ecomm/98_2liv/fdefault.htm., 200.

Livermore, J. & K. Eurjai. 'Electronic Bills of Lading: A Progress Report'. *J Mar L&Com* 55 (1997), 200.

Livermore, J. 'Deviation, Deck Cargo and Fundamental Breach'. *JCL* 2, 241 (1990), 169, 170.

Livermore, J. 'Siemens Ltd v. Schenker International (Aust) Pty Ltd: High Court of Australia Determines Air Waybill Limitation Clause Extends Beyond Destination Airport to Road Carriage'. *Korean Journal of Air and Space Law* 19, 1 (2004), 341.

Livermore, J. 'The Legal Status of the Two Airline Agreement'. *Air Law* 90 (1983), 392.

Livermore, J. *Exemption Clauses and Implied Obligations in Contracts.* Sydney: LBC, 1986, 189, 192, 269, 277.

Livermore, J. *Laws of Australia: Transport* 34.1,211.

Livermore, J. *Limitation of Liability in Laws of Australia: Shipping.* Ch. 8, 34.3. Sydney: LBC, 1999, 211.

Macmillan, C. 'Elder, Dempster Sails on: Privity of Contract and Bailment on Terms.' *LMLQR* 1 (1998), 189.

Malcolm, J.O. 'The Negligent Pilot and the Himalaya Clause: A Saga of Disagreement.' *ALJ* 67, 14 (1993), 192.

Marine Cargo Liability Working Group. *Report to the Federal Minister of Transport.* Canberra: The Working Group, 1995, 150.

Marston, J. 'The "Near" Clause in Charter Parties'. *JBL* 42 (1966), 55, 56, 58.

May Report. *The Independent Review of Economic Regulation of Domestic Aviation.* Canberra, 1986, 242.

McCarter, P. 'Redefining the Function(s) of the Notice of Readiness', *LMCLQR* 483 (1997)67.

Mcgregor, H. *McGregor on Damages.* Thomson Reuters 2009, 69.

McMeel, G. 'Straight Bills of Lading in the House of Lords'. *LMLQR* (2005)104, 155.

Meeson, N. & J.R.K. Kimbell. *Admiralty Jurisdiction and Practice.* 4th edn. Informa.

Miller, R. *Miller's Annotated Trade Practices Act-Australian Competition and Consumer Law*. Thomson Reuters, subscription service, at [1.74.5]-[1.74.15].

Mills, C.M. 'The Future of Deviation in the Law of Carriage of Goods'. *LMCLQR* 4, 587 (1983), 169.

Ministry of Transport. Wellington 1979, *Aircraft Accident Report* No. 79 – 139; *Report of the Royal Commission to Enquire into the Crash on Mount Erebus Antarctica, of a DC 10 Aircraft operated by Air New Zealand Ltd* (1981); 'The Erebus Inquiry'. *NZLJ* 8, 189 (1981).

Mocatta, A.A., M.J. Mustill & S.C. Boyd. *Scrutton on Charterparties.* 19th edn. London: Sweet & Maxwell, 1984, 64, 84, 162.

Nair, A. 'A Note on Norden: Voyage Charterparties, the Hague Visby Rules and Enforcing Foreign Arbitration Awards'. *AANZMLJ* 27, 2 (2013), 90–95.

National Bank. *Finance of International Trade.* 1985, 145.

Nikaki, T. 'The Statutory Himalaya-Type Protection Under the Rotterdam Rules: Capable of Filling the Gaps?'. *JBL* 4, 403 (2009), 192.
Ogilvie, A.S. 'Courts of Marine Inquiry in Australia'. *ALJ* 53, 129 (1979), 238.
Okake, S. 'Aviation Personal Injury Claim Settlement in Japan'. International Conference on Air Transport and Space Application in a New World, June 1993. Tokyo, 359.
Palmer, N.E. & P. Davies. 'The Eurymedon; Aground or Afloat?'. *Mod LR* 41, 747 (1978)191.
Palmer, N.E. 'Subailment on Terms'. *LMCLQR* 177 (1988)189.
Palmer, N.E. 'The Stevedore's Dilemma: Exemption Clauses and Third Parties'. *JBL* 101 (1974), 189.
Palmer, N.E. *Bailment.* 2nd edn. Sydney: LBC, 1991, 131, 263, 265, 275, 281.
Paton, G.W. *Bailment in the Common Law.* London: Stevens, 1952, 265.
Payne, W. & E.R.H. Ivamy. *Carriage of Goods by Sea.* 12th edn. London: Butterworths, 1985.
Pengilley, W. 'International Liner Cargo 11 Shipping Amendments to the Trade Practices Act'. *ABLR* 5, 29 (1989), 203.
Philippides, A. *Laws of Australia: 34.3 Shipping*, 255 (2013), 259.
Powles, J. 'Title to Sue, Problems of Consignees and Others'. *JBL* 313 (1987)202.
Rares, Q.A. 'Safe Port Promise by Charterers: Rethinking Outstanding Complications'. *AANZMLJ* 29, 2 (2015), 111–121.
Reynolds, F.M.B. 'The Significance of Tort in Claims in Respect of Carriage by Sea'. *LIMCLQ* 97 (1986), 132.
Reynolds, R. 'Again the Negligent Stevedore'. *LQR* 95, 183 (1979), 191.
Rose, F. 'Withdrawal Clauses in Time Charters'. *Cur Leg Prob* 30, 213 (1977), 71.
Rose, F.D. (ed.). *International and Commercial Law Year Book 2010.* Lloyd's List Law, 2010, 1.
Sakamoto, T. 'The Fate of Passenger Liability under the Warsaw Convention'. International Conference on Air Transport and Space Application in a New World, June 1993 Tokyo, 359.
Sheen, B. 'Limitation of Liability: The Law Gave and the Lords Have Taken Away'. *J Mar L & Com* 18, 473 (1987), 211.
Stanculescu, D. 'Recovery for Mental Harm under Article 17 of the Warsaw Convention: An Interpretation of Leison Corporelle'. *Hastings International.& Comparative Law Review* 8 (1985), 382.
Stewart, A. 'The Owner's Vulnerability to the Liability of the Demise Charterer'. *Australian and New Zealand Maritime Law Journal* 29, 2 (2015), 85.
Street, A.W. 'Collisions and Groundings'. In *Australian Maritime Law*, edited by M.W.D. White. 2nd edn. Federation Press 2000, 234.
Sturley, M., T. Fujita & J. van der Ziel. 'The Rotterdam Rules: The UN Convention on Contracts for the International Carriage of Goods Wholly or Partly by Sea'. *ANZ Mar LJ* 27, 1 (2013), 42–45.
Sullivan, A. 'The Interaction Between the Law of Salvage, the Law of Contract and the Salvage Convention'. *ANZMarLJ* 30, 1 (2016), 70–74.
Sutton, K.C.T. *Sales and Consumer Law in Australia and New Zealand.* 3rd edn. Sydney: LBC, 1983, 43.
Sutton, K.C.T. *Sales and Consumer Law.* 4th edn. Sydney: LBC, 1995, 45, 280.

Tedeschi, M. 'Consideration, Privity and Exemption Clauses: Port Jackson Stevedoring Pty Ltd v. Salmond and Spraggon (Australia) Pty Ltd'. *ALJ* 55, 876 (1981), 191.

Tetley, W. *Marine Cargo Claims.* 3rd edn. Montreal: Blais, 1988, Chapters 5, 31, 169.

Tettenborn, A.M. 'The Carrier and the Non-owning Consignee – An Inconsequential Immunity'. *JBL* 12 (1987), 202.

Todd, P.N. 'Contract with Consignees and Indorsees'. *LIMCLQ* 476 (1984), 132.

Trappe, J. 'Laytime Problems and Comparison of Law'. *LlMCLQ* 2, 251 (1986), 67.

Treitel, G. & F. Reynolds. *Carver on Bills of Lading*. 2nd edn. London: Sweet & Maxwell, 2005, 104.

Walpole, S. & L. Rees-Murphy. 'Back on Course-Excluding the Right to Limit Liability under the 1976 Convention: A Discussion of the *Cape Bari* Case'. *ANZMarLJ* 30 (2016), 12.

White, M. (ed.). *Australian Maritime Law.* 2nd edn. Sydney: Federation Press. 2000, 150.

White, M.W.D. & A.I. Philipides. *Shipping: Laws of Australia.* 34.3, 205.

White, M.W.D. *Laws of Australia: Shipping.* 273, 283, 242, 243.

White, M.W.D. *Shipping: Laws of Australia* 34.3. Ch. 9. 263, 271 (2013), 243.

Wilford, M., T. Coghlin & N.J. Healy. *Time Charters.* 3rd edn. London: Lloyd's of London Press, 1982, 70, 71, 84, 89.

Wong, J. 'Container Transportation and Anomolies in the Law'. *ABLR* 21, 340 (1995), 163.

Yiannapoulos, A.N. (ed.). *Ocean Bills of Lading: Traditional Forms, Substitutes and EDI Systems.* Kluwer Law International, 1995, 199.

Yim, C.W.B. 'Port Promise by Charterer: Rethinking Outstanding Complications'. *NZMarLJ* 30, 2 (2016), 1.

Ying, C. 'The Himalayan Clause Revisited'. *Mal LR* 22, 212 (1980), 191.

Zhoa, L. & F.W.H. Chan. 'Incorporating the Charterparty's Applicable Law Clause into Bill of Landing'. *LMCLQ* 48 (2012).

Table of Cases

(The references in this table are to paragraph numbers)

Table of Cases

Table of Statutes

(The references in this table are to paragraph numbers)

COMMON WEALTH STATUTES

Table of Statutes

AUSTRALIAN CAPITAL TERRITORY STATUTES

NEW SOUTH WALES STATUTES

NORTHERN TERRITORY STATUTES

QUEENSLAND STATUTES

SOUTH AUSTRALIAN STATUTES

TASMANIAN STATUTES

VICTORIAN STATUTES

Table of Statutes

Regulations

Index

The numbers here refers to the paragraph number.

Index

Index

Index

www.ingramcontent.com/pod-product-compliance
Lightning Source LLC
LaVergne TN
LVHW021038011026
849160LV00008BA/542